The filmic representation of finance is intimately connected to how we understand, analyse and resist financial markets. This wonderful anthology presents a cultural analysis of finance film and documentary from its earliest days to the present, showing our enduring fascination and repulsion of speculation. It offers a detailed reading of the narrative and visual themes of financial representation, and a novel perspective on its politics.

Marieke de Goede, University of Amsterdam,
author of 'Virtue, Fortune and Faith.'

This book, the first of its kind, provides a cogent, multifaceted account of the collision of two great dream machines that define our era: film and finance. The first has become our global society's most powerful form of storytelling; none of us can deny the second's extensive and intensive power over almost everything in this interconnected world. In addition to the rigour and diversity of the approaches taken by its authors, what I find especially admirable about this collection is that, by bring film and finance into critical proximity, we come to learn much more about the power and the limits of each. As we struggle today to grasp the nature of global finance before it further destabilizes our precarious world, this book will help us hone our critical imaginations. For this reason, I highly recommend it not only to scholars but to film-makers, artists and activists seeking new ways to represent the terrible power of money, and offer the alternative visions we so dearly need.

Dr Max Haiven, Lakeland University, Canada.

The essays in this pioneering and timely book make a major contribution to our understanding of finance on film. The collection discusses how films of all kinds have registered the growing dominance of the financial sector over our political cultures and everyday lives in the years leading up to and after the near-global financial crisis of 2007-2008. Acutely aware of how cinema helps to shape and inform popular opinion and understanding, the writers here argue that recent 'finance films' offer us a crucial sphere for reflection on the economic state that we're in and show us routes to forms of critical intervention in the name of economic and social justice. This collection makes essential reading for anyone concerned with understanding how we have come to explain the contemporary financial sector to ourselves. *Global Finance on Screen* will be indispensable to anyone wanting to make sense of contemporary capitalism and of the stories we tell about it.

Dr Alasdair King, *Queen Mary University of London, UK.*

Global Finance on Screen aligns itself with the struggle for an effective critique of financial capitalism across the social sciences and the humanities. The concern-driven approach of this volume assembles research on finance film at a moment in contemporary financial capitalism when filmmakers assume a deliberately critical view on finance. The volume reconstructs and re-interprets these critical social analyses from a wide range of filmic genres and formats, including documentaries, feature and television films and spanning a period of 100 years of filmmaking. The contributions touch upon finance-related issues represented in film that address much broader audiences in cultural economy and the social study of finance, such as the temporalities of finance, orders of economic and financial knowledge, or social-structural polarizations conditioned by finance. The volume is thus powerfully placed as a contribution to economic history from a Cultural Studies perspective, but it articulates also highly nuanced contemporary diagnoses of financialized societies.

Professor Andreas Langenohl, *Justus Liebig University, Germany.*

GLOBAL FINANCE ON SCREEN

Global Finance on Screen is the first collection exclusively dedicated to the growing body of multi-format and multimedia audiovisual work that this book designates as the finance film. Finance film presents both the lives and deeds of bankers and the effects financial transactions, money, credit, greed, and economic recessions have on communities in general, on men and women's well-being, desires, values, and actions.

The chapters for this book are written by European and North American scholars in film studies, anthropology, business ethics, cultural studies, political economy, and sociology. Their contributions reveal the potential of film to document financial cultures, spread finance and capitalist mythology; trace economic, cultural and political transformations; inform, raise awareness, express public outrage, and provide insightful criticism of the alienating and exploitative consequences of the growing role played by financial services in the economies of the Western world. The collection offers in-depth interdisciplinary investigations of feature films such as *Wall Street*, *Freefall*, *Margin Call*, *Justice&Co*, *The Wolf of Wall Street*, and *The Big Short*, and documentaries such as *Inside Job*, *Capitalism a Love Story* and *In a Strange Land*.

Constantin Parvulescu is research fellow at the Institute for Culture and Society, University of Navarra, Spain and guest lecturer at the University of St Gallen, Switzerland. He has published articles on the audiovisual representation of financial services and the intellectual interventions of European cinema. He is author of *Orphans of the East: Postwar Eastern European Cinema and the Revolutionary Subject* (Indiana University Press, 2015) and the co-editor of *A Companion to the Historical Film* (Wiley-Blackwell, 2013).

GLOBAL FINANCE ON SCREEN

From Wall Street to Side Street

Edited by Constantin Parvulescu

Routledge
Taylor & Francis Group
LONDON AND NEW YORK

First published 2018
by Routledge
2 Park Square, Milton Park, Abingdon, Oxon OX14 4RN

and by Routledge
711 Third Avenue, New York, NY 10017

Routledge is an imprint of the Taylor & Francis Group, an informa business

British Library Cataloguing-in-Publication Data
A catalogue record for this book is available from the British Library

Library of Congress Cataloging-in-Publication Data
A catalog record for this book has been requested

ISBN: 978-1-138-04527-9
ISBN: 978-1-138-04528-6
ISBN: 978-1-315-17203-3

Typeset in Bembo
by Out of House Publishing

CONTENTS

FIGURES

TABLES

BOXES

CONTRIBUTORS

Robert Burgoyne is honorary professor in film studies at the University of St Andrews and senior research fellow at Cinepoetics, Center for the Advanced Study of Film, Free University, Berlin. His work centers on historiography and film, with emphasis on American cinema and national identity. Publications include *Film Nation: Hollywood Looks at U.S. History* (revised edition, University of Minnesota, 2010) and *The Epic Film in World Culture* (Routledge/AFI, 2011). He has also published on memory and contemporary American culture; cinephilia in the work of Douglas Gordon and Corey Arcangel; and the imagery of haunting and spectrality in the war film. Much of his recent work investigates the cinematic rewriting of history, and film's power to illuminate the present by reconceiving dominant fictions that have formed around the past.

Pablo Castrillo obtained his M.F.A. in Screenwriting from Loyola Marymount University (US) under a Fulbright Scholarship (2010–2013), where he also worked in development at production companies such as Jeremy Renner's The Combine (*Kill The Messenger*, *The Founder*) and Kurtzman & Orci (*Sleepy Hollow*, *Now You See Me*). He received his PhD from the University of Navarra where he currently works as a lecturer in the Department of Film, TV, and Digital Media. His current research focuses on the American political thriller film in the post-9/11 era, from the perspective of genre and narrative analysis.

Michael Chanan is a seasoned documentarist, writer and professor of film and video at the University of Roehampton, London. He has written books on early cinema, Cuban cinema, the social history of music, and the politics of documentary. As a director, he began with films on contemporary music for the BBC in the early 1970s, and filmed extensively in Cuba and Latin America, mostly for Channel 4, in the 1980s (and on occasion since then). Most of his films since the turn of the millennium have either been academically funded, or else no-budget videos for the web and educational use. See www.mchanan.com and his blog, Putney Debater (www.putneydebater.com).

Pablo Echart is a professor in screenwriting and script analysis at the University of Navarra, where he has also been the Head of the Screenwriting Master's Program. He has published extensively on the classical Hollywood romantic comedy, and on filmmakers such as Alexander Payne, Woody Allen, Hirokazu Koreeda, John Huston and David Mamet. He also carries out screenwriting consulting services for production companies.

Ignacio Ferrero is professor of business ethics and Dean of the School of Economics and Business Administration at the University of Navarra. He has been visiting scholar at Bentley University, at Harvard University (Real Colegio Complutense) and at Notre Dame University (Mendoza College of Business). He has published several books on the history of economic thought and articles in academic journals such as *Business Ethics Quarterly*, *Journal of Business Ethics*, *Business Ethics: A European Review*, and *Business and Society Review*. He is currently working on virtue ethics and the common good in finance, and he is co-founder of the research group on virtue ethics in business and management, with a worldwide network of collaborators. He is coeditor of the *Handbook of Virtue Ethics in Business and Management*, Springer.

Karen Ho is a cultural anthropologist at the University of Minnesota. Her work ethnographically and historically examines the ethos, values, and practices of finance, its role in transforming our social economy and in producing massive socio-economic inequality and precarity. She researches and teaches on the anthropology of economy, with specific foci on finance capital, capitalism, globalization, corporations, socio-economic inequalities, and comparative racial and feminist studies. Her ethnography, *Liquidated: An Ethnography of Wall Street* (Duke University Press, 2009) was based on three years of fieldwork among investment bankers and major financial institutions. Her latest book project attempts to excavate an alternative cultural history of financial risk through the ethno-historic investigation of three central sites – corporations, investment practices, and investment funds – from the mid-twentieth century until the present moment.

Scott Loren is a postdoctoral fellow at the University of St Gallen's School of Humanities and Social Sciences. His areas of specialization, teaching and supervision include film studies, genre studies, narratology, posthumanism, psychoanalysis, social semiotics and visual cultures of migration. He is co-editor of *Melodrama After The Tears: New Perspectives on the Politics of Victimhood* (Amsterdam University Press, 2016). His current research deals with digital epistemologies from media and cultural studies perspectives.

Jens Maesse is sociologist at University of Giessen. His research focus is on discourse analysis, sociology of science and education, economic sociology, and political economy. From 2011 to 2015, he was the leader of the research project Financial Expert Discourse. His expertise and scholarship includes the analysis of economic expert discourses, higher education and academic cultures. His publications include: "Economic Experts. A Discursive Political Economy of Economics." *Journal of Multicultural Discourses*, Vol. 10(3), 279–305 (2015); "The Elitism Dispositif. Hierarchization, Discourses of Excellence and Organisational Change in European Economics." *Higher Education*, DOI 10.1007/s10734-016-0019-7 (2016).

Daniel Marcus is the author of *Happy Days and Wonder Years: The Fifties and the Sixties in Contemporary Cultural Politics* (2004), and co-editor, with Selmin Kara, of *Contemporary Documentary* (2016). He also edited *ROAR! The Paper Tiger Television Guide to Media Activism* (1991). He is professor of communication and media studies at Goucher College in Baltimore, Maryland, USA. His current research involves an analysis of media's roles in depicting political and economic developments in the contemporary United States, and on documentary and media activist projects.

Robert E. McNulty is director of programs at Hoffman Center for Business Ethics, Bentley University. He is also the founder and executive director of the nonprofit organization, Applied Ethics, Inc., the main work of which is the Pax Populi people-to-people peacebuilding initiative, which offers educational services to students living in conflict zones, especially Afghanistan. He is the founding co-chair of the UN Global Compact's PRME Business for Peace Working Group. He has published numerous journal articles on business ethics and business for peace and is on the editorial board of the journal, Business, Peace and Sustainable Development. The focus of his work is theoretical and applied ethics, as well as ways to advance peace amid growing international tensions and global threats from war and terrorism.

Graham Murdock, professor of culture and economy at the Department of Social Sciences at Loughborough University and visiting fellow in media and communication at Goldsmiths London University, is internationally known for developing a critical political economy approach to the analysis of culture and communication. He has held the Bonnier Chair at the University of Stockholm and the Teaching Chair at the Free University of Brussels and been a Visiting Professor at the Universities of Auckland, Bergen, California, Curtin Western Australia, and Wuhan. His writings have been translated into twenty-one languages. His recent books include: as co-editor, *The Blackwell Handbook of Political Economy of Communication* (2011) and *Money Talks: Media, Markets, Crisis* (2014). His next book, *Carbon Capitalism and Communication: Confronting Climate Crisis*, with Benedetta Brevini, brings together researchers and activists to explore the multiple ways that communication systems are implicated in global warming and the struggle for feasible alternatives.

Elena Oliete-Aldea is associate professor at the Department of English Studies at the University of Zaragoza, Spain. Her research centers on film genre and cultural studies, more specifically on filmic representations of cultural identities. She is currently working on the analysis of global connections in the context of the economic crisis in contemporary transnational cinema. Her recent publications include a monograph on British cinema and culture, *Hybrid Heritage on Screen. The Raj Revival in the Thatcher Era*. Basingstoke: Palgrave Macmillan, 2015, and a co-edited book on transnational Spanish cinema: *Global Genres-Local Films. The Transnational Dimension of Spanish Cinema*. New York: Bloomsbury, 2015.

Constantin Parvulescu is research fellow at the Institute for Culture and Society, University of Navarra, Spain and guest lecturer at the University of St Gallen, Switzerland. He has published articles on the audiovisual representation of financial services and the intellectual interventions of European cinema. He coordinates the research project Finance and the Moving Image, is author of *Orphans of the East: Postwar Eastern European Cinema and the Revolutionary Subject* (Indiana University Press, 2015) and the co-editor *of A Companion to the Historical Film* (Wiley-Blackwell, 2013).

Marta Rocchi is research fellow and vice director at the Markets, Culture and Ethics Research Centre (Rome), and lecturer of Corporate Social Responsibility at ISSRA, Pontifical University Santa Croce. She has been visiting scholar at the *Hoffman Center for Business Ethics* at Bentley University (MA, USA), and member of the *Academy of Management*, the *Society for Business Ethics*, the *Research Group on Virtue Ethics in Business and Management*, and the *International Society for MacIntyrean Enquiry*. She is on the organizing committee of the series *Colloquium on Christian Humanism in Economics and Business*. She earned her PhD from the University of Navarra. Her research interests are finance ethics, virtue ethics in business, MacIntyrean ethics in business and finance, teaching ethics in business curricula, shared value, and corporate social responsibility.

Araceli Rodríguez Mateos earned her PhD with European Mention in communication sciences at University Complutense of Madrid. Currently, she is senior lecturer in photography and film studies at University Rey Juan Carlos (Madrid, Spain), where she has also held the position of vice dean of the Communication Sciences Faculty. She was visiting lecturer in film studies at University of Lancashire (United Kingdom) and at University of California Los Angeles. Her fields of expertise are photography and documentary cinema, as well as history of social communication in Spain. Nowadays she is working in the research project "Imaginaries of the crisis: Visual depictions of the economic, social and geopolitical collapse (1929–2012)," supported by the Spanish Government. She has published four monographs and several articles on politics and cinema in Spain and in the United States, especially in relation to the terrorist attacks of September 11 in the US and March 11 in Spain.

ACKNOWLEDGEMENTS

Global Finance on Screen is the editorial follow-up to the international workshop Global Finance and the Moving Image that took place in Pamplona, Spain in October 2016. I organized this event with generous support from the Institute for Culture and Society at University of Navarra, Pamplona, the Social Trends Institute, Barcelona, and the University of St Gallen. I use this opportunity to express my gratitude to them and to all the people involved in shaping and completing this wonderful intellectual encounter. The Social Trends Institute (STI) is a non-profit international research center dedicated to fostering understanding of globally significant social trends. To this end, STI brings together the world's leading thinkers, taking an interdisciplinary and international approach. Carlos Cavallé, Ph.D., is president of STI. Founded in New York City, STI also has a delegation in Barcelona, Spain. Visit www.socialtrendsinstitute.org.

INTRODUCTION

Constantin Parvulescu

This collection studies a growing body of multi-format and multimedia audio-visual work that I call the finance film. This body of work is comprised of feature, documentary and short films, and television productions. It is a diverse body that includes Oscar-winning dramas (*Wall Street*, O. Stone, 1987), slapstick comedy (*The Saphead*, H. Blaché and W. Smith, 1920), star-driven blockbusters (*The Wolf of Wall Street*, M. Scorsese, 2013), militant documentaries (*Capitalism: A Love Story*, M. Moore, 2009), road movies (*Justice&Co* [Justi&Cia], I. Estaregui, 2014), action films (*Trader Games* [Krach], F. Genestal, 2010), thrillers (*99 Homes*, R. Bahrani, 2014), television dramas (*Too Big to Fail*, C. Hanson, 2011), reality shows (*Downsized*, T. Bruce, 2010), mini-series (*Madoff*, R. De Felitta, 2016), television series (*Billions*, B. Koppelman, D. Levien, and A. R. Sorkin, 2016 and ongoing), investigation journalism (*Inside Story Special: £830,000,000 – Nick Leeson and the Fall of the House of Barings*, A. Curtis, 1996), biographies (*The Forecaster*, M. Vetter, 2015), educational projects (*The Ascent of Money*, A. Pennick, 2008), and YouTube wonders (*Zeitgeist*, P. Joseph, 2007).[1]

In their chapters, contributors to this collection refer to finance film and its content in various ways. They talk about "Wall Street film" or "films about banking"; distinguish between "financial crisis film" and "great recession cinema"; and trace "subprime life stories" and narratives of economic vulnerability. For this volume, I propose an inclusive approach that demands taking into account all lexical variations of the concept of finance, and consequently its ideological collaterals. Such an approach emphasizes that it is critical to envision finance not only as a set of economic operations, but also as a rising generator of cultural and political transformations. Having a strong impact beyond the borders of the corporate universe, the financialization of capitalist economies informs personal identities, human interactions, and discourses on community and emancipation.

The definition of finance film cannot thus limit itself to the representations of finance as "the management, creation and study of money, banking, credit, investments, assets and liabilities that make up financial systems, as well as the study of those financial instruments."[2] The definition needs to take into account the effects money, banking, credit, liabilities, etc. have on men and women's thoughts, desires and actions, as well as on the organization and ethos of the communities they are part of. A comprehensive definition of finance film needs thus to make room for audiovisual representations that reflect the whole spectrum of global cultural and political transformations triggered by the increased economic centrality of financial services in Western economies in order to inspire research that traces detailed pictures of the financialization of cultures around the world.

Nevertheless, the significant contingent of finance films that are set in financial institutions perform an important cultural function. They investigate the secretive universes of such organizations, exposing their mores and operations to public scrutiny. Some of these organizations are economically mainstream, as suggested by the title of the film *The Bank* (R. Connolly, 2001). But on the radar of finance film enter other types of firms, located at the geographical, anthropological and legal margins of the sector – as indicated by the title of the film *Boiler Room* (B. Younger, 2000). The environments of financial services located between these examples are also presented. *The Big Short* (A. McCay, 2014) offers glimpses into the biotopes of many of them: investment banks, state regulators, insurers, hedge funds, various types of brokerage institutions, including the now infamous adjustable-rate mortgage peddlers. The film even enters the headquarters of the American financial media (*The Wall Street Journal*) and the offices of the so far cinematically unexplored credit rating agencies (Moody's).

Finance film also responds to a public interest in the psycho-intellectual, corporeal, social, and professional profiles of finance people. This interest is both critical and appreciative, as financiers are wealthy and influential people. Incontestably, the most impactful banker figure of the finance film of the twentieth century is Gordon Gekko (Michael Douglas) of Oliver Stone's 1987 *Wall Street*. His and his cinematic successors' archetypal features are investigated in Echart and Castrillo's contribution to this volume. The Gekko-Douglas icon provided both a repelling and seductive face to America's and the world's new economic exploiter. It offered a chilling perspective on the mindsets of financiers and at the same time inspired, through a combination of aristocratic looks, professional know-how and smart talk, generations of educated young Americans to seek a career on Wall Street. Gekko's massive cultural impact is reflected in the way the media treated him, often reporting on him as if he were a real-life person. It quoted his lines – such as his (in)famous "greed is good" pronouncement – calculated his wealth, pasted his portrait on the covers of business magazines (including twice on *Fortune*), applauded his return in *Wall Street II*, and used his cultural capital in FBI messages that warned against insider trading.

Even if inspired by notorious corporate raiders of the time, Gekko was fictional. Financial feature and documentary film, however, brought on screen real-life bankers as well. Most of them were sharks or crooks, in a perhaps questionable interchange of glamor between filmic presentation and real-life person. The stockbroker Nick Leeson, who bankrupted a landmark of the British banking establishment, was among the first. His feature film avatar was embodied by Ewan McGregor in *Rogue Trader* (J. Dearden, 1999).[3] Preceded or convoyed by documentary films, books and shorter audiovisual media materials, other finance biopics followed. American legend actors such as Richard Dreyfuss and Robert De Niro lined up to interpret the financial crook Bernard Madoff, and other more or less notorious real-life bankers were offered screen immortality by major Hollywood stars such as Christian Bale, Brad Pitt, Steve Carell, George Clooney, and Ryan Gosling. Nevertheless, the most visible post-Gekko-Douglas marriage between a finance and an acting icon and perhaps the most symptomatic of the public perception of Wall Street in the twenty-first century was that of Jordan Belfort and Leonardo DiCaprio in a cinematic ceremony officiated by legend director Martin Scorsese (*The Wolf of Wall Street*).

As interventions in the public sphere, finance films articulate an expected critique of the financial industry. Slightly cynical, Edward J. Epstein (2010) argues that the salience of the cinematic villainous banker figure can be understood as a marketing decision responding to given predicaments in the current global distribution of film. Epstein's indirect defense of corporate capitalism against filmic representation went viral in the mainstream financial media – in the *Wall Street Journal* it was voiced under the telling title "The Corporate Exec: Hollywood Demon – Nazis are getting old, moviemakers don't want to offend foreign audiences, so corporate types top the list of evil stereotypes" (Epstein 2011). For Epstein, the corporate villain has become the universally accepted, cinematic bad guy of the globalization era, replacing the jihadist terrorist, various types of warlords, Nazi officers, Chinese apparatchiks, or Soviet secret agents. Audiences in all film cultures around the world, Epstein argues, can accept a financial crook as evil conspirator against the well-being of the many, his or her identity not hurting local sensibilities and thus not affecting the international sales of the film telling his or her story in that particular culture.[4]

Epstein's and the film industry's commercial realpolitik notwithstanding, I argue that critical filmic presentations of financiers perform other vital cultural tasks. They indicate popular culture's way of articulating class warfare. Films like *Capital* (Le capital, Costa-Gavras, 2012), *The Human Capital* (El capitale umano, P. Virzi, 2013) or *Margin Call* (J. C Chandor, 2011) are perhaps emblematic in presenting the financiers of the Western world as an intangible aristocracy or as heralds of what a now infamous internal report of Citibank announced as the age of plutonomy (that will replace democracy). As Karen Ho, Elena Oliete-Aldea, Daniel Marcus, Michael Chanan, and Jens Maesse argue in their contributions to this volume, the 2008 financial crash has inspired filmmakers to present bankers as an overclass which has secured for itself a global hegemonic position that can no longer be challenged through traditional economic means. Chanan indicates that one of the lines of his documentary *Money Puzzles* (2016) that greatly impacts its audiences is of a trader declaring that the world is no longer ruled by governments, but by Goldman Sachs.

Because it generates high public impact, finance film educates people about the past – both by reconstructing it on screen and by proposing a certain reading of it. As such, finance film is part and parcel of economic history and initiator into the understanding of the present world of finance. No surprise then that its educational use value has been exploited by finance journalism and corporate governance publications. Many have made it their task to classify finance films according to the financial operations they shed light on. For example, a posting (Hyat 2013) on one such a blog with name claiming respectability, Chartered Finance Analyst Institute, informs its readers eager to learn more about Wall Street that the 1983 comedy *Trading Places* (J. Landis, 1983) teaches viewers about commodity futures transactions, the documentary *Billion Dollar Day* (H. Sykes, 1986) about the secrets of forex trading, the romantic dramedy *Working Girl* (M. Nichols, 1988) about mergers and acquisitions, the television movie *Barbarians at the Gate* (G. Jordan, 1993) about leveraged buyout, and the post-crisis *The Warning* (M. Kirk, 2009) about securities regulation.[5] To these classifications one can add the on- and offline recommendations carried by almost every financial publication bearing titles such as investopedia.com's "The 10 Must Watch Movies for Finance Professionals" or Fortune's "7 Movies that Tell the Real Story behind the Financial Crisis."

These recommendations run in parallel with reading lists, ads for online MBA programs, media publicity, internship offers, and online trading platform pop-ups, and show that supply of know-how on banking transactions is a key ingredient in the marketing of finance film. It is as important as finance film's star-driven casts and the attractions it offers – rich people's lifestyles, downtown skylines, stunning offices, designer clothes, and sophisticated shop talk. The imperative of providing know-how on the world of finance also explains why the storylines of finance feature films include several motivational speeches explaining company philosophy and operations, expository monologues describing the state of the business, dialogue sequences reflecting on ethical issues, and various scenes of trade virtuosity.

Wall Street, *Boiler Room* and *Margin Call* include memorable sequences of this kind – some analyzed in this volume. Additionally, the first-person narratives of *The Wolf of Wall Street* and *Madoff* make use of reality-show explanatory interludes to reach their initiation targets. Characters no longer deliver insights to other characters, but turn away from the plot, look into the camera and explain banking practices directly to viewers. Some films such as *The Big Short* even include speakers from outside the diegesis to perform this task.[6] For the same reason, finance films narrating in both the first and the third person set up dialogue scenes in which one character asks another to explain to him or her a financial transaction or situation as if he or she were a rookie in the business, "a child or a golden retriever," as a dialogue line from the more technical *Margin Call* has it.[7]

The civic mission of delivering insights into the operations of banks informs the frameworks of finance film's storytelling in other ways as well. Graham Murdock's and Robert Burgoyne's contributions to this volume show how fiction supplied finance films with successful procedures of representation that combined entertainment and information. One such widespread procedure was the Bildung story – narratives of emergence such as Bud Fox's (Charlie Sheen), the protagonist of *Wall Street*. This formula served particularly well the finance films of the twentieth century. As I show in my contribution, the integration of the narrative of emergence into the late twentieth-century film testifies to a broader transformation of American culture that started in the late 1980s, labeled sometimes as the American financial revolution. Boosted by artificially created bull markets and by the rise of the audiovisual financial media, this so-called revolution created an image of American society as an *emerging* community of investors, animated by financial literacy and the entitlement to a share of the investment pie.

The twenty-first century finance film, as Robert Burgoyne's chapter argues, developed a different chronotope. Its presentations materialized in "post-revolutionary" times, in the wake of the bursts of the tech bubble of 1999–2001 and especially the housing bubble of 2007–2008, and needed extra ingredients to make their insights marketable. Morality tales became hard-to-sell cinematic assets, as testified by the lukewarm reception of the 2010 *Wall Street II: Money Never Sleeps* (O. Stone) and the contrived plots of films such as *Papadopoulos & Sons* (M. Markou, 2012). The approach that better responded to the growing public frustration with finance added to its rhetoric not an extra dose of judgmentalism, but of disillusionment (*Equity* [M. Menon, 2016]), self-reflexivity (*The Fall of Lehman Brothers* [M. Samuels, 2009]), cynicism (*The Wolf of Wall Street*), quest for the absurd (*The Big Short*), anthropological eeriness (*Margin Call*), moral paradoxes (*Client 9: The Rise and Fall of Eliot Spitzer*), and conspiracy theory (*Zeitgeist*). It also paid more attention to the spectacular aspects of the trade (*Money Monster*, J. Foster, 2016) and showed more concern with the so-called magic of traders and their skills to make money out of air (*The Wolf of Wall Street*).

Metaphors of the successful financier changed accordingly. The twentieth century eulogized alpha male dominance – the corporate shark (*Wall Street*), the big swinging dick (*Boiler Room*), brass balls (*Glengarry Glen Ross*, J. Foley, 1992), and the master of the universe (*The Bonfire of Vanities*, B. De Palma, 1990). In contrast, twenty-first century tropes put more emphasis on speculation and mental superpowers of banking "whizzes." This probably responded to the disappearance of exchange floor traders, the increased sophistication and speed of electronic transactions, and the replacement of the rogue brokers of the 1980s and 1990s with Ivy League graduates. Twenty-first century money makers were introduced as rainmakers (*Madoff*). Jordan Belfort was said to have a shamanic method in his drug-induced madness (*The Wolf of Wall Street*). A financier in *Equity* calls himself a magician, while the titles of documentaries such as *The Forecaster* (M Vetter, 2014) or *Quants: The Alchemists of Wall Street* (M. Meerman, 2010) say it all.

The way the emergence story was delivered also changed. Third-person storytelling was predominant in twentieth-century finance film, in the first *Wall Street* or in *Barbarians at the Gate*. Impersonal narration indicated the possibility of identifying an epistemological and ethical point of view outside the increasing financialization of society. This perspective assumed that film narrative could provide a picture of finance that was not contingent upon the continuous flows of capital shaping worldviews and desires. In contrast, many twenty-first century finance stories abandoned this aspiration. First-person narration supported by long voiceovers and confessional monologues delivered directly into the camera became the new standard set by *The Fall of Lehman Brothers*, *Capital*, *The Big Short*, etc., and documentaries like *Master of the Universe* [Der Banker, M. Bauder 2013] or *Wall Street Code* (M. Meerman, 2013). Finance stories turned out to be predominantly character centered, and the increase in epistemological ambiguity brought by first-person narration went hand in hand with an increase in moral relativity in the judging of the virtues of bankers and the industry.

In this context, fourth-wall-breaking monologues were articulated, in feature films, with the vigor of sales pitches. This indicated, on the one hand, that, in the neoliberal culture of generalized marketization of life, the elementary function of asserting the existence of a person or a phenomenon could no longer be disentangled from the marketing of what iconic function that individual or thing might possess – in other words, that a point of view was a point of marketing. On the other hand, these narrative procedures reminded audiences that, as a creator of meaning and value through stories, filmic discourse replicated a growing post-bubble public perception of financial operations as nothing but a grand game of generating value out of air, and of persuading others to buy it. Monologues self-reflexively suggested that, like many purchasable financial products, the plots of films were speculative fabrications marked, as finance, by information-era modes of production. They created value not by producing something genuinely new, but by repackaging and re-selling the already existent.

In order to achieve this goal, financial and cinematic products employed similar symbolic instruments and persuasive procedures. Believable stories were one such instrument financial and film industries shared. Stories exploited emotions, created visions of success and triggered investments of desire. A film like *The Wolf of Wall Street* shows how storytelling and storyselling are almost synonymous terms. An analysis of its sales scenes reveals that buyers of stock follow similar emotional patterns of identification with the ups and downs of their assets as film audiences that root for the gains and losses of protagonists. Both buy paper to participate in this game, a ticket or a share; both are driven by the desire to immerse themselves into the dramas made up for them by the magicians of movie – and respectively money – making; and both expect to be delivered a happy ending.

In the secretive environment of banking industries, with their massive reliance on storytelling and public relations, first-person narratives also gained capital because they often seemed to provide the insider story. The commercial success of written memoirs like Greg Smith's *Why I Left Goldman Sachs* (2012) appeared to prove it, as did hosts of insiders' memoirs that flooded the post-crisis book market with dramatic titles such as Henry Paulson's *On the Brink: Inside the Race to Stop the Collapse of the Global Financial System* (2010) and John LeFevre's *Straight to Hell: True Tales of Deviance, Debauchery and Billion-Dollar Deals* (2015). This success was based on the problematic assumption that an employee of a financial organization was more than just another indoctrinated subject of the neoliberal order, and that he or she could accede to a sharper and more selfless understanding of financial capitalism than the outside observer.

An indicator of the unsustainable nature of such an assumption is the critical reception of this literature. In the case of the more serious accounts, like Smith's or Mike Mayo's *Exile on Wall Street* (2011), the predominant reaction was that the insider did not reveal anything jaw-dropping, and that his account was only confirming already circulating allegations about investment banks. In the case of the others, they were denounced as either works of public relations, as is the case of Paulson's effort to build his own legend, or as stereotyping and exploitative, feeding "the public's hunger for proof that Wall Street is full of degenerate sociopaths, while also glamorizing that degeneracy" (Levine 2015).

Insightful post-crisis finance film understood this predicament, and looked for insider-story models farther down into the past, all the way to the year 1989. Not surprisingly the book that proved to have the Midas combination of entertainment, know-how, wit, intriguing characters, original situations, and astute critical thought, was more than just a self-glamorizing or exploitation story, as its author would become one of the most influential Wall Street commentators of the twenty-first century. This book was Michael Lewis's classic and mega-bestseller *Liar's Poker: Rising through the Wreckage on Wall Street*, which curiously was not adapted for the screen in its days – and probably fortunately, as its days were not prepared for it. But Lewis's storytelling perspective returned in the post-2008 film and informed, I argue, the insider-story framework of the most visible finance feature films of the decade, *Capital*, *The Wolf of Wall Street*, *Madoff*, and *The Big Short*, the latter being not only an adaptation of another book by Lewis, but also one including tribute scenes to *Liar's Poker*.

Finance film's supply of characters, settings and plots gained more public attention after the financial crisis of 2007–2008. Since, in my opinion, this is the event that, with its colossal devaluation of assets, astonishing bailouts and painful long-term global consequences, marks the end of the twentieth century and of the faith in the apparently successful marriage of capitalism and democracy, the importance of filmic reactions to it cannot be underestimated. Like never before in history, film produced a forceful wave of negative audiovisual attention to finance and capitalism. These reactions aimed to explain the crisis, unravel its culprits and reveal the damage it inflicted, but many dug deeper into the causes of the disaster and posed questions on the legitimacy of the economic system that nurtured their cancerous growth. Aesthetically and intellectually, these representations significantly raised the quality standards of finance films. In fact, I argue that finance film would not have stood alone as a consistent and worthy body of work for critical analysis without the 2007–2008 crisis.

One should note that the 2008 crash also spurred the publication of the first concerted body of academic literature focusing on finance film. Even if to this date,

Global Finance on Screen is the first book-length academic study on finance film, journal articles and chapters in edited collections in disciplines such as cultural studies, film studies, business ethics, political economy, and business anthropology have analyzed finance films. Here I do not intend to provide a review of the literature in this field, as most of these studies are mentioned in the "References" lists of the chapters of this volume, and some of them are commented on in detail. I want, however, to express my conviction that, together with this collection, these studies have set the foundation of a corpus of scholarship that is relevant to readers concerned not only with the development of cinema but also with finance and financialization. I argue that, given the specificity of the archive it investigates, finance film scholarship offers an original contribution to economic history, as well as insightful case studies on the often pernicious ethics and politics of capitalist business culture.

The first to respond to the 2008 events were documentaries. They aimed to raise awareness, present global consequences, identify causes, make sense of the legal and cultural contexts that stimulated risky, immoral or illegal behavior, and sometimes provide solutions. In his contribution to this volume, Daniel Marcus analyzes some of the influential ones, *Inside Job* and *Capitalism: A Love Story*. One can add to the list American productions such as *The Flaw* (D. Singleton, 2010) or *Plunder: The Crime of Our Time* (D. Schechter, 2009). But the list is long and includes productions from all countries of the Western world, Canadian-French – *Meltdown: the Forces behind the Global Economic Crisis* (Krach, les dessous de la crise économique mondiale, T. McKenna and M. Gagnon, 2012), Swiss-French – *Cleveland versus Wall Street* (J-S. Bron, 2010), Spanish – *Futures Market* (Mercado de futuros, M. Álvarez, 2011), Greek – *Debtocracy* (A. Hatzistefanou, K. Kitidi, 2011), and many German television films, one of the latest being *Bank Robbery* (Bankraub, F. Genstahler and H. Vogel, 2016).

The crisis films revealed that the global population at large and not only some gullible investors had become the victims of financial speculation. Film turned its attention away from trading floors in order to investigate who were these others whose quality of life had been brutally affected by the decisions of bankers. The most visible others of the banking industry are presented in documentaries chronicling anti-finance protest movements. These others called themselves the 99% as the title of one such documentary concerned with the American protest movement has it: *99%: The Occupy Wall Street Collaborative Film* (A. Aites, A. Ewell, N. Krstic, L. Read, 2013). In Spain and in Europe, the men and women who took to the streets to protest the crisis, financialization and the way in which governments responded to the meltdown called themselves *indignados*, a denomination that entered the title of another documentary: *Indignados* (T. Gatlif, 2012). In terms of values and organization, protesters struggled to set up an antithetical environment to boardrooms of banks. This alternative space and laboratory of exploitation-free human interaction inspired the title of another documentary *The Square* (La Plaza. La gestación del movimiento 15M, A. Morán, 2011).

In contrast to the cinema of the post-Great Depression era (post-1929–1939), whose emblematic film became the eponymous adaptation of John Steinbeck's *The Grapes of Wrath* (John Ford, 1940), few post-2008 American feature finance films traced the way the crash affected the lives of the 99%. A *Los Angeles Times* critic indicated this shortcoming in 2010, expressing frustration that both Hollywood and the independent scene "have essentially ignored the stories of average Americans who have been downsized or lost their homes in the collapse of the housing bubble," and instead focused on films featuring bankers (Beale, 2010). In other words, Hollywood produced crisis films (presenting the causes and the culprits of the crash and the efforts to contain it), but not recession films – that is, stories tracing the aftershocks of the crisis away from its epicenter in metropolitan high-rises.

The critic noted two exceptions, *Up in the Air* (J. Reitman, 2009) and *The Company Men* (J. Wells, 2010). But even this honorable mention needs to be taken with a grain of salt, as neither film strays significantly away from the Hollywood model of the downtown crisis drama, and as both feature stars, George Clooney and Ben Affleck, interpreting handsome protagonists wearing expensive suits. They were, however, seen as recession films because corporate downsizing, even if of white collar personnel, played a central role in their plots. In addition, as an adaptation of a 2001 novel, *Up in the Air* did not or could not make direct references to the 2008 events, but rather focused on trimming of personnel as a common practice of finance-spurred capitalism. To this list, one could add Hollywood productions made after the publication of the article mentioned above, but again not many.

Enter American independent cinema, documentary, and television, and European film, each with a broader portfolio of incursions into the post-2008 hardships of the 99%. Television, as the *Los Angeles Times* article already indicated, produced the reality show *Downsized* documenting the everyday tribulations of a crisis-affected family. The American independent film scene reacted with family dramas, for example *Nebraska* (A. Payne, 2013), which, with its provincial, jobless and marginalized protagonists hoping to get rich by way of worthless paper (but instead getting poorer), reveals how the American dream has been perverted by greed and financialization. Another example is *99 Homes* (R. Bahrani, 2014), exploring foreclosures and standing out for its moving presentations of forced home evictions.

A variety of European documentaries on the topic of recession are discussed in Araceli Rodríguez Mateos's contribution to this volume, while Elena Oliete-Aldea's chapter shows how, as response to the crisis, post-2008 European recession features developed the theme of loss – loss of jobs, opportunities, property, home, family, hope, and happiness. Rodríguez Mateos and Oliete-Aldea refer to works such as *In a Strange Land* (En tierra extraña, I. Bollaín, 2014) and *Whoever's With Me* (A quien conmigo va, A. Mejías, 2014). To these one can add documentaries such as the Austrian *Land Robbery* (Landraub, K. Langbein, 2015), and British and respectively Spanish features, *Freefall* (D. Savage, 2009) and *Justice&Co*. Some of these examples reveal that, in recession films, banks and bankers are no longer visible.

Their acts of exploitation become depersonalized. The power exercised by finance upon economic environments has become financialization and informs the very production of growth and perhaps life itself. Exploitation is no longer localized in a person or organization (a rogue speculator or a ruthless bank), but is a systemic evil, whose perhaps most euphemistic denomination is "moral hazard," and most obvious acknowledgment is that money is not neutral (one of the central arguments of the documentary *Money & Life* [K. Teague, 2013]).

One should add here that American film, both Hollywood and independent, and European cinema also present the revenge of the 99%. Hollywood produced *Money Monster*, which keeps bankers and their media servants at gunpoint, but, for marketing and ideological reasons, discredits and eventually kills the rebellious 99%er who besieges them. Independent and European film, however, challenged such mainstream conventions. While their heroes also take justice in their hands and use violent means to get back at their oppressors, morally (*Justice&Co*) and even legally (*Assault on Wall Street* [U. Boll, 2013]) their heroes get away with murder. Had it not been too tributary to genre conventions, one could have added a horror film to the list, *Drag Me to Hell* (S. Raimi, 2009), in which the callous banker protagonist is not only killed, but also doomed to eternal suffering by a spell put on her by the victim of a foreclosure she had ordered.

Rodríguez Mateos's chapter indicates that symptomatic of finance-driven economies is the growing number of economically vulnerable citizens around the world, whose hardships are documented in the post-2008 cinema of precarity (a concept Rodríguez Mateos borrows from Alice Bardan and Lauren Berlant). Yet also symptomatic of financial crisis film is the presentation of economic and legal invulnerability at the other end of the social pyramid. While the 1987 *Wall Street* or the 2000 *Boiler Room* send their villains to jail, post-2008 films no longer follow this scenario. In *The Wolf of Wall Street*, Belfort goes to prison, but the film presents serving time as a joy-ride and as a place of reinventing oneself. *Capital* shows how a big financial firm manipulates prices and commits insider trading with no punishment. The analysis of *Margin Call* by Ferrero, Rocchi and McNulty for this volume reveals that the legal and moral set-up of contemporary finance is as such that it allows firms to sell worthless products with no legal repercussions and even feel good about their actions (that have put many people out of business and driven even more into poverty). Finally, the dark comedy *The Other Guys* (A. McKay, 2010) ironically suggests that law-breaking and money-losing investment firms and their bosses unraveled by the film's NYC cops will face no criminal charges. In fact, the companies will be bailed out by the government and their bosses awarded bonuses.

This change in the presentation of financial crime does not only gesture toward a drop in trust in social justice or a growing belief that financial services have become untouchable, but also, as Alex Gibney's documentary *Park Venue* points out, toward deeper and more haunting questions. But before reviewing these questions let us also mention that, with its presentation of the crisis and its consequences, finance film has put on stage other economic actors located in between the bankers and the vulnerable multitude, all with a certain degree of participation in the crisis. Several of these intermediaries are linked to the real estate market. As mentioned above, *The Big Short* introduces them to the public, suggesting that the crisis was not only the result of unleashed lust for profit, excessive betting, short-termist economic thinking, and rigging of the market, but also the consequence of systemic transformations that financialization and futurization of the economy had generated. In this culture of compulsive greed and wealth on debt participated not only the sellers of "toxic" assets such as mortgage-backed securities, and their evaluators who gave them AAA ratings, but also the buyers, pushed into housing scams by the sweet deals and their own unrealistic economic thought.

In relation to this, the first question Gibney's and many other finance films raise refers to the extent to which the banking sector has become a dangerous accumulation of power that controls the apparatuses of the state (legislative, executive, judicial, military, as well as the media). Populist conspiracy theory films like *Zeitgeist*, analyzed in this collection by Daniel Marcus, or fictional accounts like *The International* (T. Tykwer, 2009) express this hypothesis. In a better documented register, approaches signed by leftist filmmakers such as Michael Moore or Costa-Gavras take these doubts to a more complex level. Conspiracy is regarded as culture; rationally articulated intentions to rule the world are presented as systemic forms of exploitation serving a deterritorialized and decentralized form of global sovereignty. In this line of thought, for Moore and Costa-Gavras the evil of finance-driven capitalism is to have transformed the global economy into a grand bottom-line-obsessed enterprise, or, in euphemistic banking language, into one that puts the increase of shareholder value above all else.

Karen Ho's contribution reflects on this predicament. With her, Ferrero, Rocchi and McNulty suggest that the effects of this transformation of the economy are felt on cultural and anthropological levels. Values, human interaction and the role of community are transformed by an unrestricted legitimation of the pursuit of cash at the expense of other human individual or collective endeavors. Consequently, the finance-driven transformation of capitalism has made the system more exploitative than ever and has rendered it incompatible (if it ever was compatible) with authentic social justice, equality before the law and equal opportunity in personal development. The financial crisis has thus raised questions not only about reforming the banking system, but also about capitalism as a biopolitical organizing principle and about the limited power of public institutions to contain greed. Additionally, Karen Ho's and Scott Loren's contributions argue that one should doubt that traditional economic thought is able to provide the appropriate tools to analyze this transformation of human engagement in wealth production and exchange. Ho voices the growing doubt in the myth of the rational market, which underpinned "classical" economic theory since the 1960, and grants popular culture the merit of gesturing toward the irrational undercurrents informing the corporate world. According to Loren, who draws on the work of Lawrence Grossberg and Stuart Hall, a cultural studies approach to the economy is long overdue, and finance film is a useful medium to start such a rethinking effort.

In the last part of this Introduction, I want to argue that it is this unease with the effects of financialization that brings the best out of finance film. A brief look at the reception of Oliver Stone's *Wall Street* demonstrates that social commentary is the most culturally relevant public contribution of finance film. At the time of the release of *Wall Street*, the leading American critic Roger Ebert wrote enthusiastically about it. But it was not the formal aspects of the film, its art, that he found outstanding. What he and other critics of the time perceived as exceptional was the "radical critique of the capitalist trading mentality" Stone's film delivered. They commended its presentation of the "immoral and illegal" practices of "corporate raiders" and "Wall Street sharks" at the expense of the Fordist, industrial economy that produced the wealth of the first three decades of post-World War II America (Ebert 1987).

Ebert's approach is replicated in almost all critical reactions to finance films, from television productions like *Barbarians at the Gate*, through documentaries like *Inside Job*, to more recent ventures such as *The Wolf of Wall Street*. This perspective informs even the reviews of the formally more nonconformist *The Big Short*. The chapters of this volume follow suit. Coming from scholars with backgrounds not only in film studies but also anthropology, business ethics, cultural studies, political economy, and sociology, contributions take formal aspects into consideration, but their approach shows that it is intellectually more relevant and ethically more acceptable to analyze finance films in terms of their intervention in the public sphere and their expression of a collective desire to change specific aspects of the current cultural and economic order. As Ebert's reaction points out, what finally counts more is finance film's critical edge, its historical anchoring and the acceptable scenarios of resistance it, more or less explicitly, articulates.

Consequently, I suggest that we identify the body of work that I described in this Introduction and termed *finance film* as a set of public artistic and intellectual manifestations that share a similar *preoccupation*, rather than narrative and stylistic aspects constituting the nucleus of a developing genre or subgenre of the business or corporate film. The preoccupation that brings this stylistically diverse body of films under the same roof is, as suggested above, predominantly critical and interested in presenting the growing economic, political and cultural power of financial services in Western economies. Finance film makes visible, on the one hand, the way the banking world looks, talks, thinks, desires, and acts; and, on the other, it shows how finance's muscle and the consequences of its hegemony – the centrality of money, markets, risk management, and debt – impact the definition and production of human wealth, worth, values, and community.

One argument in favor of this choice of categorization is to stimulate those who study finance film to resist regarding it primarily as a marketing category, which, at the end of the day, is what genres mostly are in capitalist commodity culture. It is intellectually limiting to approach finance film with the main interest of revealing how it creates branding and audience expectations, and how it aims to generate material profit or cultural capital from the public distrust with financial services. Such a research goal would mostly remain confined to aesthetic and commercial aspects of film. Findings would predominantly indicate how popular culture adapts to transforming economic and cultural realities, and how it engages these transmutations in order to generate cultural and economic value. Such an approach would have to assume that even a militant documentary like Michael Moore's *Capitalism: A Love Story* functions as a simulacrum of public opposition to various forms of expropriation specific to our era of knowledge capitalism, and thus mainly as a cultural merchandise benefiting from the outrage produced by the financial crash of 2008 and the loss of jobs, property and human development it engendered.[8]

The other problem with the genre approach is a more general one and specific not only of finance film. It is a problem encountered by all formalist approaches, a problem which just becomes both more acute and more loaded with ethical undertones in the case of finance film. According to Rick Altman, framing research in terms of genre tends to imply transhistorical specificity, narrative and visual predictability, and shared formal features (Altman 1999, 14, 19, 20). While these formal characteristics may apply to some finance films, exceptions are many. Staple characters and settings can be easily noticed in finance film. But not unifying ones. Thus, given the diversity of the body of work presented above, it becomes methodologically less relevant to identify finance film according to situations, plot patterns, staple characters, and settings without providing long glosses on genre blurring and instability (King 2007, 136–146), and support one's taxonomy with paradoxical pronunciations such as "hybridity is itself a landmark of genre" (Berry-Flint 2004, 39).

A content-driven approach also pays more attention to the ethics of representation. The rise of finance and speculation in Western economies in the last three decades has generated immense damage to human well-being around the globe. In the case of finance films, a strictly formal definition might not be able to warn those who reflect on these films against the visual pleasure, attractions and redemptive situations that the storylines of these films (both fiction and documentary) inherently articulate, as well as their stereotyping and the exoticization of victims and the offering of facile closures that divert attention from deeper problems. It is a concern-based approach that, for example, reveals the main historical testimony of *The Wolf of Wall Street* and the ethics underpinning its representation of financiers. Such an approach reminds the viewer that the main cultural stake of Scorsese's film is not to show the rise and fall of an *enfant terrible* of finance, but to provide a profound reflection on America's and perhaps the world's sadomasochistic fascination with its seductive exploiters. In this lies the true value of *The Wolf of Wall Street*. It unravels a tragic and undemocratic predicament of late capitalism. Ruling classes have managed to expand their hegemonic role from their traditional effort to define the values of mainstream culture. They tap into and appropriate for their benefit countercultural discourse, including practices previously belonging to the artistic bohemia and avant-garde.

The example above also indicates that, in spite of film's financial, professional and commerce-imposed limitations, a concern-driven approach highlights its relevant historical testimony. In the era of post-truth, self-reflexive approaches driven by progressive, democracy-supporting values write the good history. They provide an example of constructive reception that emphasizes the historically relevant and distinguishes it from both informational sensationalism and exploitation. A concern-driven approach addresses issues of form as testimonies of the way in which a historical period makes sense of the cultural and economic phenomena of its time, and as a strategy to provide critical public impact. Aesthetic pleasure is tackled from a similar angle. Powerful performances or intelligent plots are testimonies, superior means of offering insightful views into a world (of finance) known for its secrecy, its multiple lobbying efforts and its grand public relations attempts to rewrite history, which probably culminates in both Henry Paulson's and Lloyd Blankfein's pronouncements (both CEOs of Goldman Sachs, one Neo-protestant the other Jewish) that finance does the work of God on earth.

I will close this Introduction, however, by mentioning one limitation of finance film. When taking a look at the titles, themes and companies producing finance feature films, one notices immediately that, like stock peddling or financial expertise, finance film is a global venture in terms of distribution, but not production. In terms of production it is an almost exclusively Western cultural artifact. And like the industry it represents, the leading position belongs to American producers, their cultural products being from time to time replicated by British or European competitors. The same observation applies to documentaries, with the coda that Western Europe's contribution to the field is larger and more diverse – but not necessarily more influential. As a topic of reflection, finance is almost inexistent in East European, Latin American, Asian, or African film – as even the few finance films that are set in the bustling stock markets of East Asia are British or American productions.

One can provide various explanations for this cinematic silence around the world, some quite predictable. The leading investment banks are North American and Western European, and the grand housing bubbles of the first decade of the twenty-first century were also a Western phenomenon. Yet smaller housing bubbles and austerity policies marked national economies around the world, and so did issues of privatization, increased foreign debt, and currency speculation. Let us hope that this silence will be broken, and that other parts of the world will more extensively reflect through the audiovisual medium on the new forms of exploitation imposed by financialization. This is not a call for imitations of *The Wolf of Wall Street* in Iranian cinema, or for a Nigerian version of *Inside Job*. Even if the financialized economy is globally interconnected, the films mentioned above are profoundly American in terms of topics and approach. My observation aims to gesture toward the limitations inherent in film as Western-centered contribution to economic history. Financialization looks and feels different in the second or third world. This is why it is important that the 99% in terms of global cultures also voice concern and provide testimonies on their particular experiences, and even more importantly, that they are able to have access and show interest in these representations. I express the hope that Western corporate hegemony does not translate into a global grand discrepancy in filmic testimonies on a phenomenon that seeks to impact without discrepancy the entire global order.

Notes

1 One can also talk about finance-related horror films: *Drag Me to Hell* (S. Raimi, 2009) and *Fired* (S. Warrier, 2010). The pornography industry also brought its contribution. The better known productions are, as their titles indicate, parodies of finance film classics. *Screwing Wall Street* (M. Ferrara and K. Kross, 2015) builds upon Oliver Stone's *Wall Street*, while the *Whore of Wall Street* mini-series (B. Brando, 2014) uses situations from Martin Scorsese's *The Wolf of Wall Street*.

2 Finance definition on Investopedia, www.investopedia.com/terms/f/finance.asp#ixzz4aB3No4Vb

3 His documentary representation is *Inside Story Special: £830,000,000 – Nick Leeson and the Fall of the House of Barings* (A. Curtis, 1996).

4 A convincing piece of evidence to support Epstein's argument could be the global success of *The Wolf of Wall Street*, which was declared the most pirated film of 2014 (Child 2014).

5 The list goes on, referring to operations such as insider trading, community banking, option pricing, corporate takeover, securities fraud, and the use of alternative monetary systems.

6 Not surprisingly, this narrative gadget was inaugurated in the television film (*The Fall of Lehman Brothers*, M. Samuels, 2009). Television film develops in a production context that is more multi-format, more interactive and lower-budget than that of the feature film, and thus more suited for formal experimentation. Its storytelling exploits spectators' familiarity with investigative journalism's on-site narrators, talk-show confessions, reality-show soliloquia, and advertising endorsements. Even when the gadget of breaking the fourth wall was transferred and flamboyantly developed in feature film, for example in *The Big Short*, its director, Adam McKay, served a long apprenticeship in television as well, and made full use it, including his experience in sketch comedy (*Saturday Night Live*).

7 In earlier films, the interlocutors who needed clarifications in plain English were family members of the banker protagonists – often their wives. Films like the deeply business-embedded *Barbarians at the Gate* offer insightful material for a feminist approach to this aspect of finance film, as does, of course, the absence of female protagonists from such films – the two main exceptions being *Working Girl* and *Equity*.

8 Such cultural pessimism can find confirmation in the high fees Moore charged for making his film.

References

Altman, Rick. 1999. *Film/Genre*. London: BFI.

Beale, Lewis. 2010. "Recession-themed Films? Not at the Multiplex." *Los Angeles Times*. November 7. http://articles.latimes.com/2010/nov/07/entertainment/la-ca-recession-movies-20101107

Berry-Flynt, Sarah. 2004. "Genre." *A Companion to Film Theory* (eds.). Toby Miller and Robert Stam. Malden: Blackwell Publishing, 25–44.

Child, Ben. "Rogue Trading: *The Wolf of Wall Street* Named Most Pirated Film of 2014." *The Guardian*. December 29. www.theguardian.com/film/2014/dec/29/the-wolf-of-wall-street-most-pirated-2014-frozen-gravity

Epstein, Edward J. 2010. *The Hollywood Economist*. New York: Melvin House.

Epstein, Edward J. 2011. "The Corporate Exec: Hollywood Demon – Nazis are Getting Old, Moviemakers Don't Want to Offend Foreign Audiences, so Corporate Types Top the List of Evil Stereotypes." *The Wall Street Journal*. October 10. www.wsj.com/articles/SB10001424052970204524604576610762349124314

Hyat, Usman. 2013. "Top 20 Films about Finance: From Crisis to Con Men." *Enterprising Investor*. September 20. https://blogs.cfainstitute.org/investor/2013/09/20/20-finance-films-for-entertainment-and-education/

King, Geoff. 2007. *New Hollywood Cinema: An Introduction*. London: I.B. Tauris.

Levine, Matthew. 2015. "A New Wall Street Memoir Full of Hookers, Cocaine, and Other Clichés." *Bloomberg Businessweek*. July 7. www.bloomberg.com/news/articles/2015-07-07/john-lefevre-s-wall-street-memoir-full-of-hookers-cocaine-and-other-cliches

SECTION 1

Telling finance stories

1

NARRATING FINANCE CAPITAL

Explorations in speculation, crisis and austerity

Graham Murdock

The abject failure of mainstream economics and journalism to anticipate the severity of the Financial Crash of 2007–2008 or to foresee the depth and durability of its social consequences has prompted sustained questioning of what went wrong, how it was allowed to happen, and where responsibility lies. Feature films and documentaries have played a central role in helping to shape public perceptions. It is tempting to take this body of work as a response to a unique set of circumstances, but I want to argue here for a historical perspective.

The years between 1850 and 1929 saw fundamental changes in the organization of both the financial system and popular culture. Over that period financial institutions moved to the center of the leading capitalist economies with minimal regulation of their activities, but far-reaching impacts on the system's stability as the promised arc of upward economic and social progress was punctuated by periodic crises. At the same time, popular accounts and representations of economic and social life were revolutionized with increasing readerships for naturalist novels and illustrated magazines, the popularity of stage melodramas, experimentation with photography, and the launch of silent cinema.

The space available here allows for only a very preliminary sketch of popular culture's engagement with this first expansion of relatively unregulated financial institutions. This initial laissez faire regime came to end after the Wall Street Crash in 1929 when banking was subjected to strong regulation. A full economic and cultural history of popular representation of finance is long overdue. But an exploration of recent films suggests that the core images, narrative devices, and characterizations developed during that initial formative period have proved remarkably durable providing resources that filmmakers have tapped into when confronting the return of the laissez faire financial capitalism that produced the Crash of 2008 and its aftermath. I want to suggest that this is because they dramatize the enduring imagined tension at the heart of modern capitalism between a "real" economy manufacturing tangible goods and a "fictitious" economy making money from money. These terms are more than economic categories. They support a series of moral and social oppositions.

Borrowing is not a simple question of repetition however. It is shaped in fundamental ways by changing cultural and political climates. We have traveled some considerable distance from the Victorian promotion of probity and suspicion of speculation to the present neo-liberal celebration of financial institutions and risky trading as central planks of the economy. Moral inquiry and censure have been steadily displaced by admiration for the rewards of rule-bending. In developing this argument I have chosen to focus on the most commercially successful or critically acknowledged instances since their currency suggests that they tap into widely held assumptions.

"Fair enterprise and extravagant speculation"

By the time Marx began drafting the third volume of his magnum opus, *Capital*, in the 1860s, it was clear that financial institutions had become central to the operation of capitalism. In Britain, investment had been boosted by the Limited Liability Act of 1855, the removal of restrictions on futures trading in selected securities in 1860, and the proliferation of "bucket shop" share brokers. Marx followed his contemporaries in seeing finance playing a double role. On the one hand, by opening channels for businesses to expand by borrowing money and issuing shares it was "driving capitalist production beyond its own limits." On the other hand, by giving rogue financiers a platform to defraud unwary investors it was creating "one of the most effective vehicles of crisis and swindles" (Marx 1974: 607). In practice, as one of the leading bankers of the time, Alexander Baring, pointed out, the line between lending to "fair enterprise and extravagant speculation" was often difficult to draw since all loans and investments carried risks (quoted in Itzkowitz 2002,125). However, the Protestant insistence that wealth should be earned by honest work and prudent calculation continued to pitch the positive role of finance in supporting the material economy against negative images of financiers who behaved little better than peddlers of patent medicines, promoting worthless schemes and appealing to investors' greed.

This institutional dichotomy was mapped onto a psychological dualism. On the side stood the idealized bourgeois individual as both borrower and lender, carefully weighing up risks and rewards, making rational judgments, and playing a long game. On the other stood the individual submerged in the crowd, swept along on a collective tide of emotion, persuaded to part with their money by charismatic tricksters selling a fraudulent dream of substantial and sudden gain. This association of speculation with crowd psychology had been given popular currency by the Scottish journalist Hugh McKay in his best-selling book of 1841, *Extraordinary Popular Delusions and the Madness of Crowds*, which featured two famous historic financial crises, the South Sea Bubble and the tulip bulb mania.

In 1720 shares in the South Sea Company which had been granted a monopoly on trade with the Spanish Americas rose spectacularly on the back of reports of its success. Their value peaked at 1,000 in August only to crash to 124 a month later amid accusations of political corruption, unfounded rumors, and fraudulent selling. One of the casualties was Sir Isaac Newton, the country's preeminent scientist and mathematician, who invested at the top of the market and lost his life savings prompting him to remark that "I can calculate the movement of stars, but not the madness of men" (quoted in Raworth 2017, 145).

Narrating finance capital: naturalist fictions

The rise of financial speculation was a central theme in some of the most successful novels of the second half of the nineteenth century devoted to interrogating contemporary life. Propelled by rising rates of literacy and the practice of serial publication, alongside press reporting, they became the dominant source of popular images of the corruptions of financial capitalism. Leading novelists were often also well known as journalists. Through his magazine articles Dickens was arguably the most read financial commentator of his time (Poovey 2002, 24). He and his contemporaries drew on recently reported events for plots and used the novel's extended space to explore their causes and consequences in a more complete and nuanced way.

The mid-1850s saw a series of financial scandals in Britain with board members of the Royal British Bank granting themselves unsecured loans and John Sadler, the Irish MP and founder of the Tipperary Bank, forging shares and deeds, bankrupting the bank with a personal overdraft of over a quarter of a million pounds, and committing suicide before he could be brought to trial. Sadler's career and demise provided the model for Merdle, the unscrupulous financier at the center of Charles Dickens's darkest novel, *Little Dorrit*, published in serial form between 1855 and 1857. The calculated associations of speculation with filth and excrement, "merde," were underlined by descriptions of Merdle "oozing" around his drawing room and casting him as the origin of a "moral infection" of greed that spread through the society like a physical epidemic, contaminating everyone it touched (Barrett 1970, 203).

As Anthony Trollope noted in his autobiography, commenting on his 1875 novel *The Way We Live Now*, the lavish lifestyles built on speculation were deeply seductive and silenced awkward questions about their sources and legality.

> If dishonesty can live in a gorgeous palace with pictures on its walls, and gems in all its cupboards, and can deal in millions, then dishonesty is not disgraceful and the man dishonest after such a fashion is not a low scoundrel.
>
> (*Trollope 2013 [1883]: Chapter XX*)

Like Dickens, Trollope was responding to events. 1873 saw a major financial crisis in North America and across Europe fueled, among other factors, by a surge in speculative investments, particularly in railways. In September, having failed to secure the credit needed to underwrite its plans for a second cross-continental route, one of the major US investment banks, Jay Cooke and Company, was forced to declare bankruptcy sparking a run of bank failures. In Britain the crisis precipitated an economic depression that lasted for over two decades with sustained cuts in public investment and high levels of unemployment.

The Way We Live Now recounts the rise and fall of the financier, Augustus Melmotte, recently arrived in London from Europe who persuades a number of well-placed persons to invest in a scheme to build a railway from Salt Lake City to Vera Cruz in Mexico, hoping to increase the share price and line his own pocket whether or not the construction of the line is actually completed, or even begun. He is revealed as a fraud when he forges his daughter's signature on a paper releasing her money so that he can pay for the country estate he has bought. He tries to persuade his clerk to endorse his signature, but he refuses and resigns his post. With his creditors closing in and the railway shares almost worthless, Melmotte takes his own life.

Trollope weaves together several themes here that have proved remarkably resilient. There is the central figure of the charismatic individual, seemingly arrived from nowhere with no established connections but able to secure entry into elite circles through sheer force of personality and persuade people to sign up to dubious enterprises with the promise of immediate gain. There are the betrayals within the family and the conflicts of conscience among previously loyal employees. But above all there is the lesson that "greed is good." This amoral spirit of possessive individualism, detached from any sense of social responsibility, has resurfaced in recent films of finance as a central animating impetus in representations of the rewards and penalties of unbridled speculation.

While Trollope's novels focused on the upper reaches of society and the expanding professional class, Dickens offered panoramas of an entire society where the ascendency of individualism was creating new openings for the enterprising and unscrupulous but consigning those left behind to lives of poverty. In this bleak view accumulation was always accompanied by dispossession. The fullest exploration of this process at work was provided by Emile Zola, who in 1868 launched a cycle of twenty novels charting the transformation of social and economic life in Paris under the Second Empire (1852 and 1870) through the intertwined lives of two families, the Rougons and the Macquarts.

The series structure allowed him to range widely across contrasted social milieu while anchoring the general relations between accumulation and poverty, biographies and histories, in the lives of related characters. In 1872 in *The Kill* he introduced the speculator Aristide Rougon who later changes his name to Saccard, a title that combines connotations of both "money bags" (sac d'écus) and violent upheaval, "saccager" – "to sack" (Nelson 2004, xxi). Following the suppression of the popular insurgency of 1848, Napoleon Bonaparte's nephew, Napoleon III, seized power in a coup in 1851 hiring Eugene Haussmann to clear the old working-class quarters and reorganize the city center around wide boulevards lined with expensive apartments. Saccard makes a "killing" from speculating in properties earmarked for demolition surrounded, in Zola resonant phrase, by "the sound of crumbling neighborhoods and fortunes made in six months" (Zola 2004 [1872]: 112). 35,000 people were dispossessed and the average worker was spending between a third and two-thirds of their income on bread.

We meet some of the displaced in the next novel in the sequence, *The Belly of Paris* (1873) set in the new glass and iron market of Les Halles, one of the centerpieces of Haussmann's "modernization" of the city. They may have been forced out of their old areas but they continue to trade in basic foods, meat, vegetables, and cheeses in the traditional way. The commodities offered for sale are tangible, even sensuous. Cheeses exposed to the sun are described as "melting and glazing in rich reds and greens of exposed copper, looking like badly healed wounds" (Zola 2009 [1873]: 238).

This is in stark contrast to the immaterial paper promises of financial speculation. Having made his initial killing in the property market, Saccard reappears in a later novel, *Money* (1891) bankrupt and hoping to re-establish his standing on the stock exchange by generating funds to build a network of railway connections in the Middle East. He launches a new vehicle for the purpose, the Universal Bank, modeled on the Crédit Mobilier that crashed in 1870, artificially inflating the share price by secretly, and illegally, buying stock and setting up a dummy account. After several years of soaring share prices his deception is discovered by a rival financier who releases large volumes of the bank's stock onto the market, causing the price to plunge and creating chaos on the exchange floor as investors jostle to sell, becoming an animalistic mob, "snarling and howling…like one of those fits of madness that can seize a crowd" (Zola 2014 [1891], 287–288). There are strong contemporary resonances in Zola's general characterization of the crash as a:

> periodic epidemic that ravages markets,…the "black Fridays" as they are called, that strew the ground with wreckage. It takes years…for the great banking houses to be rebuilt, rebuilt until the day when the passion for gambling….blazes up, setting the whole process in motion again, bringing new crisis.
>
> *(Zola 2014: 336)*

In common with Dickens and Trollope, Zola presents the world of finance as riddled with dishonesty and practices that cross the border of legality, but he places particular emphasis on the temptation for insiders to use their privileged position and knowledge to advance their own interests at the expense of ordinary investors. Again, the conflict between opportunity and obligation, personal gain and social cost, has re-emerged as a major theme in recent films of finance, including Oliver Stone's *Wall Street* (1987) where, as we will see, it operates as the central plot device.

Naturalist novels developed a number of devices that were later to be adopted in early cinema. Establishing passages describing general environments were intercut with scenes set in closed interiors. Dramas of intimate life were set against urban panoramas in which the luxurious life styles of the rich and privileged sat alongside the abject poverty of the dispossessed and left-behind. Characterizations of individuals were fixed by detailed descriptions of their appearance and clothing, proto close-ups. These techniques of description drew heavily on innovations in pictorial representation.

Picturing finance capital: popular imagery

The second half of the nineteenth century saw painters in Paris intent on capturing "impressions" of a world in incessant motion and the people at the center of this vortex of change. Portraits migrated from the studio to natural environments. The 1879 Impressionist exhibition in Paris included Edgar Degas' *Portraits at the Stock Exchange*, showing the banker Ernest May on the exchange floor listening intently to a fellow trader. The canvas is almost totally filled by the central figures but the solid stone pillars behind them suggest that financial dealing, previously conducted in the streets and coffee houses, now fully merited a dedicated monumental space.

Images of the new financial system achieved more general circulation through the new illustrated magazines of contemporary life. The full-page illustration of business being conducted on the floor of the New York Stock Exchange featured in the American publication *Harper's* for September 10 1881 typifies the new iconography. Again, the detailed rendering of the grand cathedral-like vaulted interior celebrates an institution that now occupies a central place in organizing economic and social life, as the church once did. It is not, however, a public space open to all, but a private enclave, a gentleman's club, insulated from popular experience by restricted membership and arcane rituals. This sense of being at the heart of the new order of power but removed from the mundane grind of everyday labor and deserving of special treatment has proved remarkably durable. It underpins contemporary claims to stratospheric salaries and bonuses, the refusal to take full responsibility for the social costs of financial crashes resulting from "extravagant speculation," and demands that the costs of miscalculations be met from the public purse with bail-outs that decimate welfare budgets.

The material economy depicted in nineteenth-century illustrations of factory interiors typically featured rows of machines invested in for the long term and workers standing at their stations. The *Harper's* image shows a world in motion, with individuals avidly following movements in prices and groups of traders huddled together striking deals. This mobility and immediateness of financial dealing hinted at a world permanently on the edge of instability and chaos, a potential dramatized in images that achieved wide circulation in illustrated magazines picturing traders battling to sell falling stocks and panicking depositors fighting to withdraw their money from banks about to crash. These dramatic scenes were reproduced in popular theater. In 1896, the year the Lumière brothers mounted the first commercial cinema show, in Paris, the American popular author, Charles Turner Dazey, brought an adaptation of his successful novel, *The War of Wealth*, to the New York stage. The show's attraction pivoted on a climactic run on the bank at the center of the drama with promotional posters promising that the spectacular staging of "the crisis in the affairs of a great financial institution" was the "most animated and realistic scene ever shown."

In their search for ways of capturing the textures of everyday life more completely and accurately, leading painters and novelists, including Degas and Zola, were drawn to the new technology of photography. Zola had a long-standing interest in new techniques of visual representation. He was a childhood friend and supporter of the painter Paul Cézanne and after completing the Rougon-Macquart cycle in 1894, he devoted himself entirely to taking photographs viewing it as an extension of the naturalist style of observation that informed his fiction. As he noted in an article for a photography magazine in 1900: "you cannot say you have thoroughly seen anything until you have got a photograph of it, revealing a lot of points which otherwise would be unnoticed, and which in most cases could not be distinguished" (quoted in Newhall 1964:94).

Only a few of the 7,000 photographic plates he produced have survived so we will never know how many of the settings of the novels he returned to, but by then an increasing number of social observers were using photography to document contemporary life and conditions. When Zola died in 1902, cinema-going was just emerging as a major popular pastime, and filmmakers were building on existing cultural forms to craft a distinctive mode of representation. Popular fiction provided a ready source of plots, *Little Dorrit* appeared on screen for the first time in 1913 and *The War of Wealth* in 1914. Popular illustration and photography demonstrated the narrative power of telling details and compositions that anchored perceptions of general qualities and processes in memorable images. Popular theater suggested ways of staging dramatic action. Initially this was a more or less literal transposition with the actors moving while the film camera position remained fixed. As cameras became more mobile, however, directors employed close ups, tracking shots, and crane shots from above, to replicate the multiple viewpoints pioneered in naturalist novels.

Visualizing finance capital: early cinema

The rise of cinema coincided with a further consolidation of financial economic power. In 1910 the Austrian economist, Rudolf Hilferding published *Finance Capital*, updating Marx and arguing that capitalism was now effectively controlled by banks. His thesis applied with particular force to the United States, personified by the banker J. P. Morgan who, at his zenith, controlled two-thirds of US steel production, a sixth of the railway system, and companies central to the next industrial revolution based on electronics and networked communication: General Electric and AT&T. The new corporate moguls' drive to monopolize or "corner" key resources had been explored in Frank Norris's 1903 novel *The Pit*, the second volume in a projected, but unfinished trilogy, exploring the exercise of economic power through the journey of wheat, the staple ingredient of bread, from farmers' fields to domestic table. Set in the Chicago futures market it is informed by a fierce moral critique of the consequences of untrammeled market speculation for mass living conditions. As one character notes:

> it is simply betting...on the conditions of the market, weeks, even months in advance...if we send the price down so far, the farmer suffers...if we send it up so far, the poor man in Europe suffers, the fellow who eats it.
>
> *(Norris 1994 [1903]: 115–116)*

These connections were dramatized by D. W. Griffith in his 1909 film, *A Corner in Wheat*, based on Norris's novel. Griffith draws on the imagery of everyday labor developed in French art and naturalist fiction's juxtaposition of honest toil against speculation, to trace the destructive social consequences of decisions taken in the hidden enclaves of financial power. As a review written at the time noted:

> beginning with an animated reproduction of Jean Francois Millet's masterpiece, "The Sowers."....two bent and knotted forms are seen trudging wearily over the plowed ground, their arms swinging in perfect chronometry with a slight gush of wheat grain pouring forth at each advance of the arm. [....] How little do those poor honest souls realize the turmoil the fruit of their labors will incur. What a contrast is shown in the office of the Wheat King, surrounded by his lieutenants, waiting for the word as he engineers the great corner whereby he will obtain absolute control of the entire produce, not only of the present, but the future.
>
> *(quoted in IMDb 2017)*

The immediate impact of this intervention is dramatized in images of frantic activity on the trading floor intercut with scenes of riots in queues to buy bread that had doubled in price.

By then financial institutions had begun to invest in movies as a business (see Wasko 1982). Griffith's adaptation of *The Pit* was made for the American Mutoscope and Biograph Company that had financed its expansion by borrowing $200,000 from the Empire Trust Company bank. When Mutoscope failed to meet expectations the bank installed their own representative as President and demanded more saleable short films rather than the longer films Griffith wanted to make. His later experience of bankers in Hollywood, as a board member of the Bank of America, was more positive and it was Bank of America that financed one of the best-known American films about banking, Frank Capra's *It's a Wonderful Life* (1946) with James Stewart in the lead role.

The project was the latest in a long line of investments in film which had their origins in 1904 when a recently arrived Italian immigrant, Amadeo Giannini, launched the Bank of Italy to service the working class, mostly Italian, residents of the North Beach area of San Francisco. This democratization of finance was a major break with past banking practice that had concentrated on servicing the wealthy. Almost destroyed in the city's 1906 earthquake and fire, the bank re-emerged to

FIGURES 1.1 AND 1.2 Rational economic calculation is overtaken by the "madness" of crowds as the Wheat King's aggressive push to monopolize the market and fix the price in D. W. Griffith's 1909 film *Corner in Wheat* prompts panic on the stock exchange floor and riots in queues for bread that has doubled in price.

become a major lender to reconstruction projects and later developed a strong interest in cinema, financing a range of films. In 1928 the bank merged with the Los Angeles-based Bank of America to form a much larger enterprise, adopting the Bank of America name to signal its wider ambition to become a nation-wide service catering to all Americans. The drive to build a comprehensive service had been there from the outset however. In 1909 Giannini moved quickly to take advantage of a change in state law allowing banks to establish branches in other Californian towns, opening an office in San Jose. By 1929, he was operating 453 branches across the state. In 1921, he was among the first to establish a division expressly catering to women, a rapidly expanding income group who had been mostly passed over by the banking establishment. That same year, he helped finance *The Kid*, Charlie Chaplin's first full-length film as director. His commitment to film continued throughout the Depression and War years with significant investments in major projects, including Walt Disney's first full-length animation feature, *Snow White and the Seven Dwarfs* in 1937, and *Gone With the Wind* in 1939. The investments in film included two major productions about banking, both directed by Frank Capra, *It's a Wonderful Life* and the earlier *American Madness*, released in 1932.

American Madness tells the story of the upright director of a small bank, Thomas Dickson (played by Walter Houston), who is pressured by his board to merge with a major banking trust, but refuses. One of his employees, who is having a romantic relation with the banker's wife, and has run up substantial gambling debts, robs the bank of most of its reserves to settle his account, precipitating a run which is only halted when supporters of the banker rally round to find funds. Capra employs several devices here adapted from naturalist novels and popular stage melodramas, the dishonest and jealous employee, the run on the bank by anxious customers, and the eventual reward of virtue, but the plot is set in motion by the central opposition between commercial banking serving the community by taking in deposits and making modest loans, and a banking trust oriented to speculative investment.

This tension is moved center stage in Capra's much better known and still widely shown film, *It's a Wonderful Life*, which recounts how a ruthless local banker, Henry Potter, who invests in property, gambling and prostitution, sets out to bankrupt George Bailey, the proprietor of a modest savings and loan company who lends money to workers in an idealized small American town, so that they can move out of Potter's substandard rented accommodation and own their own house. The turning point occurs when Bailey's uncle mislays the bank proceeds he is due to deposit in Potter's bank. Potter finds them and keeps them. Again there is a run on the bank by anxious depositors, but it is followed by a concerted show of community support from all those who Bailey has helped, who donate money to restore the bank's funds.

The film's negative view of the dishonesty and anti-social practices of the big banks and its resolute defense of the social value of a commercial banking system serving the interest of ordinary people, reprised some of the founding tenets underpinning Giannini's original business venture, the Bank of Italy.

By the time *It's a Wonderful Life* was released, the regulations put in place in the wake of the 1929 Wall Street Crash and the rush of bank failures had installed a solid wall separating commercial from investment banking. The Banking Act of 1933 included the Glass-Steagall provisions which required commercial banks to focus on accepting deposits and making loans and barred investment banks from owning them. Institutions were given a year to decide how they wished to be classified. The result was a sharp separation based, as the Nobel prize winning economist Joseph Stiglitz later noted, on the clear understanding that:

> Commercial banks are not supposed to be high risk ventures; they are supposed to manage other people's money very conservatively... Investment banks on the other hand, have traditionally managed rich people's money – people who can take bigger risks in order to get bigger returns.
>
> *(Stiglitz 2008)*

Banks choosing the investment route, however, remained free to engage in speculative ventures and bets on movements in the price of shares, commodities, and currencies. This division between commercial and investment banking continued until regulations were relaxed in the 1980s, and it is this return to a laissez faire regime that provides the essential context within which recent films of finance need to be viewed.

Anatomies of greed: feature films

From the mid-1970s onwards, the leading capitalist economies confronted a structural crisis in profitability. The perceived failure of state economic intervention and management opened a space for neo-liberal economic arguments that painted regulation as holding growth back and celebrated unfettered competition as the solution. This market fundamentalist view, moved to the center of policy with the election of Margaret Thatcher in the UK and Ronald Reagan in the USA, generated concerted drives to sell state assets, open protected markets, and relax regulations on corporate activity. Financial services were seen as a key motor of future growth that could only be realized if "unnecessary" restrictions were removed and the system reorganized to take full advantage cutting-edge computer technologies. The UK moved first. In 1986 the London Stock Exchange abandoned the "Open Outcry" system of face-to-face dealing on the exchange floor and installed an advanced computer network to support screen-based trading over the telephone. That same year, building societies, which had been confined to granting loans to home buyers, were freed to offer a comprehensive range of financial services, sparking a rapid consolidation as banks moved to shore up their competitive position. In 1999 the Financial Modernization Act in the US removed the Glass-Steagall provisions.

As a result, in both major centers of global finance, Wall Street and the City of London, the divisions between commercial and investment banking, and between banking and insurance and home loans, dissolved. New financial institutions, focused solely on investments and speculation, typified by hedge funds and private equity firms, proliferated, creating a shadow banking system entirely divorced from the mundane business of accepting small deposits and making loans, free to speculate in whatever areas delivered the maximum gains and to devise new financial instruments. Tagging London's move to computer trading as the "Big Bang" perfectly encapsulated the widespread sense in political and financial circles that a new universe of possibilities was being created.

In his speech to the Republican Convention in 1984, accepting the party's nomination to run for a second term as President, Ronald Reagan reaffirmed the Founding Fathers' "dream on an America that would be a Shining City on a Hill" (quoted in Reagan and Denny: 1997). By then the deregulation and cuts to public expenditure of his first term had translated the original ideal of just government into a celebration of unrestricted enterprise in which the booming financial sector took pride of place. The amorality underpinning this new orthodoxy was explored in Mike Nichols's 1988 film, *Working Girl*, a title that plays on the familiar slang expressions for women prostituting themselves for money and securing advancement through a combination of calculation and application.

The film opens with aerial shots over New York harbor. As the camera circles the Statue of Liberty we hear Carly Simon's Oscar-winning song, *Let the River Run*, welcoming a new generation "coming through the fog" and hailing the rise of new "silver cities" and "the New Jerusalem." The camera picks out the Staten Island ferry steaming towards the Manhattan business district dominated by glass towers reflecting the early morning light, the new shining city for the age of finance capital. It then closes in on the film's main protagonist, Tess McGill (played by Melanie Griffith), traveling from her working-class neighborhood to a temporary secretarial job in the mergers and acquisitions department of a Wall Street broker. Her horizontal movement, from one shore to another and across the city and then vertically upwards in the elevator that takes her to an office with a panoramic and commanding view, encapsulates her own fierce ambition for social mobility and control. Her opportunity comes when the female executive she works for is injured in a skiing accident and Tess discovers that she has appropriated a takeover proposal that Tess has devised. Drawing on the hard-earned skills she had acquired at night school, Tess decides to promote the plan passing herself off as her superior, assuming her identity, even wearing her dress to a cocktail party. Her deception is discovered but her superior's theft is also exposed and Tess is rewarded for her enterprise with the executive position she has always desired.

The narrative revolves around a double deception and a blatant disregard for rules and obligations that impede personal advantage. As Tess explains to her friend; "I'm not going to spend the rest of my life working my ass off and getting nowhere just because I followed the rules I had nothing to do with setting up." This strong affirmation of Tess's embrace of the financial sector's amoral creed of self-interest and disregard for social responsibility is underlined in the narrative by her increasing separation from the working-class friends she grew up with. The film's closing

FIGURE 1.3 In Mike Nichols's 1988 film *Working Girl*, Tess McGill (Melanie Griffith) is transformed in body and soul, deploying deception to move from her working-class neighborhood and her daily commute to a temporary secretarial job to an executive position in a finance house.

long shot shows her isolated in her new high-rise office a long way from the solidarities and ties of her old neighborhood.

One of the first major attempts to chronicle the changing social landscape being constructed by the unashamed resurgence of possessive individualism and detachment from social responsibility came with the publication of *Bonfire of the Vanities* by the celebrated journalistic chronicler of contemporary trends, Tom Wolfe. Borrowing from nineteenth-century practice, this fictional exploration of the New York rich was first published in serial form in *Rolling Stone* magazine in 1984 before being adapted and released as a novel in 1987. The book's central character, the successful Wall Street bond dealer, Sherman McCoy, thinks of himself as a "Master of the Universe" exercising total control over the transactions he makes and absolved from any responsibility for their possible consequences. One night he takes a wrong turn on the freeway into a poor area, and his mistress, who is at the wheel, accidently hits and injures a young black man. McCoy is discovered, arrested, and forced to take leave from his job after botching a deal with a major investor. The young man dies and as the novel closes, McCoy, who has lost everything, is awaiting trial for manslaughter.

Wolfe's novel was a commercial and critical success and hailed as one of the defining fictions of the decade. In contrast, Brian De Palma's film adaptation released in 1990 ran into problems from the outset with major disputes over casting and costs, recounted in detail by *The Wall Street Journal*'s film critic, Julie Salamon, who was given unprecedented access to the production process (Salamon 1991).

On release the film recouped only $15 million of its $47 million production budget and was widely attacked for blunting the edge of Wolfe's satire. As Roger Ebert, the influential critic of the *Chicago Sun-Times*, complained; "Wolfe's novel was savage and sarcastic in the way it dissected the motives of every single character. Brian De Palma's new movie is lacking in just this quality [and] doesn't seem to despise anyone that much" (Ebert: 1990). As De Palma explained in a later interview he was under pressure from the studio to make the central character, played by Tom Hanks, more likeable. We should, he admitted, have made the film "a lot darker and more cynical but because it was such an expensive movie we tried to humanize Sherman McCoy – a very unlikeable man" (De Palma 2006: 94). This tendency to humanize financial ruthlessness and amorality recurs in later Hollywood films of finance signaling the displacement of moral censure by entertainment and spectacle.

Despite its limitations the film does foreground the central opposition between the "real" and "fictional" economy. In a pivotal scene McCoy tries to explain to his daughter how he makes money by dealing in bonds but does not actually produce or make anything. The daughter asks him if he helps to build hospitals, institutions at the heart of conceptions of collective care, raising pointed questions about the morality of financial transactions designed for personal gain rather than social contribution. Seeing McCoy struggling, his wife intervenes with a telling metaphor.

> Daddy doesn't do railroads or hospitals, or anything really.... Now just imagine that a bond is a slice of cake. Every time you hand a slice of that cake to somebody else a little piece comes off and you are allowed to keep those crumbs. Daddy passes somebody else's cake around and takes up all of the crumbs.

1987, the year Wolfe's novel was published, saw the release of Oliver Stone's film, *Wall Street*. Both narratives center on characters who make their living in the financial system and consider that the accepted rules do not apply to them. In Stone's film the role of "master of the universe" is taken by Gordon Gekko (Michael Douglas), a legend on Wall Street for his ruthlessness and success. Gekko's detachment from the grit and labor at street level and command over others' lives is anchored visually by shots showing him standing by the window of his high-rise office with a God's eye view over the city to the horizon.

Gekko is modeled on Ivan Boesky, a hugely successful Wall Street trader who, when asked to speak at the 1986 graduation ceremony at the Business School of the University of California at Berkeley, took the opportunity to assure departing students that their ambitions to make as much money as quickly as possible were entirely justified, declaring that "Greed is all right...greed is healthy. You can be greedy and still feel good about yourself" (quoted in Martin 2016:192). His speech valorized the ideology of self-interest at the core of neo-liberalism and signaled a shift in the ambitions of graduates from elite universities. Where previously they might have considered a career in academia, or government service, or companies in the material economy, more and more were opting to seek employment in

FIGURE 1.4 The characterization of financiers as masters of the universe is anchored visually by repeated images of bankers and traders in offices with commanding views over the city, far removed from life on the streets and the consequences of their actions for ordinary people. Gordon Gekko (Michael Douglas) in Oliver Stone's 1987 film *Wall Street.*

financial services and reap the rewards of salaries and bonus packages that eclipsed anything offered in other sectors.

In *Wall Street*, a young stockbroker, Bud Fox (played by Charlie Sheen), eager to be mentored by Gekko, sets out to curry favor by relaying inside information on the company, Bluestar Airlines, gleaned from his father who is employed there as a union leader. After Bud has secured his relationship with Gekko, he proposes that Gekko buys Bluestar but later discovers that he plans to liquidate the company, sell all the assets, and make the entire workforce redundant. Bud then sets out to manipulate the stock price. Seeing his investment plummeting in value Gekko sells, only to find that his rival, who has been working with Bud, is buying the company. Bud is then arrested for insider trading, but is persuaded that he can expect a lesser sentence if he agrees to meet with Gekko and record his accounts of his illegal trades. The film ends with Bud being driven to court to face charges and his father thanking him for saving the company. Three weeks after the film's release, Boesky was himself given a three-year sentence for insider trading.

Stone made the film as a tribute to his own father, Lou Stone, a stockbroker during the Depression, and he draws on the conventions of family melodrama to anchor the narrative in an exploration of the tensions generated by two father-son relationships, between Bud and his mentor Gekko, and Bud and his father, played by Charlie Sheen's real-life father Martin Sheen. These cross-cutting personal ties are employed to dramatize the contradictions between the material economy and the financial economy, the real and the fictive, and between responsibilities owed to others and the corrosive seductions of rapacious individualism summarized in Gekko's motto, borrowed from Boesky, that "greed is good."

Gekko has much in common with Merdle and Melmotte. All three are charismatic salesmen for the temptations of easy money got at the least cost and all three are totally amoral, with no regard for the lives they may wreck. Dickens, Trollope and Stone all offer morality tales, of a virus that enters the body politic but is eventually expelled and normal relations restored.

Tom Wolfe modeled both the structure and initial serial publication of *Bonfire of the Vanities* on William Makepeace Thackeray's panoramic novel of the London rich in *Vanity Fair*, which appeared in nineteen monthly installments between 1847 and 1848. *Wall Street* too builds on popular representations of speculation developed in the initial phase of modern finance capital detailed earlier, and has in turn provided locations, scenarios, and phrases that have reappeared in later films. Texts offer images, scenarios and dialogue that directors may reference as homages to admired practitioners of their craft or "in" jokes shared with the audiences. In *Boiler Room* (B. Younger, 2000) the financial traders at the center of the narrative are shown watching *Wall Street* together during their bonding sessions, paying homage to Gekko by watching his scenes in absolute silence and repeating his words. These quotations from other movies may also intersect with the associations carried by actors' past performances. Melanie Griffith had already established a fictional reputation for amoral ambition as Sherman McCoy's mistress in *Bonfire of the Vanities* before playing Tess in *Working Girl*.

The iconic figure of Gekko returned in person in *Wall Street II: Money Never Sleeps* released in 2010, shortly after the financial crash. Having served eight years in prison he appears to be a reformed man but is soon revealed as very much his old self when he uses the money in the trust fund he established for his daughter, originally earmarked for an alternative energy firm, to set up a new financial business. He later uses the profits he generates to fund the energy company, apologizes to his daughter and is forgiven. Tapping into funds set aside for a daughter reprises the main plot device in Trollope's *The Way We Live Now*, but unlike Melmotte, who takes his own life, Gekko resumes business as usual.

As Anja Peltzer (2015) has pointed out, this excessively harmonious resolution leaves Gekko free to continue with his speculations while squaring his conscience by channeling some of the profits into ethical ventures. Here again, we see the moral censure that informed early fictions of finance displaced by Hollywood's valorization of humanized characters and positive endings. The result is a thoroughly individualized view of both the sources of financial corruption and the solutions, in which individual redemption eclipses engagement with an underlying structural organization of finance that tolerates rule-bending as the unavoidable price of dynamism and innovation.

Anatomies of crisis: documentary film

The problem is that the crash of 2007–2008 was a systemic failure with far-reaching social consequences that are still reverberating as a result of the austerity programs pursued by governments to address the drain on public finances caused by the huge sums devoted to bailing out failed banks. The consequence has been to transfer the costs of mismanagement from the financial institutions to the public at large, and more particularly to the poorest sections of society, in the form of reduced welfare payments and eroded public facilities.

As Araceli Rodríguez Mateos shows in this collection, documentary films offer the possibility of tracing these connections, but if we look at two best-known productions that have explored the 2008 Crash, Michael Moore's *Capitalism: A Love Story* (2009) and Charles Ferguson's *Inside Job* (2010), we see the same disconnect between operations within the closed world of finance and their consequences for everyday lives. Moore positions himself as a representative of the "ordinary" man and woman deceived and cheated by a corrupt financial oligarchy. The film opens with scenes of laid-off workers struggling to be paid the wages they have earned and people being evicted from their homes for failing to meet the repayments on their loans. The blame is laid firmly at the door of the major financial institutions, and in a typically bravura piece of theater, Moore cordons off part of Wall Street with police crime scene tape and demands that the banks return the public money paid to bail them out. Later, he returns to his home town of Flint, Michigan, devastated by the collapse of traditional manufacturing with no effective replacement, and persuades the local catholic priest to condemn capitalism as "evil" and "contrary to the common good," a statement that summarizes the film's position. Moore offers a powerful moral critique of the social damage done by unregulated finance, but he does not provide an analysis of how this was allowed to happen or how it might be addressed. Locked out of capital's inner sanctums he is reduced to shouting up at bank buildings through a megaphone in the street.

In marked contrast, as its title suggests, Charles Ferguson's *Inside Job* makes extensive use of specialized information and insider accounts to anatomize the multiple failures of perception and prediction that led financial professionals, policy makers and academic economists to collude with, or refuse to recognize, the reckless speculation and outright fraud that prompted the crisis. The result is an entirely convincing account of the causes of the Crash but as the Norwegian cultural critic Jostein Gripsrud points out, the often technical language employed may cause problems for viewers with little or no knowledge of how the financial system operates (Gripsrud 2015). Their symbolic exclusion is compounded by their absence from the text. Their voices are not heard and the impact of the crash and the subsequent austerity measures are left unexplored.

This self-enclosure is reproduced in the growing number of films dealing with the rise of high-speed trading and the reliance on computer algorithms to fix the price points at which assets are automatically offloaded. The move from on-floor to on-screen trading and the increasing reliance on computer modeling has created a new financial elite of numbers experts, nicknamed Quants. Their portrayal on film has tended to be uncritical even celebratory. In Marije Meerman's 2010 documentary, *Quants: The Alchemists of Wall Street*, for example, their possession of advanced mathematical skills is explicitly compared to the arcane knowledge of the medieval alchemists searching for the secret of turning base metals into gold. Algorithms can produce the opposite transformation however, as Meerman's 2011 docudrama, *Money and Speed: Inside the Black Box*, demonstrates by dissecting the flash crash of May 2010 when the New York stock index saw its fastest ever drop, as computer programs triggered mass automatic selling. The ensuring crowd panic and frantic shouting may have migrated from the open exchange floor to the private enclaves of company dealing rooms, but it is a scene Zola would have readily recognized. Except that deals on the exchange floor depended on trust in the judgment and probity of known individuals whereas computerized trading conveniently shifts responsibility to the impersonal logic of machines, a move that studiously ignores the fact that algorithms embody human assumptions.

Restorations: business as usual

Faced with the minimal punishments levied on the major financial institutions for their irresponsible and sometimes criminal actions it is difficult to avoid the conclusions that business very much as usual has been restored and that the ruling ethos that greed is good continues to exercise both powerful attraction and political endorsement, generating steadily widening gaps in income and wealth. In 2015, the Wall Street bonus pool was roughly double the total earnings of all Americans working full time on the federal minimum wage (Woffers 2015). But as the Governor of the Bank of England, Mark Carney, has pointed out "such high income inequalities are dwarfed by the staggering wealth inequalities" with the proportion of wealth held by the richest top 1% of Americans, which includes almost all those working in executive positions in financial services, "increasing from 25% in 1990 to 40% in 2012" (Carney 2016, 5).

In living memory, accumulation by the few has never been so securely tied to the straitened circumstances of the many. As Thomas Picketty's work has demonstrated (Picketty 2014), after a period of increasing equalization between 1930 and 1970, we are returning to relative levels of economic inequality that would be readily recognized by Dickens and Zola. Government support for the financial system has played a central role in creating this situation by reducing welfare spending and holding down wages while releasing more money to banks through quantitative easing and cutting taxes on the wealthy.

The continuing seductions of ruthless individualism and its rewards were explored in Martin Scorsese's 2012 film *The Wolf of Wall Street*, based on the autobiography of Jordan Belfort (played by Leonardo DiCaprio) who supported a lavish life style for years by selling worthless shares to unsuspecting investors, before being arrested in 1998 and convicted in 2004. Scorsese has claimed that the film is intended as satire, but as the critic Alynda Wheat has argued it presents the world entirely through Belfort's eyes, we "hear only his point of view…and see only his perspective. Who cares about the schnooks he's fleecing? We never see them" (Wheat 2013). This divorce of speculation from its social consequences is a recurring feature of recent feature films dealing with finance. We witness the impact of their negligence and criminality on the protagonists and their immediate social circle but the consequences of their deceptions for their victims remained unexplored. Nor is the underlying philosophy condemned. On the contrary, the film's final scene shows Belfort released from prison and addressing a rapt audience eager to learn the techniques of persuasion that will part people from their money.

Since 2005 these techniques have been popularized on a weekly basis on the American network broadcast show, *Mad Money*, hosted by Jim Cramer who dispenses investment advice in an entertainment format that celebrates risk taking as a source of excitement and pleasure. Cramer provides the role model for Lee Gates (played by George Clooney), the egotistical host of a similar show in the 2016 film *Money Monster.* Gates's exuberant performance, which includes a dance in celebration of unfettered financial capitalism against a backdrop of dollars, is interrupted by an angry truck driver, Kyle Bradwell, who has lost his entire savings investing in a stock that Gates had tipped. Holding Gates at gunpoint and forcing him to wear a semtex suicide vest he demands answers and an apology. The studio team, concerned for Gate's safety, hires hackers to trace the missing money and discover the present whereabouts of the CEO. Their probes reveal that the collapse in value was sparked by the company's failed covert plan to manipulate the price of shares in a South African mine they had invested very heavily in. Discovering that the company's CEO is now in a building near the studio, Kyle demands to meet him, parading Gates, who himself now wants answers, through the streets at gunpoint broadcast live on screen. After putting the suicide vest on the CEO, Kyle succeeds in extracting an apology, but is shot by police although he has no intention of harming anyone. The film offers a glimpse into the global circuits linking financial accumulation to social dispossession, but no resolution or restitution. Kyle's desperation and death becomes a momentary media spectacle, while the continuing causes of his misery in the underlying structures of speculation are left untouched.

The secretive city

The concerted attention paid to Wall Street in both feature films and documentaries since the 2008 Crash contrasts markedly with the almost complete invisibility of the City of London, a Square Mile of buildings housing the other major center of global financial capital. The two television dramas made for the BBC by the award winning director, Dominic Savage, are rare exceptions. *Born Equal* (2006) recounts the intertwined stories of a disparate group of characters living in contemporary London. They include the City banker Mark (Colin Firth). Despite having made substantial gains on a financial deal he initially refuses a request for spare change from a homeless man he encounters on his way home but later regrets his callousness, seeks out the man to give him £100, and volunteers as an outreach worker for the homeless. Savage returned to the City in his 2009 drama, *Freefall*. Set in 2007, the mood is altogether darker, presenting the amorality and social destructiveness of modern finance as deeply embedded in institutionalized practices and self-perceptions that preclude any possibility of individual changes of heart or redemption.

Savage began work on this later project in 2008 with a growing sense that a major crisis was gathering momentum. As he later recounted:

> I think those in the know saw it coming [but] Freefall felt slightly ahead of the game when I was writing it. Things hadn't started happening at that point, but later in the year came the full-on collapses such as Leeman Brothers.
>
> *(Gilbey 2009)*

Freefall explores the crisis and its social impacts through the stories of two contrasted financial services workers. City banker Gus (played by Aidan Gillen) deals in corporate mortgages and displays an all-consuming obsession with making money that has opened deep emotional rifts with his daughter and partner. His counterpart Dave (played by Dominic Cooper) works for a firm on the northern fringe of London, selling mortgages to people denied credit, including his old school friend, Jim, knowing they will not be able to meet the repayments. Increasingly stressed by his escalating debt, Jim is sacked for falling asleep at work and has his new house repossessed. Gus loses his position in the financial crisis, and finding himself isolated and alone, takes his life. Only Dave survives unscathed, moving on to apply his sales skills elsewhere. *Freefall* is a contemporary melodrama that employs the familiar Victorian devices of family ties and friendships sacrificed for unbridled accumulation and the suicide of a protagonist for whom money has become the measure of all worth.

In the course of conducting background research for *Freefall* Savage interviewed a number of bankers and brokers who recounted incidents and opinions that found their way into the script, but as he notes, his characters were "a composite of the people I met," not identifiable individuals (Gilbey 2009). Securing permission to film interviews with named people or portray the City at work in key locations is altogether more difficult.

Visually, the City dominates the contemporary London skyline with a series of high-rise office complexes towering over St Paul's Cathedral and the area's other traditional landmarks. Constructed in the wake of financial deregulation, they mimic Manhattan asserting the preeminent economic role of financial services. This appearance of plate glass modernity, however, rests on an ancient and entrenched foundation with rights dating back to the Norman Conquest. As its website notes, the financial district's governing body, the City of London Corporation, has "a special role and wide remit that goes beyond that of an ordinary local authority" (City of London 2016). Like the Vatican, it is in effect a city state within a state, enjoying unique privileges. These allow the financial institutions based in the City to vote in elections for officers alongside residents, and grants the ancient post of the Remembrancer privileged access to drafts of parliamentary legislation and the provision of comment and advice. These channels of influence allied to the substantial annual expenditure on lobbying and public relations ensure that any documentary filmmaker wishing to address the City's activities in situ can only do so on terms set by the London Corporation. This results in productions that are constructed around insider accounts. The only voices in the two-part documentary, *The City of London – Money and Power* produced for the BBC World News in 2011, for example, come from individuals working in the Square Mile or making their living from commenting on it. They admit mistakes but are adamant that the City must continue to be left alone to regulate itself.

One notable exception to this closure is Michael Chanan's 2012 "outsider" documentary *Secret City*, which combines archive footage with contributions from radical academics and interviews with activists in the Occupy Movement. Made on a shoestring budget of less than £11,000 it is an unashamedly campaigning intervention. As Chanan notes, he set out to launch a critical "investigation into the history and constitution of the City of London" with the aim of contributing to "the process of reform or abolition of Corporation and a taming of financial capitalism" (*Secret City* 2016). Despite winning a major film festival prize it has never been shown in mainstream cinemas or on a major television channel. It circulates on DVD subtitled in major European languages and is available on YouTube (in a version with Spanish subtitles), but its absence from the major arenas of public culture points to the relative lack of general access to a diversity of popular representation of finance.

Conclusion

This instance, and the general analysis offered here raises questions about both the limits of dominant audio-visual cultural forms and the present political economy of public communications. Recent films of finance tend to uncouple the operations of financial institutions from both the overall context in which they operate and the full range of their social consequences. One way to address these disconnections is to adopt the approach of Austrian filmmaker, Erwin Wagenhofer, in his 2008 documentary *Let's Make Money*, and move from a focus on fixed locations to tracking the investments that ordinary people hold through their savings and pension funds as they move across the circuits of global capitalism, from the mines and oilfields of Africa to the sweatshops and construction sites of Asia, exploring the ways value is created, transformed, and appropriated. Another option is to build on Zola's example, and explore the interactions of conditions, causes and consequences through the interlinked lives of a continuing cast of characters as they move across a series of social milieux, from the privileged enclaves of the rich and powerful to neighborhoods of poverty and dispossession.

The current political economy of distribution, however, militates against making the full diversity of possibilities readily available. Cinema ownership is becoming increasingly concentrated and is heavily skewed towards films that are likely to generate maximum returns to the exclusion of more challenging material. Online streaming, typified by Netflix, excludes those unable to afford the subscription fees and encourages patterns of viewing that are both segmented and non-cumulative. Access to commercially driven internet sites is increasingly designed around users' existing tastes and preference locking them into self-defining enclaves where they only encounter views and forms of expression they have already endorsed. These "filter bubbles" allow no room for the unfamiliar or challenging (Pariser 2011).

This suggests that public broadcasting, free at the point of use and removed from promoting financial products, has a central role to play as the core cultural space where productions tackling questions around finance in a variety of forms and styles can be organized into streams or seasons and linked to a web presence that provides access to further sources of information and interpretation, encourages audience contributions, and supports platforms for debating ways of reorganizing the financial system. The BBC has sketched a variant of this project in its recent manifesto for change, *British, Bold and Creative.* This imagines an online platform that would bring together contributions from multiple sources, offer access to a wide range of relevant representations and analyses, host users' creative contributions, and encourage participation in debates around core issues and possible alternatives (BBC 2015:70). The authors concede that this proposal is still currently on the drawing board, but the argument I have advanced here suggests that thinking seriously about ways to create a cultural commons for the digital age may go some way to addressing the enduring silences, gaps, and partial viewpoints that continue to characterize the most widely circulated fictional and documentary films on finance.

References

Barrett, Edwin B. 1970. "*Little Dorrit* and the Disease of Modern Life." *Nineteenth Century Fiction*, Vol. 25, No. 2, 199–215.

BBC, 2015. *British, Bold, Creative: The BBC Programmes and Services in the Next Charter.* BBC: London. September.

Carney, Mark 2016. *The Spectre of Monetarism.* www.bankofengland,co.uk/publications/Documents.speeches/2016/speech946.pdf

City of London Corporation. 2016. www://cityoflondon.gov.uk/about-the-city/about-us/Pages/default.aspx

De Palma, Brian. 2006. "Interview." *Empire Magazine*, No. 93, 94.

Ebert, Roger. 1990. Review of Bonfire of the Vanities. http://rogerebert.com/reviews/the-bonfire-of-the-vanities-1990

Gilbey, Ryan. 2009. "Television Industry Saturday Interview: Everyone is a Party to what Happened." *The Guardian*, July 18. www.theguardian.com/media/2009/jul/18/dominic-savage-freefall-banking

Gripsrud, Jostein. 2015. "Covering the Crisis: Politics and Culture." In *Money Talks: Media, Markets, Crisis*, edited by Graham Murdock and Jostein Gripsrud. 131–148. Bristol: Intellect Books.

IMDb. 2017. "A Corner in Wheat: Plot Summary." www.imdb.com/title/tt0000832/plotsummary?ref_=tt_ov_pl [accessed February 1, 2017]

Itzkowitz, David C. 2002. "Fair Enterprise and Extravagant Speculation: Investment, Speculation, and Gambling in Victorian England." *Victorian Studies*, Vol. 45, No. 1, 121–147.

Martin, Ian. 2016. *Crash, Bang, Wallop: The Inside Story of London's Big Bang and a Financial Revolution that Changed the World*. London: Sceptre.

Marx, Karl. 1974. *Capital: Volume Three*. London: Lawrence and Wishart.

Nelson, Brian. 2004. "Introduction to Emile Zola *The Kill*." vii–xxix. *Oxford World's Classics*. Oxford: Oxford University Press.

Newhall, Beaumont. 1964. *The History of Photography*. New York: The Museum of Modern Art.

Norris, Frank. 1994 [1903]. *The Pit: A Story of Chicago*. New York: Penguin.

Pariser, Eli. 2011. *The Filter Bubble: What the Internet is Hiding from You*. London: Penguin Books.

Peltzer, Anja. 2015. "No Guns, No Rules, Just Pure Capitalism: Hollywood's Portrayals of Wall Street." In *Money Talks: Media, Markets, Crisis*, edited by Graham Murdock and Jostein Gripsrud. 151–168. Bristol: Intellect Books.

Picketty, Thomas. 2014. *Capital in the Twenty-First Century*. Boston, Mass: Belknap Press.

Poovey, Mary. 2002. "Writing about Fiction in Victorian England: Disclosure and Secrecy in the Culture of Investment." *Victorian Studies*, Vol. 45, No. 1, 17–41.

Raworth, Kate. 2017. *Doughnut Economics: Seven Ways to Think Like a 21st-Century Economist*. London: Random House Business Books.

Reagan, Michael and Denny, Jim. 1997. "The City on a Hill: Fulfilling Reagan's Vision for America." www.nytimes.com/books/first/r/reagan-city.html

Salamon, Julie. 1991. *The Devil's Candy: The Bonfire of the Vanities Goes to Hollywood*. New York: Random House.

Stiglitz, Joseph E. 2008. "Capitalist Fools." *Vanity Fair*, December 9. www.vanityfair.com/news/2009/01/stiglitz200901-2

Trollope, Anthony. 2013 [1883]. *An Autobiography*. www.gutenberg.org/files/5978/5978-h/5978-h.htm

Wasko, Janet. 1982. *Movies and Money: Financing the American Film Industry*. Norwood, New Jersey: Ablex Publishing House.

Wheat, Alynda. 2013. "See This/Skip That: From *Wolf of Wall Street* to *Walter Mitty*." *People*, September 27. www.people.com/pepole/article/o,,20769902,00.html

Woffers, Justin. 2015. "All You Need to Know About Income Inequality, in One Comparison." *The New York Times*, March 13.

Zola, Emile. 2014 [1891]. *Money*. Translated by Valerie Minogue. Oxford World's Classics. Oxford: Oxford University Press.

Zola, Emile. 2009 [1873]. *The Belly of Paris*. Translated by Mark Kurlansky. New York: Random House. Modern Library Edition.

Zola, Emile. 2004 [1872]. *The Kill*. Translated by Brian Nelson. Oxford World's Classics. Oxford: Oxford University Press.

2

FORMS OF TIME AND THE CHRONOTOPE IN THE WALL STREET FILM

Robert Burgoyne

The challenge of representing global finance in the dramatic fiction film can be seen as a case study in the difficulty of what Fredric Jameson calls cognitive mapping, which I understand, in this context, as a way of imagining the connections between our individual lives and the liquid forces of capital that shape the fates of peoples and nations today. Although certain films such as *Wall Street* (O. Stone, 1987), *Wall Street: Money Never Sleeps* (O. Stone, 2010), and *Margin Call* (J. C. Chandor, 2011) offer a catalogue of familiar scenes – the ubiquitous horizontal scroll of the stock ticker, the sotto voce communication of the insider deal, the rapid fire dialogue freighted with opaque vocabulary that Franco Moretti and Dominique Pestre have labeled "bankspeak" – the deeper symbolic structures of what I will call "the Wall Street film" have been largely unexplored (Moretti and Pestre 2015). With themes of greed, corruption, and outsized ego dominating the foreground of these works, the deeper critical questions that these films solicit have not yet been considered.

To begin, I would like to offer a rough but hopefully revealing comparison. In his well-known book, *Imagined Communities*, Benedict Anderson framed the question of community and nation in terms of an imaginary connectedness – the illusion that the lives of the people were moving in unison along parallel pathways, linked by a sense of simultaneity – a reassuring impression of a population moving together into history. This sense of parallelism and simultaneity was expressed in the realist novel and the newspaper, both of which brought a welter of different experiences and different spaces together in a single frame, placing the nation, in its moment-by-moment unfolding, into a comprehensible order and system (Anderson 2006).

In the early twentieth century, the sense of social parallelism, of a population moving together in homogeneous time, metamorphosed into another kind of community of feeling. Although it seems hard to believe today, at the turn of the century the invention of the "stock ticker" was celebrated as a symbol of inclusiveness, of democracy and transparency, a device that allowed every American to "follow the market" (Staheli 2013, 210). Perceived as a medium that gave everyone access to the financial world, the stock ticker allowed anyone to become a speculator. The instantaneous dissemination of stock prices and market movements to the public at large broke the hold of the closed-door trading houses on speculative commerce. As Staheli describes it: "the [stock] ticker made possible a mode of inclusion that produced an overarching sentiment…the ticker was crucial to the promise of universal inclusion into the stock market, and it became a medium creating transparency… the entire country became an audience of critics who could follow every transaction without delay" (Staheli 2013, 210–211).

In the contemporary period the stock ticker and the market trend line have acquired a very different connotation. Although these icons of financial practice have become ubiquitous features of modern life – with market reports disseminated on an hourly basis and real-time updates placed at our fingertips on the screens of our smartphones – the transparency once promised by the medium of the stock ticker has been replaced by an anxious chiaroscuro. Rather than immediacy and inclusion, the market is now frequently identified in films and other popular media as impossibly intricate and obscure, involving levels of complexity that are essentially beyond the power and control of human agency. The discourse of democratization, of universally and instantaneously accessible information, is now cross-hatched with the mystifying discourses of "bankspeak." Where Staheli describes the social imaginary of early twentieth-century markets as a zone where individuals could "develop and pursue their interests," where "risk taking was considered to be intrinsic to a democratic economy," the contemporary period has brought with it a new symbolic construction, with the discourse of global finance now overlaid by themes of seduction, elusiveness, and threat (Staheli 2013, 4).

In Staheli's perceptive analysis of the cultural imaginary that formed around American markets in the first decades of the twentieth century, the emotion associated with the stock ticker itself, as a machine and as a medium, was paramount. The machinery of the ticker commanded the imagination, crystallizing a sense of communicativeness and collectivity in its physical, phenomenological operation, a sensation that extended to the sonic register: "The rising and falling sounds of the ticker – sounds with their own beat and volume – acted as indicators of the current situation of the market." The rhythm of the ticker not only linked individuals to the market but also gave rise to an impression of collectivity experienced as immediate. "Each vibration of the ticker corresponds to an identical vibration in the hearts of millions of individuals who are united across space in the same wish or in the same disillusionment" (Staheli 2013, 230).

What I would like to emphasize here is the way a new media form – the stock ticker – provided a framework for a novel remapping of space and time, in which transparency, simultaneity, and speed, oriented to the pace of the market, defined an imaginary collective experience in a certain period of American life. Staheli observes that "the ticker transformed a spatial order founded on representation into a temporally organized order founded on simultaneity. Speculative communication no longer required spatial presence. This implied a crucial shift from space to time" (Staheli 2013, 207).

The invention of the new technology of the ticker, in Staheli's formulation, both liquidated an earlier tradition of closed room, proxemic communication, and created a new set of potentials organized around collectivity and simultaneity.

In several ways, Staheli's description summons ideas first set forth by Mikhail Bakhtin in his discussion of the chronotope, which he describes as the particular figurations of space and time that shape artistic genres, and that provide the ground on which plot events and character interactions unfold. Although Bakhtin's model is specifically directed to the artistic genre of the novel, I feel Staheli's interpretation of the shifts in spatial and temporal perception in the early twentieth century – the emergence of a new social imaginary grounded in changed experiences of space and time – suggests a useful way of approaching the Wall Street film. In contemporary finance films, the depiction of the markets is dominated by an almost tactile sense of space and time. The second-by-second movements of the market, the fraught anticipation that attends a trade, the adrenalized countdown to the market's opening and closing bells dominate the narrative flow, charging the space of the trading room floor with visible energy. In the Wall Street film a unique sense of time and space permeates the social world, imposing a specific rhythm and style of social interaction, and providing a framework in which parallelism, simultaneity, and speed create the conditions for the dramatic events of the market plot to occur.

The particular forms of time and space that govern the Wall Street film may be understood as a contemporary variant of the chronotope. As Gary Saul Morson and Caryl Emerson write in their comprehensive study, "Bakhtin's crucial point is that time and space vary in qualities; different social activities and representations of these activities presume different kinds of time and space" (Morson and Emerson 1990, 167). And as Bakhtin says, "the chronotope is the place where the knots of narrative are tied and untied. It can be said without qualification that to them [chronotopes] belongs the meaning that shapes narrative" (Bakhtin 1982, 250).

The two films that will serve as my principal examples, Oliver Stone's *Wall Street* and Martin Scorsese's *The Wolf of Wall Street* (2013), offer templates for chronotopic analysis, illuminating the way the narrative world of the Wall Street film is built from specific spatial and temporal patterns. In *Wall Street*, for example, the synchrony that Staheli discovers provides the main switchpoints of the plot, shaping the events of the narrative and organizing the resolution, which turns on a cascading series of trades. Here, parallelism and simultaneity are materialized and made concrete. *The Wolf of Wall Street*, by contrast, develops a very different set of chronotopic potentials, upending the conventions of space and time set forth in the earlier film, and redefining the range of what may happen and what types of characters may act in this world.

I am using the term "Wall Street film" as a kind of shorthand to indicate works that center on the dramatic representation of the market culture of New York City, a location that has gained an iconic status in popular culture as the epicenter of finance. In the ending credit sequence of *Wall Street: Money Never Sleeps*, for example, the Manhattan skyline is embellished with a moving market trend line connecting the most prominent buildings, giving graphic expression to the image of New York City as a place where fortunes are made and lost, where risk and reward are present in equal measure, and where the splendor of the speculative market is equated with the grand architectural profile of the metropolis. My use of the phrase, "the Wall Street film," is thus intended to signal the popular identification of Wall Street – and New York City – as the symbolic locus of global finance.

Although electronic trading has largely detached capital exchange from any specific location, the iconographic status of Wall Street as the site of capitalism's most intensive manifestation has, if anything, been magnified in the contemporary period. The anti-capitalist movement Occupy Wall Street, for example, which originated in New York City, quickly proliferated across the globe, as sites of protest sprang up in financial capitals around the world, merging vernacular expressions of discontent with what has become a universal signifier of capitalist domination.

The difficulty of modeling the abstract networks of global finance and speculative risk – as Oliver Stone has said, "I don't know how you show a credit default swap onscreen" – provides the rationale and the starting point for my analysis. Rather than attempting to represent the invisible domain of capital flows and retreats, the films I consider here explore the temporal and spatial framework that provides the essential ground for narratives of Wall Street, the topology around which a cultural imaginary has now coalesced.

As one writer says, the central aspects of the Global Financial Crisis of 2008 "appear to defy audio-visual representation" – a statement that I feel applies to films of finance generally (Meissner 2012, 98). Despite the large number of films, documentaries, television programs, and hypermedia websites that have attempted to frame and represent the events of the crash, the symbolic and pictorial languages available to explain the interrelated failures of global capital are few: "The first results when typing the words 'financial crisis' into Google…are pictures of falling market index curves. Arrows and zigzag lines dominate the immediate visual imagery of financial crises. Simplistically, financial crises are portrayed in the way they appear to business insiders – as indexes" (Meissner 2012, 113). Rather than attempting to portray the workings of capital markets, the visual vocabulary of financial crisis has instead drifted to metonymy – to the portrayal of the geographic location where the crisis was, imaginatively, centered. As Meissner writes, films of the 2008 crash give an exorbitant amount of attention to the New York City landscape, as if to locate a symbolic correlative in the glass, steel, and concrete architecture of the city. In films of the crisis, the New York skyline is featured nearly as often as computer screens and virtual ribbon tickers that dominate the interior scenes of the trading floor.

Meissner's juxtaposition of the architecture of the city and the abstractions of the financial markets suggest a specifically cinematic approach to the genre that I wish to explore more deeply here. My method of analysis, derived from Bakhtin's attempt to define the governing poetic structures of space and time in various genres of the novel, is intended to provide a preliminary sketch of a film form in which temporal and spatial relations take on vivid materiality, even as the objective of the game, the immaterial medium of capital itself, remains invisible. As Bakhtin describes it, "In the literary, artistic chronotope, spatial and temporal indicators are spelled out and given concrete expression. Time, as it were, thickens, takes on flesh, becomes artistically visible; likewise space becomes charged and responsive to the movements of time, plot and history. This intersection of axes and fusion of indicators characterizes the artistic chronotope" (Bakhtin 1982, 84).

For Bakhtin, different genres of the novel are organized according to different chronotopic schemes. For example, the "novel of historical emergence" was designed around the chronotope of the road, a structure that condenses aspects of space and time. Here, the emergence of the protagonist from youth to maturity over the course of the novel is folded into the depiction of the changing historical world. In this type of novel, the protagonist is shaped by his adventures on the road; as the protagonist emerges, a new historical order evolves along with him.

Bakhtin discovered several other major chronotopes in different genres as well, including the chronotope of the Medieval market square, in which the space of ordinary daily life, a space of free and familiar contact, gives way in certain moments to the carnivalesque. Ordinarily a place dedicated to commerce and the pursuit of profits, the town square erupts during designated periods of carnival, when heteroglossia rules, hierarchies are overturned, and the disruptive energy of laughter prevails. Importantly, the carnivalesque overflows the boundaries of the town square, permeating the home and the whole of society. The events that occur in the village square expose a dual historical world, in which the somber, religiously ordered medieval sense of time and space are overturned in favor of laughter, inversion, and spontaneity.

In the Wall Street film, I argue, traces of both these types of chronotope can be discerned, articulated in a way that recalls past usages and provides resources for the present. In *Wall Street* we can readily find traces of the novel of emergence, which Bakhtin considered to be a form of Bildungsroman. The young protagonist of the film, Bud, played by Charlie Sheen, finds the path of his own personal narrative of emergence only after taking several near disastrous detours, misdirected by the charismatic Gordon Gekko (Michael Douglas). As the young hero gains power and influence, he ultimately discovers Gekko's devious designs on his father's company, Bluestar Airlines, and experiences a critical turning point. As Bakhtin writes about this type, the entire plot is now reinterpreted and reconstructed. Pirouetting from what appeared to be a Faustian tale dominated by the credo "Greed is good!" Oliver Stone's *Wall Street* becomes instead a story of filial redemption, the return of the prodigal son – a point that is reinforced in the closing credits when David Byrne sings the main verse of the song, "Home. It's where I want to be, but I think I'm already there."

Bakhtin described this type of plot as a "punctuated equilibrium," where emergence is highlighted by heightened moments of recognition and change (1982, 386). In *Wall Street*, Bud experiences three such turning points – his seduction by Gekko, his moment of revelation as he discovers Gekko's destructive intentions, and his orchestrated actions to repair the harm – a pattern of guilt, recognition, and redemption. With its highly marked turning points – its dramatic moments of "punctuated equilibrium" – the overall structure of the plot is shaped by a linear temporality consonant with the linear structure of the market trading day.

In *The Wolf of Wall Street*, by contrast, a very different chronotope can be sensed. The personal emergence of the protagonist is reduced to a few perfunctory gestures at the very beginning. Instead, we view – at length – the release of the exorbitant energies of carnival. Here, the grotesque – the throwing of dwarves at targets, the ribald and erotic, and the overturning of all hierarchies of status and behavior is celebrated, exaggerated, and raised to the level almost of a formal system. The trading desk floor in *The Wolf of Wall Street* becomes an emblematic site of Rabelaisian disorder, an exemplary carnival square, with marching bands, spectacles of every sort, a space where no one says no. The somber world of daily life in this film gives way to a carnal utopia where appetite rules. As Bakhtin has it, "Carnival misalliances – a free and familiar attitude spreads over everything…Carnival brings together, unifies, weds, and combines the sacred with the profane, the lofty with the low, the great with the insignificant, the wise and the stupid" (Bakhtin 1984a, 123).

Wall Street

In *Wall Street*, the image of time and space in the world of high finance is strikingly concrete, an almost perfect realization of Bakhtin's formula for the chronotope, where time is understood in its interconnection with space, and where space is understood as "saturated" with time (Morson and Emerson 1990, 374). Perhaps the most distinctive characteristic of the film is its temporal organization. The governing trope of the film is the trading day – the seven and a half hours between 9:30 am when the market opens and its 4:00 pm close. A great deal of narrative expectation, anxiety, and euphoria is built into this structure, which compresses extremes of dramatic intensity into a fixed and unalterable unit of time. Here, the opening bell of the trading day is greeted like the start of a race, as traders are hurled into a frenzy of activity. Speed is the governing principle – speed of talk, speed of movement, and speed of intellectual process – as frenetic speech and gesture convey an energy expenditure that is perhaps analogous to a World Cup final, or better, a high-scoring game of pinball. Moreover, in this chronotope, as the closing bell approaches, the imminence of the finale brings even greater pressure to bear, as deals that seemed tantalizingly near closing somehow resist being consummated. The heightened drama associated with the end of the trading day is met with an ovation once the markets have closed, or a pronounced diminuendo.

As in the novel of historical emergence, the protagonist, Bud, is instructed, challenged, and shaped by the pressurized environment of the market, with its deadlines, social competition, and its atmosphere of adventure. A young climber, the character attempts to define himself as the agent of his own history, as Bakhtin says, "maintaining his initiative," pulling away from the fixed compass point of his father – the much-loved head of an airline union – to embrace the tutelage and the corporate

FIGURE 2.1 Bud. Still from *Wall Street*, 1987.

raider style of a competing father figure, Gordon Gekko. Increasingly involving himself in illegal schemes and the trading of insider information, Bud soon learns to manipulate stock prices, and moves to the top of the trading desk hierarchy, a move lubricated by the large stock purchases and the instructions in slippery forms of practice given him by Gekko. The protagonist, nonetheless, retains a kernel of integrity despite the shadiness he exhibits around the edges, holding back from the most reprehensible acts that Gekko is involved in – the buying of distressed but functional companies in order to strip them of their assets, break them up, and sell the pieces. When Bud realizes he has led his father's company, Bluestar Airlines, into a trap, and that Gekko has used him to set the scene for a corporate raid that will disassemble the airline, he directs his talent and energy to working his way back to the high road. Utilizing the full resources of his trading firm, and initiating an ingenious scheme to manipulate the rise and fall of Bluestar stock, Bud finds a way to preserve the survival of the airline, while simultaneously double dealing Gordon Gekko, who in a few hours loses millions. Moreover, Bud's machinations also, somehow, put Gekko in the frame of a Federal investigation.

In *Wall Street*, the diurnal unit of the trading day defines the major symbolic dimensions of the text, marking the positive space so that the negative, shadow space can unfold. Juxtaposed to the frenzied dealing of the day, the film details a nightworld of secret negotiation and insider dealing, conversations cloaked in shadow, conceived and carried out in the nocturnal zones of cocktail bars, private jets, and luxury compounds. Under the influence of Gekko, Bud becomes an increasingly nocturnal creature, isolated, masked: a Fantomas figure rifling through the files of target companies at night. When he moves into a penthouse apartment decorated in a neo-expressionist style, he spends most of his time sitting in darkness, peering into computers, and ignoring his expensive girlfriend.

FIGURE 2.2 Gekko. Still from *Wall Street*, 1987.

Bud's return to the diurnal cycle of the trading day occurs when he turns the tables on Gekko. The character drives a frenzied series of stock purchases of Bluestar, functioning full throttle on the trading desk floor, with his work colleagues fully and enthusiastically involved – a scene that dramatizes a sense of collective excitement and emotion that we associate with a densely populated market square. The space of the trading desk floor is here saturated with time, and time is fully connected to space. With its emphasis on simultaneous, collective activity, in which everyone is within earshot of each other or connected by landline, the scene of the "turning of the tables" is staged as a return to the communal space of democratic inclusion, a diurnal world of open architectural spaces, in which every decision Bud makes is confirmed by a frenzied crowd on the trading floor, an audience connected in simultaneous rapport with the up and down movements of Bluestar stock, registered in the rhythms of the stock ticker.

Wall Street reorients the chronotope of emergence to a specific period sense of history, registering the social style of a mid-1980s subculture – the gestures, costumes, language, speed, and exuberance that dominates the film. It provides a picture of a world, a given locality, a terrestrial space – a world where face-to-face communication, voice commands over landline telephones, and the stealing of company secrets from hard copy file cabinets are the currency of the day. The film's portrayal of a world of capital that may still be seized by human initiative, a world that remains subject to individual human agency, brings a human scale to its picture of global finance, a perspective that we recognize as sentimental today. Rather than analysis, Stone's *Wall Street* offers a purely symbolic, narrative solution to what we now understand as the unmappable atopia of the capitalist global system.

Nevertheless, genres are characterized by their potentials, a word Bakhtin employs throughout his writings. Here, a certain proleptic foreshadowing of the world to come seeps through the frame lines of the narrative, as the hero achieves his emergence not by renouncing the market, but by a vast scheme of market manipulation. He saves his father's company by practicing his skill in the dark arts of market influence. A new economic order can be glimpsed in outline, along with the emergence of the protagonist, a world where the moral universe of Stone's tale is replaced by a very different set of themes. As a recent book on Stone's films has it, "In 1987 a clear moral high ground was outlined by Bud Fox when he challenged Gekko by asking him, 'How much is enough?' Gekko, of course, stepped around the question by alluding to it all as a 'game.' However, the audience was left in no doubt about the force of Fox's question...by 2010, as Gekko explains...*everyone* saw it as a game. Bud Fox's question was no longer relevant" (Scott and Thompson 2017, 136).

The film thus seems to be poised between two historical epochs, straddling the line that divides the concrete, human economies of the past from the invisible, ungraspable economies of present and future. The pressure the film places on the older genre of the hero's emergence, a pressure made visible in the ironic portrayal of Bud and the world he inhabits, seems now to signal not simply the final curtain of an older genre form, one predicated on virtuous becoming, but something altogether different. The imminent emergence of the global capital era to come, where the concrete space-time chronotope of the trading floor can be overturned at a stroke by profits made in the virtual realm of overseas markets, is in fact forecast in a scene in the middle of the film. As Gekko says to Bud over an old-fashioned satellite phone, while walking on the beach at dawn, "I've just made $800,000 in Hong Kong gold. This is your wake-up call, Bud. Money never sleeps!"

The Wolf of Wall Street

A different world is depicted in *The Wolf of Wall Street*, a realm dedicated not to accumulation, but to expenditure. As in Stone's *Wall Street*, a specific spatial and temporal structure provides the ground for the narrative. In contrast to the earlier film, however, the space and time of the narrative is not governed by the clock time of the market; indeed, time in *The Wolf of Wall Street* seems to subside as a chronotopic marker: instead, the narrative unfolds in the perpetual in between time of the entr'acte. As Bakhtin says about the space and time of carnival, it gives the right "to live a life in the chronotope of theatrical space, the right to act life as a comedy and to treat others as actors, the right to rip off masks...and finally, the right to betray to the public a personal life, down to its most private and prurient little secrets." (Bakhtin 1982,163). In *The Wolf of Wall Street*, the setting of the trading room floor, a space ordinarily dedicated to rampant ambition where competition rules, becomes a space where permission is granted, where excess and disorder reign, and where appetite and the grotesque are encouraged. In the chronotope of carnival, laughter rules.

François Hollande, the premier of France, recently characterized the contemporary world of global markets as "an adversary who has neither a name, nor face, nor party" (Meissner 2012, 113). The carnival chronotope of *The Wolf of Wall Street*, by contrast, gives both a face and a body to the depiction of global finance (a role that Gordon Gekko assumed in the earlier film). The key topoi for the carnivalesque – collectivity, the grotesque body, free and familiar contact, and the bodily lower stratum – are given the fullest possible expression in *The Wolf of Wall Street*. Crucially, excess is depicted here not as an aberration, nor as an import from a wholly different genre, but rather as a potential that is latent in the Wall Street subgenre, a kind of hidden surplus. Indeed, elements of the carnivalesque regularly blossom into view as well in Oliver Stone's *Wall Street* – a film that tries, and does not quite succeed, to constrain its carnivalesque impulses. In the grotesque gestures and distorted facial expressions of the trading floor, in the adrenalized frenzy of the traders given a hot tip, in the scrum of the market, carnival appetite returns in a distorted form.

Like the carnival of the medieval period, the atmosphere at Jordan Belfort's firm can be seen as a subversion and an unmasking – the faceless apparatus and obscure mechanisms of financial power are transformed into a theater of appetite, where the "lower bodily stratum" is celebrated. Here, the indexes and market trend lines that dominate the foreground of so many Wall Street films have no place. In contrast to the majority of these films, the stock ticker and the visual device of the market trend line are all but invisible in the universe of the film. Instead, Wall Street is here conceived as a space of inclusion and carnal excess, a place – and a time – in which the forces that cannot be contained are released and amplified.

In *The Wolf of Wall Street*, echoes of Rabelaisian laughter resound throughout the text. The attempts to control or contain the disorder become simply an occasion for more laughter. One of the lead characters, Donnie (Jonah Hill), exemplifies this rule of disorder. Served with multiple subpoenas, he puts the legal papers in a wastebasket, stands on his desk, and urinates, flamboyantly, on the orders of law, as the office staff and his colleagues goad him on and cheer.

The huge trading floor of the firm that Jordan Belfort (Leonardo DiCaprio) founds, Stratton Oakmont, is the spatial locus for the most exuberant expressions of grotesquery. For Jordan Belfort as lead character, however, the space of carnival extends beyond the office setting. Like the medieval carnival, in which the festivities in the town square overflowed into adjacent streets and alleys, into nearby squares, and throughout the whole of the town, *The Wolf of Wall Street* spreads the spirit of carnival well beyond the office floor. Although Stratton Oakmont serves as the core spatial zone of this alternative universe, the grotesque and the licentious pervade the whole of Belfort's world, with carnival erupting everywhere he goes, on his yacht, in his home, during his airline flights, and even while driving in his car.

In terms of temporal structure, carnival takes place over a strictly designated period of time; it has a limited and defined duration. But during carnival, it is all encompassing, involving the entire population. The collectivity and sense of inclusion that Staheli saw in a world renewed by the stock ticker comes back into view, in a different way. As Bakhtin describes it, "A carnival sense of the world does not know footlights…carnival is not a spectacle seen by the people, they live in it. While carnival lasts, there is no life outside it" (Bakhtin, 1984b, 7). Similarly, in the world of Stratton Oakmont, hundreds of well-dressed – and undressed – traders live the

FIGURE 2.3 Dwarf on target. Still from *The Wolf of Wall Street*, 2013.

carnival, as the film pictures it, with work converted to an ecstatic experience of living, with traders literally jumping for joy when a sale is consummated, wrestling each other to the ground, and having sexual encounters in bathrooms, boardrooms, and elevators. In Jordan Belfort's world, there is no such thing as alienated labor (Parvulescu 2016).

The genre memory of carnival, in fact, pervades many films, especially parodic films that unfold outside a realist aesthetic or an aesthetic of verisimilitude. Robert Stam has written extensively on the carnivalesque as a governing trope for Brazilian Cinema Novo, where films such as *Macunaíma* (J. P. Andrade, 1969), *How Tasty was My Little Frenchman* (N. P. dos Santos, 1971), and others employ an explicitly carnival logic, dominated by comic themes of cannibalism. The aesthetic tone of carnival also permeates films such as Luis Bunuel's *L'Age D'Or* (1930) and *Un chien andalou* (1929), the Monty Python series, the films of Mel Brooks, and in the current period, *Zoolander* (a carnival masterwork) (B. Stiller, 2001). As Stam writes, these types of films should not be seen as "the mere negation of the dominant tradition but rather as the perpetuators of another tradition…renovators of a perennial mode whose protean vitality…derives from…an ultimately irrepressible generic tradition" (1992, 10).

What sets *The Wolf of Wall Street* apart from the openly parodic films that Stam celebrates, however, is its naturalistic frame. The events recounted in Jordan Belfort's two memoires and re-enacted in the film are rendered in a diegetic world that is conventionally verisimilar, a recognizably "real world" that can nonetheless accommodate orgies on the trading floor, dwarves thrown at targets, and scenes of hundreds of finance professionals beating their chests in unison and chanting some kind of invented South Sea incantation of appetite and joy. The naturalism of the film creates a challenge for critical engagement and critique. The positions available in works of parody and satire, what Linda Hutcheon, in a related context, has called complicitous critique, are simply not given within the naturalistic frame of the text. Instead, the excess, sexual explicitness, and sheer vulgarity of the film unfolds in a more difficult aesthetic language – what I tentatively will call burlesque or mockery.

According to Bakhtin, Rabelais used obscenity, grotesquery, and appetite as verbal weapons against an ascetic, life-denying medieval world, where man's time on earth was conceived as a time of penance, a gloomy affair. Hence the importance of the medieval square as a site of carnival. Typically dominated by a church, the medieval square would periodically give birth to an alternative world of openness and license. The film's excess might similarly be read as a stand against the ostensibly serious, unjoyful, and closed world of the financial industry circa 1989 – or at least the way it tried to portray itself – confronting the sober, tidy universe of banking with a form of exuberant mockery, reversing its typical values. In the process, as the film illustrates, Stratton Oakmont would attract hundreds of young brokers to the firm, crushing into the office foyer trying to get Belfort's attention in the hopes that they will be hired. And, in contrast to the earlier discussion by Meissner about the shots of the cityscape providing a counterbalance to the elusive abstractions of capital, beauty shots of New York City are almost entirely missing from the film, as if there is no outside to the world Belfort creates.

Carnival, in Robert Stam's understanding of Bakhtin, was the people's true language, in which the poor, the peasant, the tradesman, and the aristocrat comingled. As Stam writes, the images created by Rabelais "have an undestroyable, non-official nature; no dogma, no authoritarianism, no narrow-minded seriousness can co-exist with [them]" (Stam 1992, 86). And as Bakhtin describes it, "the slinging in dung and the drenching in urine" represent "the gay funeral of this old world...The primary reflex of the carnival body, when it is not defecating or ingesting, is to laugh" (Morson and Emerson 1990, 443–444).

The Wolf of Wall Street locates the carnivalesque where the audience would least expect it. In a film genre that often takes on the mantle of importance and social responsibility, Scorsese's film mocks the genre codes of the Wall Street film as well as Wall Street itself. Where films such as *Wall Street*, *Wall Street: Money Never Sleeps*, *Boiler Room* (B. Younger, 2000), *The Bonfire of the Vanities* (B. De Palma, 1990), *American Psycho* (M. Harron, 2000), and *Margin Call* highlight the moral and ethical transgressions of the financial elite, with a narrative emphasis on moral sanction and public exposure, *The Wolf of Wall Street* depicts an antithesis – offering a picturesque dramaturgy of utopian, sensual liberation.

As an archive of images of global finance in the early to mid 1990s, the film is perhaps less instructive about the reference period than it is about the time of the film's production, 2013. Unlike *Wall Street*, *The Wolf of Wall Street* seems very much of the present moment, confronting, through mockery, the cultural fetishism currently associated with global capital. The present-day sense of capital as an unmappable, invisible dark energy, a force that is mysterious, all powerful, and exponentially determinative of contemporary social and political life, meets its match in *The Wolf of Wall Street*, where everything is made visible, where capital is turned into flesh and pharmaceuticals, and where the lowly pink sheets and the quotidian sneaker IPO can overturn the elite industries of banking and capital trade – in Bakhtin's words, "decrowning" one of our most vaunted cultural fetishes.

In considering the chronotope of emergence and the chronotope of carnival as aspects of the genre memory of the Wall Street film, I have tried to illuminate the way genres "remember the past, and make their resources available to the present"[1] (Morson and Emerson 1990, 297). One of the most interesting and novel permutations of recent film history, the Wall Street film is a case study in the ways popular art can refocus our perceptions of the dominant institutions of contemporary life, institutions that for all their power and ubiquity, have largely gone unchallenged. Seen through what Bakhtin calls the "eyes of genre," the image of global finance is here demystified, and situated in a historical and artistic tradition. Giving concrete and visible shape to what is sometimes called the specter of capital, the Wall Street film provides a way of imagining alternatives, just as carnival enunciated a different way of living in the face of medieval gloom. In their own way, each of the films I consider here works against the aura of fascination that surrounds Wall Street in contemporary cultural life – a fascination that suggests the reach of the finance industry's symbolic power, a power that now seems to have installed itself at the center of our historical world. Like the mythic idea of the frontier in an earlier era, Wall Street can be perceived as a topos that defines a key part of the social imaginary of our time.

In this chapter, I have tried to describe the formal logic of the Wall Street chronotope – the particular diurnal and nocturnal patterns of the subgenre as well as the distinctive spatial logic of spectacle and concealment that governs the form. The chronotope of the Wall Street film, however, has yet to be described in full. In setting forth the ancient chronotopes of carnival and of the road as elements of the Wall Street film, I am aware that I am adapting much older paradigms of analysis to a form that is emerging anew in response to fundamental economic and political changes. In his chapter in this volume, Graham Murdock argues that the narrative formats of the twentieth-century novel inform cinematic representations of finance, an argument that I find persuasive. What I suggest, however, is that the Wall Street film also carries the sedimented traces of much older novelistic traditions. The chronotope of the road and the chronotope of carnival shape the Wall Street film, I argue, in a way that illustrates Bakhtin's theory of genre memory, in which genres are seen as repositories of social and cultural memory, capable of remembering the past, and responding to the present in a new way. The concentrated spatial and temporal patterns of the Wall Street film lend themselves to chronotopic analysis in a way that few other film genres do, and perhaps a more comprehensive description may follow from this initial attempt. Bakhtin argues that genres are "the drive belts linking the history of society and the history of aesthetic form" (Morson and Emerson, 278). The Wall Street film offers an exemplary case study in the way the image of global finance is articulated in contemporary cultural life.

Note

1 For Bakhtin, genres serve as "organs of memory" for culture, a crystallization of past social experiences – structures that "remember the past, and make their resources available for the present" (Morson and Emerson 1990, 297). Genres impose their own historical

perspectives and systems of value on individual texts. Capable of both recalling past usages and responding to the present in a new way, they can be understood as crystallized forms of social and cultural memory. They embody the worldview of the period from which they originated as a strong form, while carrying with them "the layered record of their changing uses." As Morson and Emerson write, genres are the "residue of past behavior… congealed events…they remember the past, and make their resources available for the present" (297). In this way, genres are capable of a kind of double voicing.

As with many pathfinding ideas, Bakhtin's concept of genre memory emerged in the context of a heated disagreement, in this case, over the poetics of narrative form. The Russian Formalists, great champions of the innovative and the novel textual device, of defamiliarization, and the making difficult that is associated with the avant-garde, argued that literary artistic form must break with tradition, and must aggressively short circuit the pragmatic, practical functions of ordinary language through experimentation. Bakhtin, following Medvedev, disagreed, arguing that true change in literary form is "prosaic and continuous, rather than revolutionary" (Morson and Emerson: 280). Genres, the carriers of artistic tradition, were "organs of memory" that contained the potential to shape "new visions of the world" (Morson and Emerson: 280). The Formalists, in valuing only the new, ignored the potential for innovation contained in genre, and its value as a vehicle of historicity.

References

Anderson, Benedict. 2006. *Imagined Communities* (revised edition). New York: Verso.

Bakhtin, Mikhail. 1982. *The Dialogic Imagination: Four Essays*, trans. by Michael Holquist and Caryl Emerson. Austin: University of Texas Press Slavic Series.

Bakhtin, Mikhail. 1984a. *Problems of Dostoevski's Poetics*, ed. and trans. by Caryl Emerson. Minneapolis: University of Minnesota Press.

Bakhtin, Mikhail. 1984b. *Rabelais and His World*, trans. by Helene Iswolsky. Bloomington: Indiana University Press.

Meissner, Miriam. 2012. "Portraying the Global Financial Crisis: Myth, Aesthetics, and the City." *NECSUS: European Journal of Media Studies*, Vol. 1., No. 1.

Moretti, Franco and Pestre, Dominique. 2015. "Bankspeak: The Language of World Bank Reports." *New Left Review*, 92, March–April, https://newleftreview.org/II/92/franco-moretti-dominique-pestre-bankspeak

Morson, Gary Saul and Emerson, Caryl. 1990. *Mikhail Bakhtin: Creation of a Poetics*. Stanford: Stanford University Press.

Parvulescu, Constantin. 2016. "The New Bohemians: Broker Lifestyles in Finance Films." Presented to Global Finance and the Moving Image conference, Pamplona, October 20–22.

Scott, Ian and Thompson, Henry. 2017. *The Cinema of Oliver Stone: Art, Authorship, and Activism*. Manchester: Manchester University Press.

Staheli, Urs. 2013. *Spectacular Speculation: Thrills, the Economy, and Popular Discourse*. Stanford: Stanford University Press.

Stam, Robert. 1992. *Subversive Pleasures: Bakhtin, Cultural Criticism, and Film*. Baltimore: Johns Hopkins University Press.

3

FINANCIAL DARWINISM IN RECENT AMERICAN FEATURE FILMS[1]

Pablo Echart and Pablo Castrillo

The notion of a certain identity crisis in capitalist culture, along with the traditionally critical portrayal of business in American film (Ribstein 2012), becomes particularly manifest in cinematic narratives concerned with financial markets, stock trading, speculation, and the boundless possibilities of personal enrichment in such environments. The memorable Gordon Gekko (Michael Douglas) of Oliver Stone's *Wall Street* (1987) established the financial trader archetype, characterized by his charisma and magnetism, by the powerful driving force of greed and ambition, and by his lack of ethical scruples in placing his self-interest above the social common good. Ever since, Hollywood brokers have tended to appear under the light of excessive masculinities and anti-social conducts, opposed to both their families and the economy, and they are often linked to criminal activities and hypersexualized hedonism (Brassett and Rethel, 2015, 443–445). The aim of this chapter is to explore, through film analysis focused on characters and dramatic devices, the ways in which the contemporary heirs of *Wall Street* develop and reinforce the dark undertones of this archetype. In order to do so, we will focus on *Margin Call* (J. C. Chandor, 2011), *The Wolf of Wall Street* (M. Scorsese, 2013), and *The Big Short* (A. McKay, 2015).

More or less directly inspired by actual events, these three feature films have reflected upon the financial praxis – *The Wolf of Wall Street* choosing a period from the past that, in hindsight, appears as a forewarning – that has become the epicenter of the economic turmoil the world has been weathering since 2008. Their critical discourses spring in varied ways from the financial Darwinism that rules the activity of traders and other professionals of the field. Despite the potential misunderstanding and reductionism that can surround this notion,[2] we resort to it by way of metaphor, inasmuch as it graphically conveys a professional habitat dominated by a competitive logic and lack of moral criteria, designed only for the "survival of the fittest"[3] and of the strongest predators. As we will attempt to demonstrate, out of the three movies, *The Wolf of Wall Street* is the one that utilizes this biological analogy in the most overt way, by reducing its characters to animalistic caricatures, content with their self-affirmation over their clients-victims and their tumultuous indulgence in physiological and sensorial pleasures (sex, drugs). *Margin Call* can be figuratively interpreted as a narrative concerned with the radicalness of the survival instinct. This drive is perceived in the main plot of the film, which recounts how the financial firm chooses to survive at the cost of unleashing catastrophe onto the markets, as well as in the relationships among the brokers, ruled by a sense of competition within the company. Finally, and unlike the previous two films, *The Big Short* underscores the value of knowledge and smartness as necessary conditions for achieving success-survival in an increasingly abstract financial ecosystem swamped with incomprehensible instruments and terminology.

Despite their differences in tone and genre, these three films coincide in critically affirming how the Wall Street financial environment endorses Gordon Gekko's iconic statement: "greed is good." The filmic archetype of the financial broker validates this pessimistic assessment, one that MacIntyre (2015) has ascribed to an economic system that is flawed by a deep disconnection between the sphere of virtue and money, once the latter has been turned into the measuring stick for all of existence. The financial trader would be the most accurate embodiment of *pleonexia*, that is, "the vice that informs the financial sector of the globalising economy: growth both for the sake of growth and at the service of and as an expression of acquisitiveness" (MacIntyre 2015, 17). Moreover, under the current conditions, the inculcation of qualities of moral character is not only irrelevant for the purpose of success in this professional sector, but most likely even an insurmountable disadvantage (MacIntyre 2015, 12).

Be first, be smarter, or cheat (*Margin Call*)

Inspired by the survival of Goldman Sachs and the turmoil of other firms at the outset of the crisis, *Margin Call* recounts the decisions made by the executives of an investment bank in order to avoid the threat of collapse. The plot follows the rationalization process whereby the company resolves to sell off all its mortgage-backed securities (toxic assets) in record time, so as to ensure its survival. The dramatic payload of the story springs from the characters' inner struggle to align with this drastic measure with unforeseeable consequences for the economy and society. *Margin Call* presents the workplace as a locus of dehumanization and as a markedly male environment in which public speaking and rhetorical skills become a fundamental tool for professional success. The film continues the dynamics of aggressive and fraudulent stock sales ordered by cynical and cold-hearted bosses, and traders that become soulless savages as they play a kind of financial con-game of incommensurable proportions. As we discuss next, a distinctive trait of this film is its depiction of the financial corporation as a kind of alluring trap. None of the employees, regardless of their professional status, have the desire or the courage to quit their job, in spite of its vicious atmosphere.

This is because, for the characters in *Margin Call*, money represents a supreme value, and the measuring stick for personal success or failure. The insatiable curiosity of a young broker (Penn Badgley) about the salaries of the company's executives and the income of people devoted to other kinds of business (such as the strippers of the club they frequent after work) is the most obvious evidence of this fact. Money must be earned in ever-growing amounts, due to the simple reason that there will always be more – and more obscene – ways of spending it. This idea is clearly illustrated in a scene in which Will Emerson (Paul Bettany), a senior executive, breaks down to his younger colleagues how he has spent the 2.5 million USD he had earned the previous year. This permanently unsatisfied desire – this greed, ultimately – is the main flaw of the characters, one that exposes them to manipulation and domination by their superiors. As a consequence, the three characters that embody some form of dissent end up inevitably being trapped by the lure of money as well as by the interests of the firm. This inescapable logic is best perceived in the subplot concerning Eric Dale (Stanley Tucci), the firm's Head of Risk Management who is fired at the beginning of the movie. However, once the bank resolves to sell off its assets, his compliance must be purchased and therefore an offer is made: to receive 172,000 USD per hour for remaining silent while the company executes the sale, or face litigation over the terms of his severance. This choice between asymmetrical options underscores the intrinsic determinism ingrained in the system: any attempt to rebel is promptly smothered.

Along the same lines, Sam Rogers (Kevin Spacey), the executive who acts as a conduit between senior management and the traders, withdraws his resolution to depart from the company as soon as the assets have been sold: despite his guilty conscience about the fraudulent operation, he stays with the firm because he "needs" the money. Lastly, the young Peter Sullivan (Zachary Quinto), who discovers the exposure of the company, and who is taken by the viewer as the moral reference of the film – in good measure because he is the only one who verbalizes a concern about the consequences of the operation they intend to carry out – ends up assuming the rationale of the company by being rewarded with a promotion and a salary bump.

As will be seen, this worship of the god money lies at the core of a Darwinism that can be detected both inside and outside the gates of the company, that is, in the relationships among corporate employees as well as in their relationships with the clients and investors, who will end up becoming victims of their scam. In terms of the outside world, as it is known, the film's plot is sustained by the survival of the company, for which it is necessary to carry out a massive sale of toxic assets that will destroy the financial market and trigger an economic and social crisis that will impact – as it does still today – the lives of millions, both in the US and the rest of the world. As is made manifest by the firm's CEO John Tuld (Jeremy Irons), the traders' mission is to get rid of "the biggest bag of odorous excrement ever assembled in the history of capitalism." The goal is to survive and, as MacIntyre maintains, such a goal does not contemplate any ethical qualms. Once the decision is laid out, and its consequences calculated, the traders bend to the will of their superiors fueled by the expectation of spectacular bonuses. As stated by Sam, the money will also compensate the loss of their professional reputations (which, as it can be clearly seen, have their price as well).

As Werner has explained (2014, 649–651), the film employs various strategies of "social distancing" that allow the salesmen to neutralize the moral implications of their acts, to detach themselves from their consequences, and to place the focus of attention on their own survival. Specifically, Werner describes such strategies along three main lines: (1) an impersonal, instrumental culture, which suppresses emotional bonds; (2) language resources that neutralize actions; and (3) detachment from society. The first one affects the relationships between both the brokers and their clients, and among the employees themselves, as we will show below. Regarding the second strategy, Werner identifies the following techniques of neutralization, as established by Heath (2008): denying of responsibility over their actions, denying that any actual injury has been inflicted, denying the worthiness of their victims, appealing to a higher loyalty understood as a moral duty, finding comfort in the fact that everyone acts in the same way, and claiming to be entitled to their misconduct by placing the blame on others. Finally, these characters' detachment from society is based on both a "work hard-play hard" lifestyle and the reduction of difficult personal situations – i.e. mortgages – to cold digits and statistics.

These tools allow the traders to keep their egocentric individualism intact. Or, in the words of the film's director: "in my film most of the characters are by their nature very inward looking self-centered people so they are more concerned with their own plight than the potential effect this event [the collapse] may have on anyone else" (Choudhury 2012, 19). Thus, Peter Sullivan's questions about the social responsibility of their job in the first act of the film are answered by his boss Will Emerson in an unapologetic monologue of overcomplicated rhetoric. As another example of self-justification, he concludes that their jobs are necessary in order to preserve the status quo of a society accustomed to a wealthy lifestyle that, in fact, it cannot really afford. Will Emerson does not see "normal people" as victims of investment banking, but rather, as hypocritical beneficiaries of its risky practices. It is inferred from his stance that the clients want to profit from the system without acknowledging that it is rigged in their favor.

This dichotomy, articulated between the good of financiers versus the common good of the social body, is clearly and graphically presented in the reflection elaborated by Eric Dale, the fired Head of Risk Management, about his past work as a civil engineer, when he built a bridge that allowed commuters to save themselves thousands of miles and hours daily. Despite his partner's cynical attempts to play down such accomplishment, this scene brings up a notion that can be tracked to other films concerned with economy and corporations: the difference between the activity of capitalist marketers (who basically profit from immaterial labor) and that of other professions that create tangible contributions to the common good.[4] In the aforementioned speech with which Will Emerson justifies his work, there is an implicit recognition of this conception of finance as a kind of fantasy: what he does is a necessary job for people who "wanna live like this in their cars and big fuckin' houses they can't even pay." In this cycle of financial films, the most rotund expression of this notion is probably asserted by Mark Hanna (Matthew McConaughey), the mentor that inspires Jordan Belfort (Leonardo DiCaprio), the so-called "Wolf of Wall Street." In their eccentric conversation about how the business operates, Hanna delves in the idea of Wall Street finance being nothing more than an unreal, fictitious world in which traders do not create nor build anything and whose jobs consist of keeping clients – also captives of greed – from removing their assets from the market, which would actually make the economy "real." Ribstein mentions *Pretty Woman* (G. Marshall, 1990) and *Other People's Money* (N. Jewison, 1991) to explain this non-existent contribution of bankers to social wellness, and concludes the following: "Capitalists in films are villains because they see business as simply fungible sources of monetary gain, not places where people work, live, and create" (Ribstein 2012, 215).

On the "inside" of the company, on the other hand, the first sign of Darwinism is found in its policy of firings and promotions, which in fact are related. Portraying a common occurrence in the ordinary reality of Wall Street, the opening sequence shows the merciless arrival into the firm of a downsizing team that ends up causing a workplace bloodbath. As in Eric's case, the victims are expelled in humiliating ways and turn before the eyes of the survivors into outcasts: it is more prudent for those staying to keep a safe distance, than to overtly show solidarity or thankfulness. The warlike language employed and the recognition of the competence of those laid off may lead one to think of a certain randomness in the process, but the truth remains clear: the firings obey a Darwinist logic by which only those who can adapt to a changing environment survive. And even more: the departure of co-workers becomes an opportunity to thrive and climb up the corporate ladder, as Sam brilliantly explains to his "survivors." This manner of proceeding with regard to firings and promotions brings to light the idea that any personal feeling or circumstance is in fact irrelevant, and that the employees are valued strictly in terms of functionality, as more or less optimal resources for productivity. A clear indication of the depersonalization of the employee appears with stark clarity in the fact that the top executives are recurrently shown to be unable to remember their subordinates' names, that is, the touchstone of their personal identity.

More proof of the reigning Darwinism inside the company is to be found in the subplot that deals with the power struggle between two high-level executives of the firm to keep their status intact. The rivalry between Jared Cohen (Simon Baker) and Sarah Robertson (Demi Moore) is resolved in favor of the first one and certifies the existence of a glass ceiling inside the company (Werner 2014, 648). It is of clear symbolic value that the only victim among the senior execs happens to be a woman. In this manner, *Margin Call* stays the course of a hypermasculinized image of Wall Street, as reflected on the screen: the jungle of finance is a place for men. Robertson is not guiltier than her male counterparts, and yet, she takes the fall and becomes the necessary "scapegoat" (sic).

Greed is fun (*The Wolf of Wall Street*)

The Wolf of Wall Street fictionalizes the historical rise and fall of financial crook Jordan Belfort between the late eighties and nineties. In Scorsese's own words, the brutalization of banking that the film portrays is intended as "a provocation for the people to question what really goes on [today] in Wall Street" (Lerman 2014, 27). In his understanding, the last three decades have brought about in the US and Europe a dangerous and pernicious philosophy of search for material wealth (not even social or professional success), whose flagship is embodied by Wall Street traders: "I wanted to reenact the energy in the mentality of these salesmen, for whom it is acceptable to lie, deceive, take advantage of others, and take as much as you want just because you can" (Lerman 2014, 22).

The story, told in a satirical tone, presents Jordan Belfort as a leader who, gifted with an exuberant ability for rhetoric (Balló and Pérez 2015, 119–120), assumes, propagates, and celebrates a "greed is fun" mentality among his acolytes. As he himself recognizes, he is addicted to sex as well as all kinds of drugs, but above all he is addicted to the money that facilitates his pleasures. Contrary to the conclusions of many psychological studies denying the correlation between money and happiness (Werner 2014, 647), Belfort's faith in this pairing is unshakable. In a motivational speech for his employees, he expresses so in this manner: "I want you to deal with your problems by becoming rich!" And, coming closer to the issue of Darwinism, he concludes: "You be ferocious! You be relentless! You be telephone fucking terrorists!" According to this worldview, therefore, money does provide happiness, and it is earned at the expense of others. As in *Margin Call*, this addiction to money does not contemplate any limits but does embrace fraud, with the particularity that the victim is not subject to the perpetrator's indifference, but rather, to his scorn and contempt. In Belfort's own words, "We sold garbage to garbage men…their money was better off in my pocket, I knew how to spend it better."

Thus, *The Wolf of Wall Street* coincides with *Margin Call* in its depiction of financial traders as blinded by greed, while differing in its formal conception: Scorsese's film renounces all naturalist pretensions and chooses instead a series of generic, tonal, and rhetorical codes that result in a controversial film. The radicalness of Scorsese and screenwriter Terence Winter resides in the fact that Belfort not only seeks the allegiance of his subordinates to his "greed is fun" creed, but also the support of the viewership, to whom the film appeals through a narrative told in the first person. It is up to each audience member, then, to carry out a critical assessment of a story that, as Burgoyne points out in this same volume, is permeated by a carnivalesque spirit that aims at subverting with all manner of excess the presumably lethargic life of ordinary people. Thus, the nocturnality and asepsia of the glazed offices in *Margin Call* are transformed in *The Wolf of Wall Street* into a ludic, festive space of collective celebration. The camera travels beyond the workplace to show, in a warm color palette, the lavish, materialistic hedonism of Jordan Belfort's lifestyle. Moreover, the rivalry and coldness that infuse the character relationships in Chandor's film contrast with the portrayal of the employees of Stratton Oakmont as members of a fraternity. They are fellows united by a common faith in and blind loyalty to their leader (a loyalty that ultimately will turn out not to be reciprocal), and by the enjoyment of common vices. In this respect, while the traders depicted in *Margin Call* keep up appearances in public with impeccable manners (even if they confess to having their vices), the employees of Stratton Oakmont do the exact opposite by parading a lack of inhibition – also proper to the spirit of carnival – and obscene behavior that evince their primitive nature and absence of sophistication.

Belfort, a cheap and grotesque version of Gatsby (Anderson, 2013), is surrounded by an animal imagery that matches his hedonistic depravation, but above all, his way of developing business relationships. If Wall Street is a "financial jungle," as Belfort's company announcement reads at the opening of the film, then he is the king of such jungle: the lion that prowls around the corporate offices and sets himself up as its symbol. In a comical way, the jungle metaphor continues onto the non-verbal communication made of noises and grunts with which the financial traders express their corporatism; a series of primeval rhythms through which Belfort and his mentor seal their mutual harmony, and which reflect the euphoria of the magnate and his employees when he refuses to step down under the pressure of the FBI. Continuing this strategy of animalization, his nickname of the "Wolf" of Wall Street – attributed in the film to the *Forbes* magazine – refers in a very obvious way to the moral philosophy of Hobbes and his use of the Latin proverb, "homo homini lupus est," with which it is clearly stated that the individual naturally seeks his own benefit at the expense of others. If only the strongest survive the jungle, it is not surprising then that Belfort employ a hunting metaphor when he rallies his associates to draw in the investments of the richest men in America: they are Captain Ahab in the hunt for the largest whales. The fact that his employees do not know the literary reference, besides creating a comedic gag, illustrates a view of the financial trader that does not require any cultural refinement: in order to scam others, it is enough to be bold, to lack scruples, and to be driven by a boundless greed. Without reaching the degree of grotesque exaggeration of Scorsese's film – in which the common trait to the entire management team seems to be their underqualification – this notion can be extrapolated to *Margin Call*, in which the high-level executives do not hide their inability to interpret the computer-generated data, and where the CEO of the company demands an explanation of their predicament as if he were only a child or a dog. He even adds, without a trace of embarrassment, that "It wasn't brains that brought me here; I assure you that." The apparent acknowledgment of human relationships (also economic and social) as ruled by Darwinism also appears in the dealings between Belfort and Agent Denham (Kyle Chandler), the FBI agent who attempts to bring him down: "You know [Belfort says], every time someone rises up in this world there's always some asshole trying to drag him down." This catch-me-if-you-can plot device ends up with Belfort in prison because, trapped as he is in his own enjoyment of the financial jungle, he is unable to play his cards cleverly. Even then, the narrative shows its malicious side when Agent Denham perceives his triumph over Belfort as a kind of Pyrrhic victory: he, who has carried the seed of avarice for a long time – he tried to be a broker in the past – will continue to be one of those "losers" who travel the New York City metro system every morning.

Even though this point might seem of little relevance, it is interesting inasmuch as Denham embodies the values of a right social order. Furthermore, he is an average man in whom any citizen could recognize a version of himself, of any "good man". The melancholy of his triumph therefore confirms and even fuels Belfort's worldview, one that splits the world between winners and losers, between men who choose to drive convertibles in the company of hot chicks and those who wait in traffic inside a beat-up car by the side of their overweight wives. The relationship between money and happiness is thus extended to a bond between money and social status, or between money and power, in other words. The magnitude of one's income not only determines one's social position, but also the respect that he deserves; or conversely, the more meager the salary, the more prone to be humiliated. This is illustrated in the film time and time again by the stratification of prostitutes into categories according to the price of their services, by the tossing of midgets, or by the abuse received by the naïve Belfort from his boss at the outset of his career. When Belfort asserts that "there is no nobility in poverty," he is validating the existence of a new form of social aristocracy. To be part of the privileged class – to be among the best – no longer depends on one's knowledge, virtue, social skills, or family name, but rather, it hinges on the ability to amass exorbitant amounts of money (which are earned, needless to say, by reaching into the pockets of others). It is, therefore, a monetary aristocracy.

Fraud, not stupidity (*The Big Short*)

The Big Short follows four teams of investors as they discover and bet against the mortgage bubble that will trigger the great financial crisis of 2008. The main characters are visionaries. Within the universe of the film, they are the only ones capable of noticing a reality to which their peers remain oblivious, blinded as they are by the euphoria of an ever-expanding yet artificial economy. A distinctive feature of this film is the emphasis it places on the complexity of financial products and the intricacy of the market. In a deliberate manner, the plot seeks to create confusion in the viewer, who becomes overwhelmed by financial concepts inaccessible to common citizens. The film, on the other hand, resorts to humorously expositional and metafictional scenes in order to instruct the audience on financial concepts and thus, to a certain extent, mitigate their disorientation. This impenetrability seems to function as a protective strategy for the agents of the market, who in this way become "the fittest." The issue of Darwinism in this film offers new nuances. Among the ensemble of protagonists, the film highlights the role of Mark Baum (Steve Carrell), a character inspired by the real-life hedge fund manager Steve Eisman. In charge of an investment group under Morgan Stanley, Baum becomes appalled by and denounces the *mala praxis* that pervades the financial market, which encourages risky and speculative attitudes motivated by the urge "to get rich fast" (Peltzer 2015, 163). Baum's characterization as a sensible businessman – accentuated by a subplot of personal loss that reveals vulnerability – moderates the aggressive traits of the broker archetype, often built on the qualities of charisma, dauntlessness, lack of ethical qualms, and the strong driving motivation of greed and ambition. Nevertheless, this positive connotations in the main character have their limits: in spite of his indignation, he does not ultimately have the leeway to act against the mandates of the market.

Besides providing a more acceptable version of the broker archetype, another distinctive feature of not only Mark Baum, but also the other protagonists, resides in their ability to figure out the intricacies of the financial market. In the world of *The Big Short*, financial education, professional experience, and market information are far more relevant than sheer guts or cunning. This technical proficiency contrasts starkly with the stupidity of Belfort's underlings in *The Wolf of Wall Street* and the admitted ignorance of John Tuld in *Margin Call*. Thus, while *The Big Short* reinforces the perception of the stock market as a rigged game, it also adds the distinctive feature of knowledge as a differential value: the winners – the survivors – are not just charismatic and daring, but they rely above all on their smartness. In a certain sense, all three films validate John Tuld's criteria for success: "be first [*Margin Call*], be smarter [*The Big Short*], or cheat [*The Wolf of Wall Street*]."

The Big Short gives no room to charismatic villains, replacing them instead with a financial system that is multipolar and abstract, and from which it is not easy to exact concrete accountabilities, other than from the brokers who operate under institutional mandates (Thomason 2016, 27). Boyle and Mrozowski, in the introduction to their collective volume *The Great Recession in Fiction, Film, and Television* (2013), argue about the Michael Lewis book on which the film is based that it is the innate complexity of twenty-first century finance – rather self-evident, judging from its inextricable jargon – that guarantees the continuity of the system under a kind of placebo effect: "The key, then, is that the boom market of the early 2000s was too obscurely complex to be understood by even those closest to it – a convenient truth that allowed everyone to assume that it was working and it would continue to work" (Boyle and Mrozowski 2013, xviii). Perhaps too, as pointed out by a *Film Comment* reviewer, the film is "a cautionary tale about Americans' eagerness to believe in concepts too good to be true, like ever-expanding home ownership and increasingly easy-to-get-mortgages" (Sragow, 2015).

The apparently unstoppable profits yielded by financial speculation indeed seemed to validate this convenient truth. When Mark Baum alludes, on various occasions, to the stupidity of certain activities, he is in fact referring to the lack of realism that guides many financial operations and, as a consequence, to the irresponsibility of ignoring the potential harmful effects they could have on the real economy. In different instances, Baum employs the terms "stupidity" and "fraud" as analogous to one another, but ends up breaking this equation when he discovers that the flooding of the market with toxic and risky assets does not follow from a lack of awareness, but rather, the certainty that banks would emerge unharmed from the rubble of the market in the case of a financial meltdown. In a key moment, the character exclaims: "they knew! (…) they knew the tax-payers would bail them out, they weren't stupid, they just didn't care!" Ultimately, Baum discovers that the fraud is not a result of mere stupidity, but rather, of conscious wrongdoing.

These critical undertones of *The Big Short* are reinforced in the film's resolution. Before the closing credits, the narrator informs the audience, in a deservedly cynical tone: "Banks took the money the American people gave them and used it to pay themselves huge bonuses and lobby the congress to kill big reform (...)" And in a more urging and ominous tone, a final text card explains that in 2015 banks began to sell financial products similar, if not virtually equivalent, to the ones that caused the recession, warning the viewership about the possibility of a new bubble. Moreover, the archival footage peppered along the film retrieves the memory of those hosts of ordinary people who were completely clueless about the 2008 meltdown, and who nevertheless would end up paying its costly price (Paredes Badía 2016, 28). In a brief appearance in the film's plot, two real estate agents are judged in negative light for their Darwinist (im)morality, by which they happily exploit vulnerable sectors of society – immigrants – whom they scam and later deride. A slight glimpse of poetic justice is offered to the viewership when these characters reappear near the film's ending looking for employment opportunities at a job fair, but the film does take a jab at greedy, irresponsible brokers.

To a certain extent, not even the protagonists escape unscathed from the film's criticism. Despite their cleverness, they are not actively committed to stopping the looming disaster. Michael Burry (Christian Bale), the first one to uncover the cracks in the system, is portrayed as someone who, perhaps due to his slight case of autism, seems more concerned about proving his hypothesis rather than worrying about the effects it will have on worldwide economy. Jared Vennett (Ryan Gosling) is the quintessential embodiment of the unscrupulous opportunist, who only sees in the impending financial disaster an opportunity for personal gain. Charlie Geller (John Magaro) and Jamie Shipley (Finn Wittrock), the two young brokers "who simply want to get super-rich super-quick" (Sragow, 2015), cannot contain their excitement when they find out their dream will come true, even if at the expense of the hardships of millions of people who will lose their jobs and homes. Only their mentor, Ben Rickert (Brad Pitt), seems to have a conscience, when he tells them not to celebrate: "You just bet against the American economy. [...] Which means, if we're right, people lose homes. People lose jobs. People lose retirement savings, people lose pensions."

Mark Baum appears to be more conflicted by the decision to "bet against the market." The last sequences of the film are devoted to Baum's dilemma, and his final decision to sell his investments and thus earn over 1 billion USD for his fund, of which he will "clear two hundred mill." This decision, however, is presented in the light of a no-choice scenario: as the fund manager, Baum has a responsibility to his investors; as an individual, he has a responsibility to his family and himself; and besides, he has already attempted to unmask the faults of the system only to be met with plain indifference. His qualms emerge from the fact that "once we sell, we'll be just like the rest of them," but in the end, the imperative of survival prevails. It is thus out of necessity that he sells his assets – in this sense resembling the company executives of *Margin Call* – but always remaining clear on the moral value of his actions and strongly opposed to the recklessness that has led to the meltdown. Mark Baum is indeed a Darwinian survivor, but not so much a predator, inasmuch as the survivor acts out of necessity in order to prevent its own extinction. The predator, on the other hand, thrives at the expense of others on a regular basis, as Jordan Belfort does.

Conclusion

The banker protagonists of *Margin Call*, *The Wolf of Wall Street*, and *The Big Short* share common elements that allow for the consideration of a dramatic archetype defined first and foremost by greed as its decisive fatal flaw. Gordon Gekko's well-known motto "greed is good" had already functioned as a kind of rationalization for the character to embrace this rapacity. In a similar way, the trader archetype in these later films undergoes a process of self-justification by which his actions become vindicated. The desire for money frames the conduct of these characters, to the extent that their free will appears to be limited. This nearly behavioralist characterization is present in every major character of *Margin Call*, it fuels the hedonistic spiral of Jordan Belfort, and seals the final decision made by even the most sensible protagonist of *The Big Short*. This flaw, therefore, virtually always smothers any redeeming values, such as the moral sense of Peter Sullivan and Sam Rogers in *Margin Call*, the early love story of Jordan Belfort in *The Wolf of Wall Street*, and the awareness shown by Ben Rickert and Mark Baum regarding the difficulties soon to be experienced by American society in *The Big Short*.

Common to these characters is a Darwinian mindset that translates into a professional and personal behavior ruled by the principles of adaptation, competition, and sometimes even depredation. Directly dealing with the US economic system, these films decry its perverse drift toward a lawless capitalism, understood as "an invitation to accept once and for all the *homo homini lupus* as an all-embracing principle that sustains social coexistence" (Insausti 2004, 52).[5] Consequently, the plots and character arcs of the analyzed films convey a worldview in which "the state of human nature is precisely that of confrontation and moral disorder (as Hobbes defended) and not of harmony (as did Rousseau)" (ibid.) Surrounded by such a state of disarray, the protagonists of these films perform the role of either survivors or predators. The former ensure their preservation *in spite of* their displeasure at causing harm to others, while the latter choose to thrive precisely *at the expense of* others. In both cases, these characters end up capitulating to the rules of the financial ecosystem, and embracing and enjoying its rewards.

Notes

1 This chapter is part of the research project "Imaging the crisis: audiovisual representations of the economic, social, and geopolitical collapse (1929–2012)," financed by the Ministry of Economy and Competitiveness, Government of Spain (reference CSO2012-33782).

2 In fact, these attributes can be applied to the notion of "social Darwinism," from which ours is derived, as Hodgson (2004) has demonstrated.
3 So as to avoid further potential misconstructions, it seems pertinent to recall that the term was originally coined by Herbert Spencer, and only later employed by Darwin in his *Theory of the Species* (Hodgson 2004, 432).
4 A very clear example of this can be found in the character of the executive turned carpenter in *The Company Men* (J. Wells, 2010).
5 Insausti's words are applied in his original text to the narrative of *The Asphalt Jungle*. What Burnett's novel and John Huston's homonymous film attributed to the modern city, in the films analyzed in this chapter, refers to the financial – and also social – fabric of America.

References

Anderson, Melissa. 2013. "Balls to the Wall." *Artforum*, December 23. http://artforum.com/film/id=44562. Accessed February 7, 2017.
Balló, Jordi and Pérez, Xavier. 2015. *El mundo, un escenario. Shakespeare: el guionista invisible*. Barcelona: Anagrama.
Boyle, Kirk and Mrozowski, Daniel. 2013. *The Great Recession in Fiction, Film, and Television: Twenty-First Century Bust Culture*. Plymouth: Lexington Books.
Brassett, James and Rethel, Lena. 2015. "Sexy Money: The Hetero-normative Politics of Global Finance." *Review of International Studies*, 41(3): 429–449.
Choudhury, Nashrid. 2012. "J.C. Chandor – Margin Call." *Student Filmmakers*, 7(1): 16–20. https://es.scribd.com/document/120972293/Student-Filmmaker-2012. Accessed January 31, 2017.
Heath, Joseph. 2008. "Business Ethics and Moral Motivation: A Criminological Perspective." *Journal of Business Ethics*, 83: 595–614.
Hodgson, Geoffrey M. 2004. "Social Darwinism in Anglophone Academic Journals: A Contribution to the History of the Term." *Journal of Historical Sociology*, 17(4): 428–463.
Insausti, Gabriel. 2004. *Tras las huellas de Huston. La jungla de asfalto*. Madrid: Eiunsa.
Lerman, Gabriel. 2014. "Entrevista Martin Scorsese." *Dirigido Por*, 440: 24–27.
MacIntyre, Alasdair. 2015. "The Irrelevance of Ethics." In *Virtue and Economy. Essays on Morality and Markets*, edited by Andrius Bielskis and Kelvin Knight, 7–22. Farnham: Ashgate.
Paredes Badía, Israel. 2016. "El mal es el capital." *Dirigido Por*, 462: 28.
Peltzer, Anja. 2015. "No Guns, No Rules, Just Pure Capitalism! Hollywood's Portraits of Wall Street." In *Money Talks: Media, Markets, Crisis*, edited by Graham Murdock and Jostein Gripsrud, 151–168. Bristol: Intellect Books.
Ribstein, Larry E. 2012. "Wall Street and Vine: Hollywood's View of Business." *Managerial and Decision Economics*, 33: 211–248.
Sragow, Michael. 2015. "Deep Focus: The Big Short." *Film Comment*, December 9. www.filmcomment.com/blog/deep-focus-the-big-short/. Accessed January 20, 2017.
Thomason, John. 2016. ""We Would Prefer Not To": "The Big Short" and Liberalism's Myths." *Los Angeles Review of Books*, February 27. https://lareviewofbooks.org/article/we-would-prefer-not-to-the-big-short-and-liberalisms-myths/. Accessed January 20, 2017.
Werner, Andrea. 2014. "'Margin Call': Using Film to Explore Behavioural Aspects of the Financial Crisis." *Journal of Business Ethics*, 122(4): 643–654.

4

"FINANCIAL WISDOM" AS DISCURSIVE POSITION

How financial expertise is constructed in documentary film

Jens Maesse

1. Introduction

This chapter analyzes the discursive rules and performances that make possible the emergence of financial expertise as a discursive strategy in documentary films. The term "financial wisdom" points to a hegemonic position that claims to be superior to other perspectives. It is a communicative device that opens up unequal imaginary relations and positions for further communicative impacts at different points in time and space. The chapter will show how, in documentary film, different discursive and narrative strategies come together and establish a communicative mechanism. Whereas hermeneutic approaches tend to work out the inner meanings and messages of a text, I demonstrate how a text itself can be understood as a formal discursive apparatus.

The chapter focuses on the 2012 BBC documentary *The Great Euro Crisis* by Michael Portillo, a filmmaker and storyteller who is a British Conservative, a former minister in the Major cabinet and an advisor to the Thatcher government, who presents himself as a "self-confessed Eurosceptic." To understand what it means to be a "self-confessed Eurosceptic" requires embedding this positioning strategy within the film's *narrative* organization, a performed *story* and a *polyphonic logic*. On the basis of a discourse analysis of the story, the narrative and polyphonic interplay of different voices, I reveal how the "financial wisdom" is the result of a series of performances of the financial expertise. My analysis shows how the film organizes the interpretation processes at the formal-material level (in contrast to the semantic level) and at the micro and macro dimension of the film as a discourse.

When financial expertise is expected to speak to audiences, how can we grasp the interrelationship between the film and society? According to Hirschman and Popp Berman (2014, 779), research on economic expertise has developed three ways to examine the way economics impacts on society: by focusing on "the broad professional authority of economics, the institutional position of economists in government, and the role of economics in the cognitive infrastructure of policymaking." The analysis of documentary films seems to be connected to the first and third levels of impact. My study is not only interested in how a certain discourse is constructed by and within the film. I am particularly focusing on the modalities which allow the film to speak to certain audiences in different geographical places (people in the UK and in Europe) and at several historical points (in 2012 when the film was broadcast, before the Brexit referendum and also after it). It seems, therefore, necessary to understand in what kinds of social fields films start to intervene.

Section 2 gives a brief introduction into the film and Section 3 introduces methodological backgrounds. I explain the analytical differences between *story*, *narrative* and *utterance*, and why this differentiation makes sense from a discourse analytical viewpoint. Section 4 conducts an in-depth analysis of the film. It presents how financial expertise is constructed as a communicative device and creates audience impact. It also analyzes how three different expert positions are created and how they organize the ways in which the film can be read, interpreted and used by social actors. The Conclusion (Section 5) indicates that the same film can create different meanings, depending on the context in terms of time and space, social background and political orientation of the audiences.

2. The structure of the film

The Great Euro Crisis film was produced in 2011 and 2012 and broadcast in 2012 as a BBC documentary.[1] The documentary film features the Greek euro crisis and the impact of European financial institutions under Lucas Papademos's transitional government (2011–2012). At that time, Greece was in deep crisis. After the onset of the euro crisis in 2007, Greece gradually slid into a sovereign debt crisis, a financial crisis, an economic crisis and, in the end, a social and political crisis. In 2011 a transitional government was formed, with so-called "economic technocrats" at the top. Papademos, a former central banker, negotiated a Memorandum of Understanding with the so-called "troika" (IMF, EU Commission, ECB). This Memorandum was intended to be an aid program for Greece, to allow it to refinance its debt. In exchange for this financial assistance Greece was expected to introduce austerity measures. These measures included cuts in wages, social welfare, education, health and other public sectors. As a result, unemployment increased and an economic downturn began.

The documentary film is narrated in nineteen scenes. It starts with Portillo's arrival at Athens Airport where he introduces us, as an expert, to the causes and dimensions of, and possible solutions to, the crisis. Afterwards, Portillo meets different people, such as political representatives, economists, workers, parents, a journalist and other people involved in the crisis from Greece and Germany, and talks to them about how they perceive the crisis in their daily contexts and what should be done to solve the various problems. It ends with a plea by Portillo to leave the euro currency.

From an analytical viewpoint, the film consists of three relevant parts. Each is important for the interpretative dynamics and meaning-making logics of the film and corresponds to the story, the narrative and the polyphonic interplay.

First, right at the beginning Portillo presents a theory of what is going on in the financial world in Greece and Europe. This theory (the *MP's story*, see Section 4.1) has an important impact on how everything that is later presented in the film will be framed in terms of economic reasoning. Second, on the macro level, the film is characterized by a certain conversational dynamic between Portillo and his interview partners. Different figures enter the scenes throughout the film and talk to Portillo about the crisis. This aspect will be analyzed with narrative theory in order to understand how arguments and claims are orchestrated for the audience. Third, at the end of the film, Portillo gives a final statement which presents his personal conclusion. This aspect will be analyzed with polyphony theory in order to see how the audience is directed on the micro level to certain problems and solutions. To understand the communicative dynamics of the entire film, all three dimensions are important and they are represented by different parts of the film as a communication device.

Against this backdrop, *The Great Euro Crisis* discusses an entire complex of financial institutions ranging from investment banking, credit businesses, cash flow and transactions to financial supervision and monetary regulatory institutions. It deals especially with the impact that investment banking practices within a certain regulatory framework (risk management with CDOs and other collaterals) has on other parts of the economy (households, growth, sovereign debt) and questions the particular role of money and currency frameworks (the euro system and the drachma) during the crisis from 2007 onwards. It particularly questions the European bailout policy and austerity measures, as well as macro-economic policies as part of the bailout mechanism (the Memorandum, ESFS/ESM). Thus, in order to explain this complex economic framework of financial institutions, the storyteller of the film, Michael Portillo, takes on the roles of different "financial expert" figures.

But what is a financial expert? The role of "the" financial expert as a single entity does not exist, because the cultural, financial, economic and political worlds have created many roles, images of "the" financial and names for financial experts. A financial expert role refers to a set of positioning practices which change from context to context. In an investment bank, for example, people can take on a role as a financial expert on a particular asset class, for example as a "trader" or an "analyst," or as a financial expert who speaks to people who want to invest their money somewhere (a "broker"). Whereas certain Hollywood films tend to present spectacular images of financial experts in spheres of risky investment and wild speculation (see Parvulescu; Loren; Ho; Burgoyne in this volume), many other parts of the financial world are less spectacular. In these worlds, bankers appear as economic experts and technicians, as well as money, financial and currency politicians. "Central bankers," for example, are figures that are related to certain questions of monetary policies or banking supervision. Even if central bankers' speeches have a certain spectacular dimension today, the bulk of their activity is related to very technical and complex knowledge areas which are opaque to laypeople.

However, a financial expert can also enter the field of politics, for example in regulatory policy debates, which are even more technical and insider-related. Hollywood-style films can only gradually feature these fields of banking expertise, since Hollywood speaks to a very big audience of laypeople from very different social milieus. The technical issues of banking and financial experts' lives are normally presented by another film genre, the documentary film, which allows for a more pedagogical discussion of what it means for a country and its people to be involved in and affected by certain banking and financial practices (see Rodríguez Mateos in this volume).

3. Sociological and methodological remarks

In order to proceed with our discourse analysis of the film in Section 4, it is necessary to make some sociological and methodological remarks. These explanations will give us an idea about the social context in which the film as a communicative device speaks to audiences.

3.1. How economic expert discourses enter communicative relations with audiences

Discourse, including language, pictures, texts and symbols, books, articles or films, circulates through a trans-epistemic field, where it builds heterogeneous communicative relations with multiple social actors and groups. These actors and groups are actively involved in financial expert discourses. A trans-epistemic field is a special sort of contextual environment. Economic experts are located at the interface of the trans-epistemic field by their discursive practices, even in film. The forms of knowledge that are relevant in these processes range from everyday knowledge to political ideology, institutional and professional knowledge, certain tacit knowledge and other forms of interpretation. On the level of the political economy, economic expertise is an important sort of knowledge (Lebaron 2014; Fourcade 2009). It provides particular interpretation patterns, helps people to classify the world into "important" and "unimportant" facts, and offers certain solutions to whatever it has learned to see as a "problem" (Fitzgerald and O'Rourke 2016). In order to get a rough idea of how economic expert discourse is constituted, Figure 4.1 illustrates the concept of the trans-epistemic field.

The trans-epistemic field represents a larger framework in which economic experts perform different roles as discursive actors. It consists of two different but interrelated dynamics (Maesse 2016). On the one hand, it is constructed around four different social fields (Bourdieu 1989) which, in contrast to Bourdieu's field theory, do not remain closed but gradually open up to each other. On the other hand, they are made up of discursive practices (Foucault 1980) that take place at the interface of the trans-epistemic field.

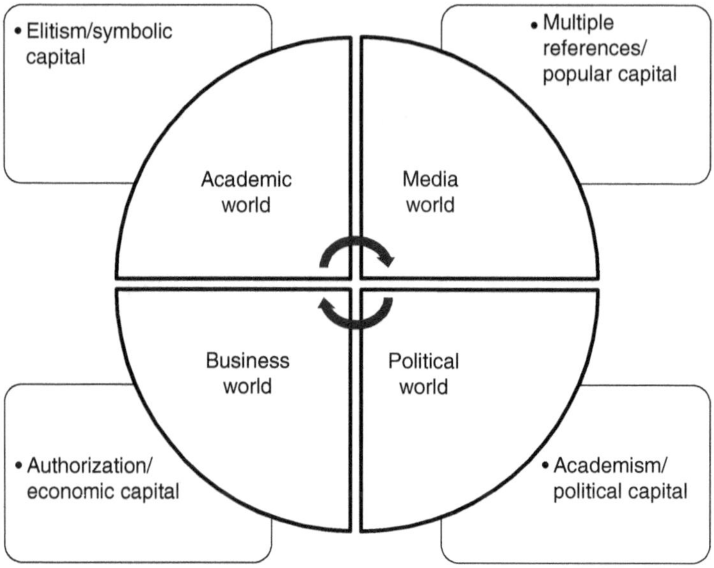

FIGURE 4.1 Trans-epistemic field of economics (Maesse 2015: 290).

This model is central to understanding how economic experts in documentary films enter into communicative relations with society. Meaning making is not represented in the film, it results rather from an interaction between film and society. Whereas knowledge is sedimented in social contexts, the film is only a formal apparatus that orchestrates the contextual knowledge. In the case of a documentary film, economic expert discourses follow a "multi-reference" logic and convert symbolic, political and moral capital into populist capital (see Table 4.1). Discourse as a communicative power device mobilizes audience knowledge. It is part of a struggle over cognitive as well as political and economic hegemonies in society.

3.2. Narrative, story and utterance as analytical units

The film lasts fifty-nine minutes and presents Michael Portillo as a storyteller. He meets different people in Greece and Germany and talks to them about the crisis. During the film, Portillo tells a story which turns out to be his *economic theory* about what happened in Greece and Europe. This story is quite simple and is presented at the very beginning of the film. It can be summarized as follows: Greece, a poor southern country, is in crisis because it is a member of a monetary union with Germany, a rich northern country. It lacks competitiveness because German industry can sell cheap products to Greece that are financed by loans coming from Germany as well (export surpluses). The middle classes were attracted by a certain "German lifestyle" (represented by German cars, such as Porsche) after the introduction of the euro, and started to live beyond their economic means. A corrupt and economically naive political elite supported this process, and so a debt crisis was unavoidable. In order to regain competitiveness, Greece must leave the euro and reintroduce the drachma.

This story will be called the *MP's story* in order to indicate that it belongs to a certain author. It is an important element of the film and should be separated from another dimension of the film, namely the *narrative*. According to Greimas (1976), narrative is characterized by two dimensions: a deep structure and a surface structure (Jameson 1976). Whereas the deep structure of the narrative is constructed around fundamental semantic units, represented by the semiotic square, the surface structure follows an "antropomorphistic illusion." This illusion is manifested in *actants* and pushed forward through a simple dynamic. According to Greimas, every narrative can be analyzed, at the surface level, using the following narrative model. In this model, for each actant, the narrative develops different entities, which can be "human" in nature or objects, situations and so forth (Hébert 2011). An analysis of the film will show what roles economic experts play in this process.

Both the *MP's story* and the *narrative* are larger units of discourse in which economic experts can appear. The smallest and, from a pragmatic discourse analytical point of view (see Angermuller 2013; Zienkowski 2016), most important and fundamental unit of discourse is the *utterance*. A phrase, a sentence, a word or a picture can form an utterance. An utterance usually consists of a proposition ("economy growth"), a speaker (an instance that is responsible for the proposition) and other voices (that oppose, support or cooperate with the speaker-voice). However, in order to grasp the multiple appearances of economic expertise in the film genre and to understand how economic expertise develops a certain discursive politics through film, it makes sense to distinguish between the *MP's story*, the *narrative* and the *utterance*. At the same time, these units represent modalities by which the film as discourse relates to the different social contexts, illustrated with the trans-epistemic field in Section 3.1.

4. Forms of expert positioning

4.1. The MP's story as a naturalizing politics of economic language

The first and most obvious level on which economic expertise operates in this film is the economic story, presented by the storyteller, Michael Portillo. Even if this seems obvious, an analysis makes sense since a certain sort of economics is of particular importance for the film's discourse. Two aspects should be recognized. First, to tell a story about apparently economic issues supports a certain naturalization or essentialization of economic frames of interpretation as "styles of reasoning" (Hirschman and Popp Berman 2014). To represent something in the world as "GDP" or "price" does not imply that "prices" or "GDP" exist naturally. On the contrary, there is a certain economic language that is used (like any other language, be it national, organizational, class-related and so forth) to transform "raw" observations (things that can be represented by many different words or pictures) into things that seem to be "economic facts."

Through the lenses of these "economic facts," particular issues appear as "problems," others are presented as "necessities" (such as Thatcher's TINA ideology) and certain political options appear as "solutions." Economic discourse, such as the *MP's story*, tends to present things in the world as causally related to each other (such as "competitiveness" to "prices," "wages" and "currencies"). Economic "facts" are part of strongly rationalized models whereby changes to one "variable" have a direct impact on all the other "variables." Even if, in economics as well as in economic policy discourse, different models and theories are controversial, each of them explaining economic facts with sometimes contradictory arguments, the proponents of the respective theories/models tend to see each model as absolute and universal, so that alternatives are often ignored and neglected. Thus, the tendency in economics to put everything into handbook form can be seen as a symptom of a certain universalizing tendency.

A *naturalizing politics of economic language* is at work throughout the film. It is expressed in many statements about Greece. The following example from the beginning (minutes 2–3) of Portillo's film illustrates this economic framing:

> It is only when you take a walk through the streets of Athens that you get a sense of the situation that this country is in. I can't believe that I'm in Europe in 2012. It's hard to imagine that such a small nation of about eleven million people could accumulate a *national debt equivalent of 31,000 euros* per man, woman and child.

As this example illustrates, Greece as a country, a geographic place, a group of people and so forth is framed in terms of "debt" as an economic category. The audience can, of course, reject this economic framing through "debt." But it is confronted with those economic languages as sense and meaning maker of what "Greece" is throughout the film. This economic framing makes it likely that audiences of this film will understand "Greece" and "Europe" as an "economic problem."

Whereas different conflicts between the narrative and utterance levels appear at various points, the underlying story is never really called into question during the documentary. As we will see later, these conflicts are about the possibilities, limits and scope of applying economic rationality (through political institutions). Economic rationality *per se*, and as represented in this neoliberal story, is not called into question.

Stories that operate on the level of economic language politics do not communicate to academic economists in the first place. Even if the stories must be consistent with the academic criteria of economics as a model-based science (at least in a very vague form), political and naturalizing effects are based on often simplified and apparently clean stories in the eyes of laypeople. Therefore, non-economists, such as the audiences of documentary films, are important communicative interlocutors. Stories as parts of discourse construct social relations between an expert figure and the audience. In order to reach the minds of educated and politically interested people, the story should be scientific in nature and easy to understand, as well as morally acceptable.

TABLE 4.1 *The Great Euro Crisis* (2012): How the film communicates within a trans-epistemic field to three different social groups.

Social group/context	**Everyday middle-class context**	**Academic context**	**Political context**
Meaning maker	Values of working-class/middle-class people	Basics in economic modeling and argumentation	Signal for political and ideological belonging
Form of power	Moral capital	Symbolic capital	Strategic-political capital
Social relations as power relations between communicative partners	Citizenship opportunism	Recognition, devotion and acceptance	Political solidarity

In the eyes of these sorts of people (usually educated middle-class members), Michael Portillo's story about Greece's "competitiveness problem" and an exit from the European monetary union through reintroduction of the drachma is not only academically authorized (through symbolic capital attached to the story itself being marked as "economic theory"), but also morally explained and legitimized. Next to "academization markers" (such as references to economic and scientific authorities), "moralization markers" work in this discourse and refer to Western middle-class value systems.

This moral legitimation is introduced in the film using pictures of soup kitchens and poor people, and through interviews with representatives of "doctors of the world,"[2] supported by numbers on rising unemployment and wage cuts. The film portrays Greece as a third-world country in the middle of the European Union. An exit from the EU is now presented not only as an economic policy measure, which would simply be part of one model among many, but also as a practical solution to a *moral* situation that seems to be unacceptable to the value system of an ordinary member of the Western middle class.

Without this moral dimension, the economic expert discourse would miss its communicative target. "Moralization" and "economization" go hand in hand. Whereas the moralization aspect of economic expert discourse is needed to inform the audience (which is a specific audience with a specific value system), the economization aspect is needed to persuade the same people to place economists in a position of political power and legitimacy. Academic and moral capital is being mobilized by the story's discourse in order to construct a certain political attitude.

Next to these *academic* and *moral* capitals, brought into play by academizing and moralizing discourse markers, *political* capital is mobilized in the discourse. From the point of view of an economic policy debate, the storyteller argues for a political solution, one that is predictably argued for by someone from the conservative-nationalist camp.

Since Michael Portillo is himself a British Conservative and the film was broadcast by the BBC, the discourse intervenes at this time in the ongoing debate on Brexit. Next to the moral and academic positioning, bestowed with academic and moral capital, that the speaker adopts in the story, he also takes at least two political positions: one in an economic policy debate and one in the Brexit debate. When we look at the relation of these three varieties of capital, the discourse develops *populist capital* that consists of interplay between the other three sorts: *academic reputation* and *moral indignation* combined with *political advocacy* is a formula that creates populist capital in economic expert discourses. How exactly this mobilization of capital (and, therefore, social relations of power) is conducted will be demonstrated in the next two sections. The narrative and utterances refer to formal communicative rules. They construct the speaker position of the discourse as an economic expert position. These positions contribute to the constitution of certain conflicts and cooperations. Whereas the story opens up a variety of possible (economized) meanings of the film, the narrative and the utterance tell us how these meaning-making processes are orchestrated around different opinions and perspectives.

4.2. Economists as actants of the narrative

As noted above, the documentary film is narrated in nineteen scenes. The storyteller meets with politicians, economists, workers, parents, a journalist and other people from Greece and Germany who have been involved in the crisis, and talks to them about their views on the crisis and what should be done to solve the various problems. The storyteller leads the audience step by step through the different dimensions, impacts, causes and historical contexts of the crisis as portrayed in the framework of the *MP's story*.

After some introductory remarks about the Greek crisis, in a first scene, Michael Portillo meets Dimitra Nousi, the director of a local food-distribution organization for poor people. She explains the disastrous consequences of the crisis and the austerity measures affecting people's lives, and the hunger and suffering they must endure. This suffering extends to more and more areas of society. This is explained as being the result of the euro crisis. In a second scene, Jason Manolopoulos, an economist, demonstrates how and why the introduction of the euro was not an economic but rather a politically motivated decision. The Greek political system is presented as corrupt and driven by clientelism. Doros Liappis, a bankrupt entrepreneur, describes in a third scene how the Greek middle classes were seduced and attracted by the "German lifestyle" (represented by a Porsche, which Liappis now has to sell due to the crisis) after the introduction of the euro currency. This lifestyle, however, was not economically sustainable because the Greek economy was always poor, as Portillo explains to us in his economic story.

The lives of luxury which the Greek middle class enjoyed between 2001 and 2010 were basically driven by cheap German imports and financed with cheap German loans (this is an important part of the *MP's story*). Such economically questionable behavior was only possible because the already recognized corrupt political class had faked the economy, as testified to in a fourth scene with the investigative journalist Tasos Telloglou. He shows Michael Portillo the ruins of the Olympic Games venues and explains why these are as a result of corruption and nepotism. In further scenes, Portillo meets Jason Manolopoulos, an economist, who again explains the corrupt tax system and moves on to discuss demonstrations, and George Papaconstantinou, the finance minister, who spells out the austerity measures which are presented as necessary and imposed from outside. In further scenes the consequences of austerity are illustrated in conversations with shipyard workers and parents who take their children to a health center where they must pay for everything, even if they are unemployed.

All these figures and scenes testify, in a way, to the economic downturn and political impotence (through corruption or austerity measures imposed from outside). Portillo moves on to Germany where he meets BMW car workers in Leipzig. In contrast to their Greek fellows, German car workers profit from cheap exports, as another economist explains to Portillo. The German economist continues and shows why reductions in wages and cuts to social welfare were necessary to make the German economy internationally competitive. Competitiveness, however, is explained as a result of cuts and waivers.

Portillo goes to Frankfurt and meets the chief economist of Commerzbank, Jörg Krämer. Krämer agrees with Portillo that leaving the euro would be advantageous for Greece. The euro in its current form is a politically motivated but economically unreasonable decision. In another scene, Andrea Ypsilanti, a left-wing social democrat and critic of austerity measures, explains why the German political establishment is split between support for and criticism of austerity, but Portillo moves quickly on to talk to ordinary German people in the street. They argue for stopping financial support to "lazy Greeks." Even if Ypsilanti is known to have a Keynesian critique of neoliberalism, her arguments are not presented as an alternative to Portillo's economic story. After an interview with Wolfgang Schäuble, the German finance minister, who explains the economic, institutional and political logic of the euro system to his British counterpart, Portillo moves back to Greece.

Everybody agrees about the disastrous economic and social consequences of austerity and the crisis, as well as the corrupt character of the political system in Greece. Even if almost everybody contributes to the different aspects or entire plot of the *MP's story* about competitiveness and the economic downturn, nobody (except Jörg Krämer) in Germany or Greece is willing to support Portillo's demand for a Greek exit from the euro area as an economically reasonable solution. And the viewer begins to suspect that economic rationality (at least what is presented as such) cannot rule for reasons that gradually become apparent. The storyteller offered each interviewee a drachma note and a euro note. Everybody chose the latter instead of the former. The Greek people seem to prefer to soldier on with the euro instead of finding an economically reasonable solution via an exit from the union.

This leads the storyteller to reach the conclusion that the Greek people prefer the disastrous economic consequences of austerity and crisis over reverting to the drachma. This would imply a return to the old corrupt political system. It is suggested that the people prefer the "hard reforms" imposed by the euro system (represented by the "Troika"), which was neither democratically elected nor otherwise legitimized, as the storyteller argues.

The film ends with a discussion over dinner with the journalist, the Greek economist and a PASOK member of parliament about the future of Greece. The discussion shows that Greece is stuck in a dilemma between "corruption, nepotism and a return to the old times of economic underdevelopment," or an "economic downturn directed by a European economic dictatorship." "This is awful to British ears," the journalist admits to Portillo, who rounds off the film with the following statement:

> The fears [about a loss of competitiveness, JM] expressed by my friends are reflected by opinion polls across the Eurozone, where the majority support the idea of a more centralized Eurozone. And yet to me they do so without any clear notion of how this new Europe would work as a democracy. Throughout the continent, governments are faltering as they face public opposition against the austerity measures. And now the voters in Greece and France have punished the politicians who try to impose them. People want the euro but don't seem prepared to accept the tough conditions attached. And in my view this means that the great Euro crisis is a long way from being solved.

For reasons of simplification and illustration, we consider only the most important figures in the film who join in twice (the journalist) or three times (the economist) in the storyteller's conversation. For illustrative purposes, we also include the entrepreneur, since all the other Greek interview partners can be added to this list in a similar manner. As victims of the crisis, they testify to at least parts of the economic story.[3] The Germans confirm the general story and complement the narrative. The narrative of the documentary film can be formalized with the actant model, as shown in Table 2.

However, the narrative of the documentary film deals with the question of how to interpret the Greek crisis and what measures should be applied to solve the problem. According to Hébert's interpretative schema, following Greimas (see Section 3), the sender position is taken by Greece/Europe in crisis sending a request to the subject (the storyteller MP) in order find an explanation (economic theory) and a solution to the problem (leaving the EU). The storyteller tells his story (about economic competitiveness and reintroducing the drachma as a solution), which can be understood as a representative of the "object" actant. The "receiver" position is represented by the "solution to the crisis," reintroducing the drachma in Greece. The storyteller himself is the hero and should be positioned as the "subject" actant. The different people whom the storyteller meets in different scenes can be understood as "helpers" and/or "opponents" of the "subject."

The important argument for understanding the role of economists in this narrative is the relationship between the subject and the helper/opponent actants. The storyteller's conversation partners are requested to help or to oppose the

TABLE 4.2 *The Great Euro Crisis* (2012): Film narrative in the actant model.

Sender: euro and Greece in crisis	→	Object: MP's story	→	Receiver: Greece leaving the European monetary union
		↑		
Helper: the economist, the journalist, the entrepreneur (by *supporting* Portillo's economic story)	→	Subject: MP	←	Opponent: the economist, the journalist, the entrepreneur (by *rejecting* Portillo's policy)

subject achieving his or her goal. Every figure acts as a helper, insofar as each one supports, illustrates or testifies to parts of the story (therefore, *helping* the subject). Interestingly, the Greek economist seems to play a superior role here, since he confirms the entire story ("joining the European monetary union was not an economic but a political decision") and testifies to parts of it (by describing the corrupt political system and flawed economic policy, giving the example of the tax system). Nevertheless, every helper appears to be an opponent, too, because each one disagrees with the storyteller's demand to leave the European monetary union (therefore *opposing* the subject). Thus, the subject is being betrayed by the helper since the very same actors oppose the subject's mission.

The Greek and German interviewees hinder the subject achieving the goal of the narrative (reintroduction of the drachma, leaving the EU). Even the economist who is in a superior position compared to the other figures, since he is presented as someone who can fully evaluate the *MP's story* in all its details, is unable to let economic rationality rule the country. The political obstacles seem to be stronger. They hinder economic rationality finding its place and leading the narrative to a happy ending. This situation is now characterized by the need for economic rationality (to which nobody really objects) that faces the political impotence of a corrupt elite (a thesis that everybody confirms). This deadlock in which Greece (and Europe) is trapped leads to the next unavoidable dilemma, whereby an undemocratic European technocratic economic leadership, taking draconic austerity measures, appears to be the only solution to achieve international competitiveness.

As the analysis shows, economic expertise is simultaneously operating on two levels: on the one hand, at the level of the *MP's story*, and on the other, at the level of narrative *actants*, where economists play a superior role in evaluating or opposing the economic story, or at least parts of it. Thus, in the *narrative*, it is the economist who confirms the economic rationality of the economic story and, simultaneously, explains why the same economic rationality cannot endure.

This is how the narrative constructs a scenario of hopeless impasse. Greek institutions are "weak" and, therefore, in a way "uneconomic." What is required to reach a happy ending is a state apparatus that is able to act according to economic needs. At this point the dramatic situation is highlighted. This entire situation is already a drama. The fact that the Greek people cannot even vote democratically for the harsh economic austerity measures makes this entire situation even worse. Thus, as the final statement by Portillo shows, the EU is able to apply harsh but necessary measures, but it cannot build on democratic legitimacy and the people of Europe are moved outside democratic participation processes. In the narrative, Europe is stuck in a dilemma of austerity and democratic expropriation, and because the people cannot even vote for the harsh measures that are presented as necessary to regain competitiveness, they remain resentful of the only actor that can modernize Greece, i.e. Europe.

4.3. The economist's and the "British" point of view in utterances

The entire deadlock in which the narrative has ended up is a dilemma, especially for those people who are discursively positioned in a place called "Europe." The Europeans are caught between a rock and a hard place, the devil and the deep blue sea, where economic rationality can only rule at the price of democratic exclusion and social disasters. This desperate situation implies a discursive standpoint from which the problems can be solved according to economic rationality (regaining competitiveness) and democratic approval (through elections, discussions and so on in a democratically healthy political system). This standpoint is not a standpoint found within the tricky situation of Europe. On the other hand, it is the only reasonable point of view of rationality itself. It is the point from which the rational economist is able to oversee the battlefield and see why economic rationality is prevented from ruling the game in Europe and Greece.

Thus, next to the first economic expert position (represented by the *MP's story*, see Section 4.1) and the second one (represented by the helper/subject/opponent actants conflict, see Section 4.2), a third sort of economic expert positioning appears at the end of the film. Whereas the first one represents the place of "idealized rationality" and the second one might be called the place of "practical dilemma," the third position seems to be the place where "theory" (first position, Figure 4.1.) and "practice" (second position, Figure 4.2.) meet each other at a place of synthesis in "ideal practice."

A look at the final statement shows how this position is constructed on the microlevel of the film's discourse. The following statement is uttered after a final discussion with the journalist, the economist and the PASOK member of parliament who explain to Michael Portillo that there is no alternative to austerity and the EU if Greece is to become internationally competitive.

This discursive utterance will be analyzed in respect of its polyphonic organization. Polyphony analysis can show how the speaker of the discourse takes a final position. The utterance constructs a speaker position by enacting many voices. Voices (pov = point of view) are positions that can be accepted (indicated by

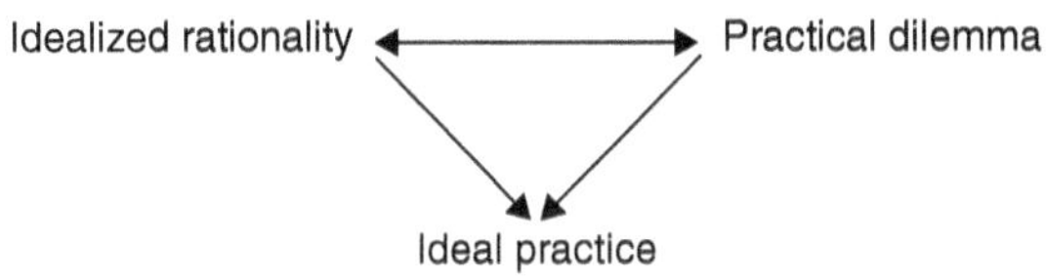

FIGURE 4.2 Different discourse positions of the film.

[m] = me) or rejected (indicated by [o] = the other). Only those voices that are accepted by the speaker of the discourse are possible candidates for the "speaker position." However, special emphasis is put on the last or final speaker position, since this particular voice is able to finalize the utterance and take the meaning to a certain point. This voice will be called [m/s]. Next to the position of the speaker [m] and the other [o], neutral voices [x] are evoked by discourse. These voices basically stand for "facts" that neither "me" nor the "other" calls into question.

> The fears [about a loss of competitiveness, JM] expressed by my friends are reflected by opinion polls across the Eurozone, where the majority support the idea of a more centralized Eurozone. <u>And yet</u> <u>*to me*</u> they do so <u>without</u> any clear notion of how this new Europe would work as a democracy.

BOX 4.1 POLYPHONIC ANALYSIS OF *THE GREAT EURO CRISIS* (2012)

pov_1[x]: the fears of Greek friends about a loss of competitiveness IMPLY a more centralized Eurozone
pov_2[o]: there is a clear notion of democracy (in Europe) (indicated by "without")
pov_3[m]: REJECTION OF pov_2
pov_4[m]: pov_1 SHOULD IMPLY pov_2 (indicated by "and yet")

In this part of the utterance an important candidate voice for the speaker position has been constructed by pov_4. With the statement "a more centralized Eurozone should imply a clear notion of Europe as a democracy," the speaker takes a view on a particular situation in Europe. But what does this situation look like in detail?

> […] Throughout the continent, governments are faltering as they face public opposition against the austerity measures. And now the voters in Greece and France have punished the politicians who try to impose them. People want the euro <u>*but*</u> <u>don't seem</u> prepared to accept the tough conditions attached […].

> **BOX 4.2 POLYPHONIC ANALYSIS OF *THE GREAT EURO CRISIS* (2012)**
>
> pov_5[x]: governments are faltering
> pov_6[x]: voters in Greece and France have punished the politicians
> pov_7[x]: people want the euro
> pov_8[m]: pov_7 IMPLIES SOMETHING (namely pov_9) THAT IS NOT CONSISTENT WITH pov_5 and pov_6 (indicated by "but")
> pov_9[o]: people are prepared to accept the tough conditions attached (austerity)
> pov_{10}[o]: NOT TRUE pov_9 (indicated by "don't")
> pov_{11}[m]: MAYBE pov_{10} (indicated by "seem")

This section develops a certain scenario ($pov_{5,\,6,\,7}$), whereby the European political system is confronted with a troublesome situation. And the speaker makes an evaluation of this situation with pov_8 and pov_{11} that can be summarized as follows: "Economic policy requires political stability and consent. This is, perhaps, not the case in Europe."

> [...] And in my view this means that the great Euro crisis is a *long way from* being solved.

> **BOX 4.3 POLYPHONIC ANALYSIS OF *THE GREAT EURO CRISIS* (2012)**
>
> pov_{12}[o]: the great euro crisis is being solved
> pov_{13}[o]: NOT TRUE pov_{12} (indicated by "long way from")
> pov_{14}[m/s]: IF pov_9 WAS TRUE, THEN pov_{12} (indicated by "and in my view this means")

With this last statement, the utterance reaches its final destination. Two things happen here. First, the troubles in $pov_{4,\,8,\,11}$ are not resolved and, second, the speaker seems to be definitively leaving this entire messy situation. "The euro crisis can be solved if the people accept tough conditions." This seems to be impossible within a heterogeneous cultural and economic system like Europe. For a citizen of the European Union, this conclusion would imply certain things (leaving the union, reform of the union etc.) in order to achieve economic rationality and reconcile it with political stability. Yet, for a member of the United Kingdom, this statement can imply completely different things. First and foremost, this implies that the UK is not in the same situation as the EU. Secondly, it can be read as an argument for no longer remaining in the EU. This conclusion can be connected with well-developed and good reasons, because the UK would be a place where economic rationality rules political stability. "Ideal practice" is what happens in the UK as a place outside the EU. At this point, the "financial wisdom" position that Portillo adopts right at the beginning of the documentary film can, through the audience's presupposition, easily be connected with pov_{14}.

However, through this kind of positioning, the economic expert is becoming separated and divorced from his expertise (knowledge). Due to political paralysis, economic rationality cannot rule in Europe and the economist as a figure is condemned to remain in a passive observing position. The narrative mission fails (because the receiver will not get the object and the subject misses his mission) and the entire film looks like being an example of what will happen to the UK if it does not vote to leave the Union in the forthcoming referendum (the Brexit campaign, that was voted on in June 2016).

Through this sort of split positioning, the economist takes the role of an admonisher: "As you can see, when economists cannot rule the country due to political chaos, rationality will not succeed even if everybody admits to it. Therefore, let's get out of this EU." Yet, this solution is only an apparent solution. The presented coherence of this "ideal practice" does not exist since pov_{14} is not a consistent position. It is rather a split place, entangled between the other voices that make up pov_{14}. As pov_{14} is a conditional clause, it opens up the discourse to different and even conflicting interpretations by different audiences in time and space. If this final position is the place of "financial wisdom" and "ideal practice" the entire film does not come to a happy end. It rather ends up in a socio-political dilemma, entangled in the contradictions that the film has developed on the macro as well as on the micro level of the narrative and of the utterance.

5. Conclusion: the film as a complex communicative device

The analysis has shown how *The Great Euro Crisis* creates a speaker position which is split between contradicting perspectives. The film does not send one coherent message. It offers an inconsistent interpretation schema elaborated through the "helper-opponent-contradiction" on the narrative level and it becomes particularly obvious at the utterance level.

As the structure of pov_{14} illustrates, the final speaker position, from which Portillo communicates to his audiences in the UK and Europe, is entirely split up through "IF" and "WAS," between pov_9 and pov_{12}. Pov_9 and pov_{12} are themselves contested by $pov_{10,11}$ and pov_{13} and the many other voices around. It is not the position pov_{14} as a single voice that forms Portillo's final statement. Rather the entire polyphonic game forms the speaker's position from which Portillo speaks to the audience. This opens up the documentary film to different interpretative scenarios, depending on the audience's position in time and space, social belonging and political orientation, professional background and educational level.

These interpretative scenarios can be analyzed when we listen and talk to people watching the film in different contexts. For illustrative purposes, let us imagine some scenarios. For example, the argument made by the film's discourse sounds, for certain British middle-class conservatives in 2012, like a "strong argument" for voting against the EU in the upcoming Brexit referendum. In contrast the film can be interpreted by Spanish, German or other European citizens as a plea for a more regulated financial system. The confident undertone in Portillo's split voice can give certain British people a feeling of supremacy and facilitation (we, the UK, have – thank God – nothing to do with this messy situation within European banking and economics) and it can be understood by Europeans as condescension about financial chaos.

At different points in time and history, the interpretative and communicative outcomes may also be slightly different. After Brexit in 2016, for example, the pound sterling fell to nearly 1 to 1 with the euro, and economic and political instability seems to be possible in the UK. Europe, in contrast, has at least solved parts of the crisis, and it seems, from a 2016 standpoint, that Europe will have a chance to build a more coherent financial and economic system. This further integration will probably be facilitated through Brexit, since the UK was always against a more integrated Europe. Now, the film looks like a "history lesson" for pro-Europeans across all countries, and like "foreboding" regarding what can happen in the UK but not in Greece.

However, the film as a financial expert's discourse now enters different communicative relations because the contexts of understanding have changed for both UK and European audiences. Yet, the formal communicative apparatus, constructed by the discourse, as analyzed above, remains the same. The scenario in the film looks from a post-Brexit viewpoint like a disaster that can happen in the UK as well. The Brexit crisis dynamic (decreases in industrial production, increases in prices for imported goods, devaluing of the pound sterling, the danger of falling housing prices etc.) can be interpreted as déjà vu, vis-à-vis the Greece crisis.

My analysis has demonstrated how the complex performances of economic expertise in the film open up space for interpretation. A film has no single meaning; it is rather a discursive apparatus for the construction of multiple meanings, changing from context to context. What we learn from this analysis is that the "financial wisdom" position, created as a complex set of inconsistencies, contradictions and open questions, is not a knowledge position. It is, rather, a political, hegemonic dispositif to reinforce a communicative message to multiple audiences in time and space that cannot be controlled by the author of the film. Economic expert discourses as well as the economization of our cognitive frames are not unilateral processes. They rather form a field of contested interpretations. The intended message of a film can quickly change meaning and might be directed against the political and ideological intentions of the filmmaker.

Notes

1 The film is available online at www.bbc.co.uk/programmes/b01hllyd
2 The film uses this designation and probably refers to MSF (Médecins Sans Frontières = doctors without borders).
3 Integration of the German interview partners into the analysis would be interesting, but it would not add any important content to the analysis.

References

Angermuller, Johannes. 2013. "How to Become a Philosopher. Academic Discourse as a Multi-Levelled Positioning Practice." *Sociología Histórica*, 3, 263–289.

Bourdieu, Pierre. 1989. *Distinction. A Social Critique of the Judgement of Taste*. London: Routledge.

Fitzgerald, Joseph K. and Brendan K. O'Rourke. 2016. "Legitimising Expertise: Analysing the Legitimation Strategies Used by Economics Experts in Broadcast Interviews." *Journal of Multicultural Discourses*, 11(3), 269–282.

Foucault, Michel. 1980. *Power/Knowledge. Selected Interviews and Other Writings*. New York: Pantheon Books.

Fourcade, Marion. 2009. *Economists and Societies. Discipline and Profession in the United States, Britain, and France, 1890s to 1990s*. Princeton and Oxford: Princeton University Press.

Greimas, Julien A. 1976. *On Meaning. Selected Writings in Semiotic Theory*. Minneapolis: University of Minnesota Press.

Hébert, Louis. 2011. *Signo. Theoretical Semiotics on the Web. The Actantal Model*. www.signosemio.com/greimas/a_actantiel.asp.

Hirschman, Daniel and Elisabeth Popp Berman. 2014. "Do Economists Make Policies? On the Political Effects of Economics." *Socio-Economic Review*, 12, 779–811.

Jameson, Fredric. 1976. "Foreword." In *On Meaning. Selected Writings in Semiotic Theory*, by Julien A. Greimas. Minneapolis: University of Minnesota Press, VI–XXII.

Lebaron, Frederic. 2014. The World of Economics: A "Strong Field" – Pegged to the Field of Power. *Presentation at the workshop "Die Soziologie ökonomischen Wissens", Jena*.

Maesse, Jens. 2015. "Economic Experts. A Discursive Political Economy of Economics." *Journal of Multicultural Discourses*, 10(3), 279–305.

Maesse, Jens. 2016. "The Power of Myth. The Dialectics Between 'Elitism' and 'Academism' in Economic Expert Discourse." *European Journal of Cross Cultural Communication, Special Issue: Culture, Integration and Communication: Issues and Approaches in Higher Education Contexts*, 4(1), 3–20.

Zienkowski, Jan. 2016. *Articulations of Self and Politics in Activist Discourse: A Discourse Analysis of Critical Subjectivities in Minority Debates*. Springer.

SECTION 2

Critical interventions

5

FINANCE, CRISIS, AND HOLLYWOOD

Critique and recuperation of Wall Street in films about the Great Recession

Karen Ho

The Hollywood "Wall Street movie" has long dramatized the practices and effects of hubris, conspiracy, and excess in destabilizing American corporations, cornering financial markets, and engendering financial crisis. Wall Street passions and machinations have always been key narrative drivers in this genre, and it might well be assumed that film has, for its own purposes, exaggerated some of the more sensational aspects of the finance industry. John Paul Rollert, who teaches business ethics at the Booth School of Business, University of Chicago, has observed that many Wall Street films, in their seemingly "reckless celebration of excess," can also lead audiences to bear witness to "the grotesqueries of greed" and thus question whether "the American Dream" should be a "nihilistic bacchanal where any excess is redeemed by the ability to be excessive" (Rollert 2014).

In the wake of the global financial crisis of 2008, however, it has become unclear whether Hollywood's focus on the "economic" desires and fantasies of elite white men has been hyperbolic at all. In fact, it might be that the dramatic amplifications of Wall Street genre films and docudramas actually capture the dizzying extent to which the dreams, anxieties, and enactments of financial actors helped to construct and catalyze multiple financial crises over the past thirty years. In this regard, these films have been terrifyingly prescient: given that the global socio-economic catastrophes of 2008 were the stunning aftershocks of a finance-instigated hypercapitalism in overdrive, the seeming exaggerations of the financial film are revealed as less fantastical and perhaps more akin to realist drama.

To what extent have Wall Street "crisis" films been able to capture the outrageousness of unsustainable and turbo-charged financialization in a way that more "measured" approaches have missed? Fantasy (and the fantastical) in Hollywood can often reinforce the kinds of hierarchies they purportedly seek to destabilize – thus it is also crucial to investigate which seemingly critical cinematic approaches to finance merely reproduce Wall Street assumptions, and which ones better diagnose the contemporary moment. This endemic problem of the inadvertent recuperation and reproduction of dominant finance, even by critics in a variety of fields, is a vital site of intervention precisely because Wall Street's fall turned out, in fact, to be short-lived. In this chapter, recognizing finance's continued grip on the global economy, I examine the politics of critical visual representations of finance, launched in the wake of the Great Recession, in order to analyze the extent to which they challenged and/or maintained dominant financial norms and assumptions.

Despite the fact that it is was precisely the major financial institutions on Wall Street that catalyzed and played the largest part in generating global financial crisis, they were bailed out, rescued, and consistently subsidized with very little pressure for reform. According to the New York State Comptroller's Office, for example, by 2009 the Wall Street bonus pool, to be distributed mainly to high-level investment bankers and traders, had already risen to $22.5 billion, the highest in history aside from the three years leading up to the 2008 crash. A crucial question, then, is why: why, after such a massive failure of financial models and practices, and after such a massive challenge to dominant finance's legitimacy in the world, was Wall Street allowed to reconsolidate its power?

It is beyond the scope of this chapter to depict the ways in which Wall Street captured and managed an increasing share of the savings of Main Street as well as the earnings of corporate America, and as such, commanded a bailout in the name of the larger social economy. However, the question of how Wall Street can continue to claim meritocratic expertise after the 2008 disaster is an issue that an analysis of recent "crisis" films can address. From blockbusters such as *The Wolf of Wall Street* (M. Scorsese, 2013) or *The Big Short* (A. McKay, 2015), to docudramas such as *The Last Days of Lehman Brothers* (M. Samuels, 2009) or *Too Big to Fail* (C. Hanson, 2011), a wide range of Wall Street films has broadly engaged with the key themes of financial crisis – the causes, the extent of financial rationality and/or irrationality, and the socio-economic effects. The rebounding of the markets, however, has led to the crucial question of why criticism of finance has seemingly been ineffective. To what extent have the various critiques and analyses of visual media failed to reframe and transform the broader cultural understanding of finance, and to what extent have they shined light on the infrastructure and inner workings of Wall Street? Specifically, it is important to examine whether or not these films inadvertently celebrate the crisis-inducing "bro culture" they claim to be indicting, and whether or not they recuperate the myth of market rationality.

Of course, these vexing questions, problematic binds, and binary traps permeate all discourse on finance, and certainly go beyond film and visual representations. Academia itself, especially given that influential subfields in economics have been key architects of such theories as the efficient market hypothesis and the imperative of shareholder value maximization, has participated in creating the very ideological infrastructure that legitimates global financial markets. Many academic disciplines, such as the subfields of economic sociology and the social studies of finance, have critiqued these developments, although, as I will detail, they fall into similar traps when they reproduce binaries of economy and society, representing "economy" as rational and self-governing and "society" as cultural and particular.

As a scholar long engaged with the anthropology of finance, I believe that the most important development in critical scholarship in the wake of the 2008 implosion is the recent focus on the ways in which the subjectivities of financial actors imbue and co-constitute the construction and trajectory of financial markets. In other words, various affects (from emotion and desire to insecurity) intersect with race, gender, sexuality, and class identities and positions, as well as with institutional and national locations, to shape financial practices, values, and models. These studies have demonstrated that finance (not to mention markets, capitalism, and the larger political economy) is always already constituted by interests, passions, relationships, and emotions, and that misrecognizing finance as acultural and dispassionate would necessarily mystify not only everyday financial norms, but the making of crisis and inequality. (See, for example, Cooper and McFall 2017, de Goede 2005b, Figlio 2011, Ho 2009, Konings 2015, Krippner 2012, McGowan 2016, Miyazaki 2013, Thrift 2001, Yanagisako 2002, Zaloom 2010. Such nuanced treatments will serve as important inspirational models for this analysis of Wall Street film.)

Problematic binaries: Hollywood excess and the othering of the irrational

Wall Street's return to business as usual in the face of critique leads me to the critically acclaimed, blockbuster films *The Wolf of Wall Street* by Martin Scorsese and *The Big Short* by Adam McKay, both exemplary in their illustration of how film can trenchantly critique Wall Street, and yet leave normative assumptions about financial markets relatively intact. With both films, it is precisely how they construct and reproduce differences and hierarchies between "rationality" and "irrationality" that in turn allows a rejuvenation of "true" market rationality. By disentangling the rational from the irrational, as well as making clear that the latter ought to be excised from the everyday workings of normative markets, the films hint that finance can perhaps be redeemed.

The Wolf of Wall Street *and the marginalization of excess*

Writing for *The Atlantic*, John Paul Rollert makes the case that while *The Wolf of Wall Street* was accused of celebrating excess, bacchanal fantasies, and misogyny (like many Wall Street films), it is "actually one of the most scathing critiques of Wall Street" Hollywood has ever produced (Rollert 2014). According to Rollert, Scorsese, by refusing to get stuck in the details of explaining financial transactions, aims higher and works on a grander scale, focusing on a larger point – that we are all getting screwed by Wall Street's decadence and excess. Without overt moralization, the film shows that excess for the sake of excess (and self-interest for the sake of self-interest) lead to moral corrosion and incoherence precisely because the audience recognizes that most people do *not benefit* from a culture of universal greed. While I am sympathetic to this interpretation and do not necessarily agree with those critics of *The Wolf of Wall Street* who are wary of the unintentional consequences of its over-the-top representations of financial excess and "bro culture," my critique diverges from both positions: I make the case that the film unfortunately reproduces the binary of rational and irrational, wherein normative finance is portrayed as rational precisely because the excessive is marginalized.

From a Wall Street perspective, the film's anti-hero, Jordan Belfort of Stratton Oakmont, is already framed as "external" to dominant finance and normative financial markets. In fact, he is more akin to a marginal huckster than an investment banker because, in the financial hierarchy, stockbrokers – as a class of workers – are not really understood as part of Wall Street at all. Because they make a living selling stocks to middle-class individuals and households, not corporate institutions, large investment funds, or sovereign entities, they are framed as inferior in both occupational status and socio-economic class. The film reproduces this sensibility: the origin story of Belfort and his fictional firm of Stratton Oakmont begins outside of Manhattan. He builds his team of scrappy stockbrokers from his childhood networks in the middle- and working-class neighborhoods of Queens. His chosen product, "penny stocks," not only harkens back to the days of unregulated bucket shops in pre-Depression Wall Street but is understood as the unvarnished financial con, the liminal "outside" to the fancy structured products of high finance. While these specific character traits and cultural contexts – Belfort's bootstrapping ambition, his transformation from average Joe into "stockbrokering" mogul – provide the narrative drive, they also place Belfort decisively outside the imaginary of dominant finance.

Specifically, Belfort's aspirational, aggressive, and masculinist class-mimicking performance catalyzes his enterprising spirit *and* carries the excess too far. As shown in the opening montage with an actual lion walking through the trading floor of Stratton Oakmont as part of a corporate commercial, Belfort's bald-faced, over-the-top embrace of hyper masculinity immediately alerts the audience that financial culture will be interpreted as excess, and perhaps more importantly, that Belfort is somehow not quite normative, mainstream, and/or "inside" dominant finance enough to take its culture for granted. In other words, by taking Wall Street's braggart masculinity at face value, Belfort betrays his own lack of fluency with the codes of normative financial markets. In dominant marketspeak, for example, official, "outward-facing" discourses attempt to project acultural-ness despite the fact that masculinity and white fraternal networks are actively and simultaneously embraced. Belfort's inability to flexibly "code switch" betrays his own lack of cultivation and reveals the "declassé" status of stockbrokers in comparison to high finance.

This class division and hierarchy matter precisely because in contemporary cultural formations, lower class (and other liminal) social categories function as the repository for "culture." As with any reductive binary formations, even though the "culture" can be "positive," (i.e. working classes and people of color are often framed as more passionate, fun, and in touch with nature), the many social ramifications include the fact that those categories understood as unmarked and acultural escape scrutiny as well as claim normativity. *The Wolf of Wall Street* is wholly in line with the discursive assumptions of dominant finance when it represents liminal, "wannabe" stockbrokers as embodying excess – hypermasculinity, heightened sexuality, and hyperconsumption, combined with irrationality and fraud. When Jordan Belfort is caught, inevitably imploding under the weight of his own excesses, it is his distance and divergence from the norm that is penalized, not the norm itself. Of course, one could certainly argue that Scorsese intended Jordan Belfort to symbolize *all* of Wall Street – yet his positionality as a stockbroker and his characterization as "marked" white ethnic social climber with over-the-top masculinity position him as the "stranger within" and thus a convenient foil for of dominant finance.

Other Hollywood blockbusters, from *Dances with Wolves* to *Avatar*, reproduce this hierarchical logic of rejuvenation. Just as the downfall of Jordan Belfort allows for a recuperation of normative markets, in *Dances with Wolves*, Kevin Costner's 1991 Oscar winner for best picture, native peoples – as the "primitive" repositories of "culture" – provide the necessary regeneration for a white nation that had grown increasingly corrupt and soulless.[1] Whereas Belfort's primitivity symbolically absorbs the irrational excess of financial markets, it is through the adoption of "Indian ways" that Lieutenant John Dunbar, the white male soldier protagonist of *Dances with Wolves*, escapes the increasing degeneracy of Euro-American society, allows his more interconnected, "true identity" to emerge, and, "cleanse[s]...the corruption of European-American life" (Huhndorf 2001, 4–5). At the end of the film, Dunbar fights heroically for his adopted band of Lakota Indians, and thus the ensuing conquest of Native America is accompanied by an assuaging of white guilt and a "regeneration of racial whiteness and European-American society" (Huhndorf 2001, 3). In both films, it is through the simultaneous appropriation and rejection of the primitive that excess and degeneracy are excised and dominant forms can regain normative legitimacy.

A similar dynamic can be found in the development of modern finance. Marieke de Goede states that the "development of finance as an academic discipline and professional practice has historically depended upon the abstraction of all that is considered to be 'human' from this domain. In other words, financial study and decision-making are supposed to exist independently from culture, society, history, sexuality and emotion" (de Goede 2005a, 22). As de Goede painstakingly demonstrates, however, the now normative understanding of the stock market as the rational epitome of financial markets was made possible by constructing a contrastive, gendered binary, where speculation and panic were relegated to the realm of the (irrational) feminine so that masculine rationality would come to be associated with measured "risk-taking," calculated using the tools of science to enact reductive economic theories and ideologies. Of course, critical scholars of finance have long shown that "rationality" is less a characteristic of actually existing finance than it is the product of "gendered discourses that contrast masculine rationality with feminine irrationality" in order to frame contemporary normative finance as properly risk-taking, not irrationally speculative (de Goede 2005a, 22). De Goede argues that Wall Street's appropriation of "rationality" was the result of political advocacy and discursive framing intended to shift influence to the financial sector and to legitimate a particular regime of financial exchange (de Goede 2005b).

This legacy (though not always marked by the same gendered representations) carries on into the contemporary moment, explaining how dominant financial actors, institutions, and practices have been able to return to business as usual by once again laying claim to meritocracy, rationality, and expertise while delimiting and segregating the crisis – characterizing it as the work of "a few bad apples," or the result of temporary "irrational exuberance." Normative markets, it turns out, have long relied on appeals to well-established binaries to return to legitimacy; by framing "the human" as a "disturbing and distorting influence on economic fundamentals," markets (which were framed through this depoliticizing device of abstraction) were salvaged (de Goede 2005a, 23).

The Big Short *and the unexpected recuperation of Wall Street from within*

In *The Wolf of Wall Street* marginalized stockbrokers concentrate and dramatize the excesses of Wall Street, and when these stockbrockers are undone, normative Wall Street rids itself of irrational liabilities. In *The Big Short*, by contrast, iconoclast investors are seen as potential saviors of Wall Street (and the US), if only people would listen to them. While these two films seem to be making opposing arguments, I would like to argue that the films actually represent two sides of the same coin – that both are implicated in the project to rejuvenate dominant finance. On the one hand, irrationality needs to be "othered" and jettisoned; on the other, rationality needs to be recuperated from within, from the center, where it belongs.

Like Belfort in *The Wolf of Wall Street*, the key protagonists of *The Big Short* are represented as a having an "outsider" sensibility – not in terms of excessive masculinity nor in terms of subpar job classification, but in terms of their iconoclastic style and "renegade" approach to investing. Unlike Belfort, however, they are not stockbrokers but high-status Wall Street traders and investors that represent institutions from large hedge funds to Morgan Stanley and Deutsche Bank. In this sense, they reside at the very center of Wall Street, but have not been seduced by the irrationality that has taken hold of seemingly everyone else in the financial sector. These "cynical investor-heroes," to borrow a phrase from film critic Andrew Barker, are all misfits and oddballs: socially uncontaminated upstarts, loners, and/or jaded elders. Dr Michael Burry (a doctor turned hedge fund investor, who is on the autism spectrum), Mark Baum (an angry, disaffected hedge fund manager with a conscience at a subsidiary of Morgan Stanley), two young "garage-finance" startups, and Ben Rickert (a former Wall Street trader who had escaped the predations of Wall Street) (Barker 2015). As *The Big Short* weaves these characters together, it becomes clear that they stand in for "the smartest guys in the room." They are deserving of their place on Wall Street because of their genius, manic energy, and adherence to market fundamentals, all of which help them to discover that the housing market is going to crash before anyone else. The film, then, seems to advocate a return to purist market fundamentals rather than a radical reform of Wall Street.

The film's recuperation of Wall Street from within only makes sense in light of the larger context of widespread recognition of failure at the center of things, at least for a few years after 2008. From the 1980s until the Great Recession, the ideological assumption that financial markets were rational, efficient, and the best allocators of capital was undoubtedly the dominant belief on Wall Street and in academic finance circles. Nowhere was this ideology more fully embraced than in the realm of stock prices and the financialization of companies: the fantastical idea, abstractly developed in the academic models of a few financial economists, was that embedded within the company's stock price was all the best and most relevant information on how to approach and invest in the corporation itself – future profit projections, corporate strategy, even the optimal way to govern the institution (Jensen 1986, Jensen and Meckling 1976, Dobbin and Zorn 2005, Fox 2009). As such, all an investor and/or an executive had to do was focus on raising a company's stock price, and *everything* would fall into place: shareholder benefits would redound to all stakeholders. The underlying assumption here, of course, is that the *number*, the stock *price*, is always already rational and "right": as an efficient embodiment of mass information and interpretation, it has already distilled the market consensus and canceled out the human factors that can be swayed by various individual proclivities or irrationalities.

Thus, one of the most earth-shattering revelations to emerge from the 2008 crisis was the recognition, even at the highest levels, that finance, and in particular these ideas of efficient markets and shareholder value primacy, was growing increasingly *irrational*, and even more importantly, the growing suspicion that the ideology of rational markets was itself a *myth*. In fact, the critical journalist Justin Fox, in *The Myth of the Rational Market*, painstakingly traces the creation of this ideal model and theory, and how it came to serve as a proxy for actually existing markets. Fox illustrates the puncturing of this worldview with a depiction of former Chairman of the Federal Reserve Alan Greenspan testifying in front of the House Committee on Government Oversight and Reform, admitting that his "view of the world… was not right" (Fox 2009, xi). Greenspan self-describes his "shock" that financial markets were not as exceptionally "smart" as he had presumed. Fox summarizes:

> [This] ideology…widely shared in Washington and on Wall Street [was that] [f]inancial markets knew best. They moved capital from those who had it to those who needed it. They spread risk. They gathered and dispersed information. They regulated global economic affairs with a swiftness and decisiveness that governments couldn't match.
>
> *(Fox 2009, xii)*

In this context, then, of dominant finance out of balance, where big investment banks have captured rating agencies and regulators, and networks of smug bankers are too busy capitalizing on their institutional advantages and cultural capital while preying on the hopes and precarities of others to bother with actual data, it is those men smart enough to belong in finance, yet eccentric enough not to be corrupted by the trappings of Wall Street, who become the new role models. In a tale of Wall Street outsmarting Wall Street, the audience witnesses financial excess, folly, corruption, and fraud from the perspectives of highly capable and nuanced actors who, in the end, represent inadvertent, "internal" checks on Wall Street madness. For example, Burry is a mathematical whiz who painstakingly does the hard work to gather mass amounts of data in order to interpret and intuit subprime's impending doom. Similarly, Baum's tracking of subprime money flows leads him to undertake a research mission in Florida where he observes mortgage brokers bragging about the commissions they make by pushing unsustainable mortgage terms on to unwitting buyers. Because of their intense eccentricity and anti-social approach to Wall Street's "bro culture," they are not fully socialized or seduced into normative practices and shortcuts – which is in fact what enables them to conduct "due diligence" research and fulfill their potential as avatars of the market. As such, they are the first to spot the warning signs of impending market disaster, figure out a "play" to bet against (i.e. "short") the market, and make a fortune in the wake of millions of people rendered homeless and jobless.

In this landscape of normative finance gone awry, then, where the majority of bankers and traders are caught up in the "irrationalities" of the business, it is the iconoclastic investor who can re-rationalize the markets: by refocusing on the data generated by financial measures and models, these actors reaffirm that market fundamentals can be used to ascertain "true" value. Such a move parallels the ideals of the efficient market hypothesis and is thus, advertently or inadvertently, a reaffirmation of the core legitimacy of rational markets. In addition, because the key protagonists are anti-social experts, they understand finance without being encumbered by its corrupting social hierarchies; as such, they showcase an underlying faith in the rational potential of the market once the noise and frivolities are stripped away. Because the heroes come from "within" finance, and are part of a shrinking minority in the industry that still abides by an old-school "rationality" – the notion that the price of securities should reflect a rigorous assessment of its value – they are fully consistent with Wall Street self-representations.

Of course, the ending of *The Big Short* has led to critical ambivalence over what constitutes the larger intervention and moral of the film. As the film's conscience, Mark Baum realizes that his and the others' actions actually reproduce Wall Street assumptions: once he and his colleagues reap the benefits of the short, "we'll be just like the rest of them," and *there is no lesson*. Specifically, the protagonists' shorting of the market does not teach or discipline Wall Street because the system does fail *and yet* the powerful are rescued. As such, Wall Street's extractive practices are not only elided, rationalized, and normalized, but also subsidized and bailed out. As Baum opines, "They knew the taxpayers would bail them out. They weren't being stupid; they just didn't care." Capturing these conflicting emotions, the *New York Times*'s A. O. Scott concludes,

> The film's final images, its abrupt shift in tone from exhilaration to exhaustion, its suddenly downbeat music (by Nicholas Britell) all combine to trigger a climactic wave of almost unbearable disgust. It offers no solutions, and no comfort.
>
> *(Scott 2015)*

The finale of *The Big Short* certainly encourages critical thought, even harkening to Audre Lorde's crucial observation that the master's tools cannot dismantle the master's house. At the same time, precisely because the narrative compels the audience to root for the central protagonists and identify with their commitment to rational markets, the film still implicitly concedes that the expertise of Wall Street is necessary to expose and rein in markets. By using their intensity in the service of the fundamentals to counter the irrationality of markets, the heroes of *The Big Short* show how markets can be reworked from within, and how a group of smart men can recoup the ideals of the rational market even if the system cannot truly be reformed. Perhaps not surprisingly, it turns out that this "saving of Wall Street" is very similar to Michael Lewis's argument in *Moneyball* (B. Miller, 2011) where a rational, data-driven approach to baseball cuts away at the accumulated biases and blind spots of the game's conventional wisdom and enables a (relatively) poor, small-market team to compete.[2]

Finally, I want to end this section with an interrogation of why critiques of Wall Street's irrationality lack staying power. I offer the explanation that "the irrational" gets translated *into* "the rational" through normatively accepted magical thinking about financial markets. In other words, the very ideological precept that financial markets take in and adjudicate the collective judgments of millions of (rational) market actors and spit out "the right" answer (i.e. the stock price) is a fantastical formula that makes possible and normalizes an alchemy that transforms the irrational into the rational. Ironically, even though this model presumes what has already been debunked, that market actors are normatively "rational," the consistency of the rational inputs does not actually matter: the collective judgment of all available information cancels out individual misjudgments and irrationalities. This rationalizing pipeline of financial information importantly dovetails with Wall Street's key moral framework, which similarly transmutes a variety of "immoral" practices and proclivities, from fraud to greed, into the larger, "moral" good via the magic of the market. Taken together, these two processes – transformation of the irrational into the rational, and of the immoral into the moral – do not simply strengthen each other, but are part and parcel of the way in which modern finance came to construct its legitimacy and its dominance in the first place (de Goede 2005b).

It is important to recognize that Wall Street, in line with well-developed tenets of conservative philosophy, has long claimed to transmute seemingly sinful interests, values, and proclivities into socially positive outcomes: thus, its assertions of productivity can be read as part and parcel of this larger transvaluation of values. Such a move is nowhere more evident than in Hollywood movies such as Oliver Stone's iconic *Wall Street*, which is illustrative of what might be called "the irrationality" of financial morality. For example, Gordon Gekko's penultimate speech exemplifies the new normative discourse of how Wall Street understands the capitalist moral order:

> The point is, ladies and gentlemen, that greed – for lack of a better word – is good. Greed is right. Greed works. Greed clarifies, cuts through and captures the essence of evolutionary spirit. Greed in all of its forms – greed for life, for money, for love, [for] knowledge, has marked the upward surge of mankind and greed – you mark my words – will not only save Teldar Paper but that other malfunctioning corporation called the USA. Thank you very much.
>
> *(O. Stone,* Wall Street *1987)*

In other words, critiques of Wall Street immorality are not only potentially ineffective on a societal level, but are also not heard as such by Wall Streeters themselves precisely because the local morality of finance – from MBA programs to Wall Street firms – already socializes participants into the neoclassical economic philosophy that "immoral" and/or "amoral" thoughts and behavior (i.e. self-interest and greed) lead to "moral" outcomes. Of course, the very fact that this assumption – that socio-economic goods such as efficient corporations and innovative allocation of capital arise from the excesses of Wall Street greed – has been soundly critiqued and shown to be an unsustainable smokescreen in the wake of massive crises has not loosened the hold of this ideology. As I have argued elsewhere, however, Oliver Stone's critique was not necessarily heeded nor even "heard" on Wall Street precisely because notions of greed, excess, and (creative) destruction are already incorporated into Wall Street's moral philosophy as central elements (Ho 2012).

Docudramas and the interrogation of rational "free markets"

In the previous sections, I made the argument that, despite the fact that finance is neither rational nor efficient, *and* despite the fact that *The Wolf of Wall Street*, *The Big Short*, and, yes, *Wall Street* (O. Stone, 1987) had intended to critique finance, the dominant logics and assumptions of financial market rationality and possibility remain intact. In a sense, movies that amplify the excesses of Wall Street ironically reinforce its fundamental norms. A necessary follow-up, then, would be to examine a more "realist" mode of representing dominant finance to analyze whether or not a deliberate attempt to approach the everyday "reality of Wall Street, might be better able to explore the actual inefficiencies and irrationalities that constitute finance. In fact, I make the observation that delving into the daily social facts of Wall Street, as opposed to pre-formed imaginaries and narratives of Wall Street that often fall prey to dominant models, allows a more nuanced and contextual understanding and representation of the actual workings of the finance industry.

Ironically, the category of the docudrama might escape the fictional overdetermination of Wall Street. *Too Big To Fail*, an HBO dramatization of Andrew Ross

Sorkin's journalistic tour-de-force by the same name, and *The Last Days of Lehman Brothers*, a BBC dramatization of the last three days before Lehman Brothers' bankruptcy, use the context of spiraling crisis to highlight the elite few who proxy for "the market" and why such a narrow band of actors, institutions, and concerns goes against most mainstream assumptions about the construction of fair, efficient, and rational financial markets. The deliberate focus on the power and influence of a few key men and institutions flies in the face of normative assumptions about the so-called "invisible hand."

Against a backdrop of impending financial doom, with key institutions refusing access to credit, both films focus on the intense negotiations and navigations between elite financial and governmental actors as they decide how and whether to rescue or jettison some of the largest investment banks in the world. Though it is unclear how self-consciously the filmmakers see investment banking CEOs and governmental leaders as *standing in for* "the system," i.e. for the entirety of the financial sector and even the economy as a whole, it becomes clear that these "few good men," so to speak, understood themselves that way, and thus equated self-preservation with saving the country – if not the world. Specifically, the viewer witnesses how a handful of privileged white men have sought, and been granted, the authority to represent institutional interests and monies, and to amass (and deny others) collective power through their own networks. Moreover, and this is crucial, both the analysis and narrative drive of these films are set in motion by the relationships and hierarchies among these men: their trust and confidence (or lack thereof) in each other, their resentments and memories of historical slights and indignities, how they turn a blind eye to conflicts of interest and regulatory capture, etc., all shape their market decisions.

In this context, I make the case that in these two films, the imagined and much-heralded free markets in finance are shown to be *irrational oligarchies*: the millions of "rational" investors that supposedly comprise the decision-making processes of the free markets, especially in finance, are revealed as nothing more than a convenient fiction. Instead, a handful of elite men decide the fate of global financial markets based on interpersonal networks, reputation, pride, and self-preservation. Is this not the epitome of irrationality and the explosion of the myth of the rational market? The "realist" portrayals within these films do not showcase autonomy, rationality, or efficiency; on the contrary, we see backroom bailouts, conflicts of interest, massive individual and institutional failures and denials, individual anxieties and proclivities, and the mobilization of undue influence.

The Last Days of Lehman Brothers begins with the desperate downward spiral of Lehman Brothers and the frantic phone calls of CEO Dick Fuld, who is attempting to stop the hemorrhaging stock price and demands for collateral by trying to broker a sale of Lehman or garner a last-minute loan. The crux of the problem is revealed when US Treasury Secretary Hank Paulson, a former Goldman Sachs CEO, calls a meeting of the major Wall Street investment bankers at the New York Fed and explicitly forbids Mr. Fuld to participate. Paulson announces by fiat that "there is *no public money*" to bail out Lehman, not even for a few days to bridge or "sweeten" a potential deal with another bank. Such an announcement not only forces the other CEOs to reckon with the precarious state of their own banks (and contemplate the possibility of themselves being "hung out to dry"), but also pushes them toward mobilizing their own networks of bankers to orchestrate a "private solution" to avert Lehman's downfall, which would expose them all. When a few of the CEOs refuse to take Paulson's bait and threaten to leave, he utters the key ultimatum of the film:

> The West is fucked. We fucked it up. Oh, not just you and me. All of us. The West, it's done; it's over. You want to call it a game, this is the game. You want your great grandchildren speaking Chinese; the dollar's gonna go. We had Rome, then Europe, then this. We screw it all up. We ran through it all. And, we come out on the other side.... We have this one weekend, where maybe we can come up with something to hold it all together a little while longer...

In this scene, it becomes jarringly evident that Wall Street investment bankers are "the we" who equate themselves (their livelihoods, their influence, their institutional power and reach) with "the West" – with the North Atlantic economy, the monetary flows and market exchanges that undergird it, and by extension, the very structure and survival of civilization itself. Beyond the sheer hubris and self-importance presumed by this statement, it is striking the extent to which the US treasury, the Fed, Wall Street – and perhaps the viewers of this docudrama themselves – have internalized and naturalized a particular financial oligarchy's presumption of power and influence, and, in turn, helped to enact a self-fulfilling prophecy. In other words, the belief that Wall Street "is" the market *and* "is" the West not only centralizes financial markets as the single most important institutional structure in and of the West, but also means that in order to prevent "the fall" of the West, Wall Street must be made whole again. Thus, Wall Street becomes the key node – as both the seat of the key decision-makers as well as the key recipient of investments – through which "we" are rescued.

The Last Days of Lehman Brothers ends with an understanding that Lehman's failure was an exception to the practice of bailout, a desperate attempt to mimic and model a "free market" approach to Wall Street-led financial crisis by refusing to shore up Lehman's toxic assets with public money, to broker a merger with a healthier bank, or to provide a loan to bridge a deal. The Treasury Department and the Federal Reserve had hoped that allowing Lehman to fall would showcase their resolve to avoid moral hazard and to bolster free market dreams – but instead they succeeded only in highlighting the orchestrated singularity of this one-time refusal. The fact that "everyone before and everyone after got bailed out" – not to mention the policy and regulatory apparatus that has favored finance over the past thirty years – demonstrated that free markets are anything but free. Moreover, the film showcases the cultural and temporal particularity that imbues market decision-making. As we are shown Dick Fuld's anxiety and isolation, as well as the timing of Lehman's freefall (after the bailout of Bear Stearns), the audience wonders how much Goldman Sachs's historical role as a competitor contributed to the sacrifice of Lehman – not to mention Hank Paulson's judgment that Lehman was poorly run and over-leveraged in its market positions, as well as his apparent personal distaste for Fuld.

Too Big To Fail extends this theme – of government's privileging of finance as the central site of its intervention – towards a more troubling conclusion. For the majority of the film, the viewer experiences the action through the affective lens of the protagonist Treasury Secretary Hank Paulson. We not only feel his agitation but also his market sympathies and overarching hope for preserving high finance in the face of impending self-inflicted destruction. Like *The Last Days of Lehman Brothers*, the film centers on the Lehman debacle and Paulson's vexed relationship with it: he desperately hopes Lehman can be rescued *without* governmental intervention, and yet the viewer also senses that he is willing to sacrifice Lehman to demonstrate the risk of moral hazard (even for one day), to bolster his own reputation for toughness, and, perhaps most importantly, to demonstrate just how crucial (or at least interlinked) finance was for the US economy and beyond.

The turning point of the docudrama arises when Paulson gets the call from the CEO of General Electric conveying that it cannot fund "day to day" operations, that business in America could be "shutting down." The post-Lehman onslaught of near-insolvencies (of multiple financial and corporate institutions, not to mention credit markets) puts Paulson over the edge, and he develops a new heroic resolve to rescue Wall Street. In fact, the viewer recognizes that Treasury and the Federal Reserve are willing to mobilize their entire arsenal of resources and strategic toolkit to make Wall Street whole again, even if it means imbuing finance with even *more* power and resources. After the failure of Lehman, the film's action turns from regulatory attempts to admonish and temper Wall Street to efforts to save it. The locus of power and attention shifts from Wall Street bankers trying desperately to establish contact and airtime with key governmental actors to Treasury and Federal Reserve officials acting as Wall Street's suitors. The cameras shift from key governmental actors (such as Hank Paulson) at the head of a table of Wall Street CEOs, to these same actors huddled outside in hallways and waiting rooms hoping for Wall Street to accept their generous offers of bailout with no strings attached. By the end of the film, Paulson and Bernanke are filmed gazing out the window contemplating whether or not Wall Street will ever think beyond their narrow and self-serving understandings of markets.

By the end of the film, Paulson, Geithner, and Bernanke are literally handing out cheap money to all the major banks whether or not they need it. *Too Big To Fail* shows that the overwhelming strategy of regulators became "giv[ing] them [Wall Street] money so they would lend it out," and promoting the fiction that all the major banks left standing were robust by offering "cover" money to both weak and strong banks, so no one could differentiate between them. In a discussion with his staff, who wants "to take the stink off" the bailout and cash handouts by inserting restrictions on how banks spend the money, or by announcing a corollary plan to also help average mortgage holders, Paulson brashly dismisses them. "Put more restrictions on it? They won't take it!" As Paulson walks away, the film pivots to Michelle Davis, Assistant Secretary, Public Affairs in the Treasury Department, who indignantly states, "They almost bring down the US economy as we know it, but we can't put restrictions on how they spend the 125 billion we're *giving* them because…they might not take it?!" Serving as a moral compass in the film, Davis's point of view drives home the film's critique: that "calming the markets" was imagined almost solely in terms of stabilizing the most powerful institutions, and that Paulson, Geithner, and Bernanke exhibited not only a spectacular failure of imagination, but also an extremely deferential attitude toward the great powers of finance. Their main strategy to fix financial crisis was to make Wall Street systemic again – in other words, "too big to fail."

Conclusion

Certainly the contemporary context shapes the construction, interpretation, and impact of film. Almost a decade after the Great Recession, the fact that finance continues to strongly shape the American economy and that Wall Street investors and bankers influence most corporate decisions should give us pause. How effective have the myriad critical approaches to finance been? In this chapter, I have argued that even though critics have widely praised films such as *The Wolf of Wall Street* and *The Big Short*, these films inadvertently bolster and replicate the cultural assumptions and norms of Wall Street, because they do not fully analyze how financial culture and ideologies possess a robust template for converting irrationality into rationality and immorality into morality. Moreover, by not fully questioning the market principles "underlying" or "before" the various excesses and bubbles of subprime and the like, these films fall prey to the normative narrative that, absent herd mentalities and the seductions of greed and gluttony, the principles of financial analysis and measurement are sound. Without the temptations and distortions of drugs, fast money, crooked stockbrokers, and greedy mortgage brokers, finance still epitomizes the smartness, creativity, and mathematical efficiency of free markets.

Of course, such analyses elide the fact that financialization has led to ever-greater socio-economic inequality, precarity, and crisis. Perhaps more importantly, it is not commonly appreciated that the very values, measures, and standards of finance, when used to govern diverse institutions, investments, and public goods, from corporations to universities, oftentimes narrows their commons, shortens their timeframe, and redistributes wealth towards the top. I make the point, then, that the very building blocks of finance and financialization need to be questioned.

By contrast, docudramas such as *The Last Days of Lehman Brothers* and *Too Big To Fail* focus on an elite cabal of men who engage in petty slights in the wake of the crisis, who negotiate with, betray, lean on, and enact retribution against their fellow financiers and financial institutions. These films highlight scenes of white men brokering the largest bailout in financial history, where the audience viscerally learns how Wall Street actions are deeply interpersonal, affective, and motivated by masculine codes of competition and fraternal bonding. The narrative strategies of these films,

I argue, demonstrate the extent to which the financial elite work within their "in-networks," forged and solidified through bonds of whiteness and masculinity, to plan and structure market action and make deals. Expertise, trust, and belongingness, as these films visually enact, cohere according to assumptions and categories of race, gender, class, and sexuality, and structure the accrual and flow of benefits and capital. As such, these films capture the extent to which financial markets are constituted by the relationships between particular dominant players and networks, and the games they indulge in.

These docudramas, seeking to detail, explain, and narrativize some of the central events and actors of the Great Recession, go behind closed doors and into boardrooms to dramatize journalistic accounts of the community of frenzied deal-making and eventual rescue that characterized the crisis. What they capture, or perhaps expose – by virtue of their attempt to explain influential moments through detailed and micro-scaled focus on the actions of key decision-makers – is the competitive white masculinist fraternity that was central to the construction, collapse, and rescue of financial markets.

While I had long researched and analyzed how the very same experts who engendered unsustainability were called upon to fix the system – in the process revealing their inability *not* to reproduce the very problems that had caused the crisis in the first place – I had *not* viscerally understood the extent to which the whole episode was heavily conditioned by categories and networks of belonging that determined who was considered deserving and capable, and who was not. I had surmised that such a framing would be too clichéd or symptomatic of an elementary analysis that looked reductively to identity politics. Yet I came to recognize that these identities, categories, and hierarchies not only help to structure networks and channels of accumulation, but also condition the kinds of relationships that get formed and the very motivations, sentiments, and passions that imbue them. In our current moment, as neoliberal, financial markets continue to be dominant, it is crucial to demonstrate that financial markets are specific, contingent, and explicitly located sites of actors and institutions. The financial genre in film has been a compelling resource to showcase how global stories are always also power-laden and particular stories.[3]

Notes

1 Native Studies scholar Shari Huhndorf, in her book *Going Native: Indians in the American Cultural Imagination*, grounds this trenchant argument in a long history of European-American appropriation of indigeneity and specifically, the practice of "going native" in order to justify and elide settler colonialism.

2 I thank Gary Ashwill (personal communication), who brought this important insight and parallel to my attention.

3 My deepest thanks to Constantin Parvulescu for organizing the wonderful conference *Global Finance and the Moving Image* at the University of Navarra, Pamplona, Spain, which served as the inspiration and impetus for this chapter. Moreover, his galvanizing abilities as an editor helped to coax this chapter into being. I also thank Jigna Desai and Gary Ashwill for their advice and editorial comments.

References

Barker, Andrew. 2015. "Film Review: 'The Big Short.'" *Variety*. November 13. http://variety.com/2015/film/reviews/the-big-short-review-1201639770/.

Cooper, Melinda, and Liz McFall. 2017. "Ten Years After: It's the Economy and Culture, Stupid!" *Journal of Cultural Economy* 10(1): 1–7. doi:10.1080/17530350.2016.1267026.

Dobbin, Frank, and D. Zorn. 2005. "Corporate Malfeasance and the Myth of Shareholder Value." *Political Power and Social Theory* 17: 179–98.

Figlio, Karl. 2011. "The Financial Crisis: A Psychoanalytic View of Illusion, Greed and Reparation in Masculine Phantasy." *New Formations: A Journal of Culture, Theory, Politics* 72. http://newformations.co.uk/abstracts/nf72abstracts.html.

Fox, Justin. 2009. *The Myth of the Rational Market: A History of Risk, Reward, and Delusion on Wall Street*. New York: HarperBusiness.

Goede, Marieke de. 2005a. "Resocialising and Repoliticising Financial Markets: Contours of Social Studies of Finance." *Economic Sociology*. http://dare.uva.nl/document/206503.

Goede, Marieke de. 2005b. *Virtue, Fortune, and Faith: A Genealogy of Finance*. 1st edition. Minneapolis, Minn.: University of Minnesota Press.

Ho, Karen. 2009. *Liquidated*. Duke University Press.

Ho, Karen. 2012. "Finance." In *A Companion to Moral Anthropology*, edited by Didier Fassin, 413–31. John Wiley & Sons, Ltd. doi:10.1002/9781118290620.ch23.

Huhndorf, Shari M. 2001. *Going Native: Indians in the American Cultural Imagination*. 1st edition. Ithaca: Cornell University Press.

Jensen, Michael C. 1986. "Agency Costs of Free Cash Flow, Corporate Finance, and Takeovers." *The American Economic Review* 76(2): 323–329.

Jensen, Michael C., and William H. Meckling. 1976. "Theory of the Firm: Managerial Behavior, Agency Costs and Ownership Structure." *Journal of Financial Economics* 3(4): 305–60. doi:10.1016/0304-405X(76)90026-X.

Konings, Martijn. 2015. *The Emotional Logic of Capitalism: What Progressives Have Missed*. 1st edition. Stanford, California: Stanford University Press.

Krippner, Greta R. 2012. *Capitalizing on Crisis: The Political Origins of the Rise of Finance*. Gld edition. Cambridge, Mass.: Harvard University Press.

McGowan, Todd. 2016. *Capitalism and Desire: The Psychic Cost of Free Markets*. New York: Columbia University Press.

Miyazaki, Hirokazu. 2013. *Arbitraging Japan: Dreams of Capitalism at the End of Finance*. Berkeley: University of California Press.

New York State Comptroller. 2009. "Wall Street Bonuses Rise Sharply in 2009." www.osc.state.ny.us/osdc/wallst_bonuses/2010/022310.htm.

Rollert, John Paul. 2014. "An Ethicist on Wolf of Wall Street: The Most Anti-Greed Movie Ever?" *The Atlantic*. February 26. www.theatlantic.com/entertainment/archive/2014/02/an-ethicist-on-em-wolf-of-wall-street-em-the-most-anti-greed-movie-ever/283806/.

Scott, A. O. 2015. "Review: In 'The Big Short,' Economic Collapse for Fun and Profit." *The New York Times*. December 10, sec. Movies. www.nytimes.com/2015/12/11/movies/review-in-the-big-short-economic-collapse-for-fun-and-profit.html.

Thrift, Nigel. 2001. "'It's the Romance, Not the Finance, That Makes the Business Worth Pursuing': Disclosing a New Market Culture." *Economy and Society* 30(4): 412–32. doi:10.1080/03085140120089045.

Yanagisako, Sylvia Junko. 2002. *Producing Culture and Capital: Family Firms in Italy*. Princeton: Princeton University Press.

Zaloom, Caitlin. 2010. *Out of the Pits: Traders and Technology from Chicago to London*. 1st edition. Chicago: University of Chicago Press.

6

BOILER ROOM AND THE FINANCIALIZATION OF THE AMERICAN ECONOMY

Constantin Parvulescu

As an economic and cultural process that started in 1980s and continues beyond the 2008 economic crisis, financialization changed Western economies and cultures at both macro and micro levels. Economically, it resulted in an increased influence of financial markets, financial institutions and financial elites over economic policy and outcomes (Palley 2007, 2). This influence shifted the main goal of corporate activity to maximizing shareholder value (Lazonick and O'Sullivan 2000, 17), boosted CEO and investment banker compensations, spread the myth of liquidity, and imposed short-termist profit strategies and the quest of higher leverage (Palley 2007, 112). It defined economies as a zero-sum game (Olson 2010), caused the increase of debt of states and populations (Montgomerie 2009, 17), spurred investing passion at all levels of society (Akerlof and Shiller 2010, 154), prioritized the discourse of quantitative risk valuation and analysis (Haiven 2013, 240), created the economic predicament of too big to fail (Palley 2013, 185), and last but not least generated a brain-drain to financial corporations (Ho 2009, 59).

Yet recent debates in critical social and cultural studies (Grossberg 2010) have raised concerns over the impact of this transformation outside the realm of the economy, enlarging the meaning of financialization to a "creep of financial ideas, allegories, narratives and measurements throughout society and culture" (Haiven 2014b, 5–6), producing specific sensibilities and subjects marked by invasive legitimizations of money and greed. Politically, financialization has been seen as underpinning the spread of neoliberal thought (Botos 2014, 265), reinvigorating individualism, increasing social atomization (Martin 2002, 45), and fueling the discourse on market triumphalism (Sandel 2012, 3). Anthropologically, it is suspected to have impacted daily life (Martin 2002), inculcated abstraction and marketization in human interaction (Lotz 2014, 113), boosted the valuation of speed in various aspects of human activity (Tiessen 2012; Davis and Meyer 1998), and created new networks of elites (Ho 2018 in this volume). Recent debates have also raised concerns regarding the impact of financialization on culture (La Berge 2014, 7), values and virtues (McDaniel 2015), social emotions (Woodward 2009), and social and artistic imagination (Haiven 2014a).

This chapter aims to contribute to this conversation by way of film analysis. It studies the presentation of brokers' lifestyles in the American financial feature film *Boiler Room* (B.Younger, 2000) in order to trace not only how financialization "crept" into the images, dialogues, situations, and character profiles of this film; but also to reveal how values linked to financialization have been embedded in the American culture of the 1980s and 1990s – known also as the deregulation era. Produced at the end of this era, whose denouement is marked by the burst of the tech bubble (starting in 1999), *Boiler Room* provides insightful testimonies as barometer of cultural financialization and as tool to better understand this phenomenon. The absorption of aspects of financialized cultures in *Boiler Room* articulates a relevant testimony on the social emotions and economic mindsets that contributed and still contribute to cultural financialization and to the production of the financialized subject around the world, thus paving the way for new means of economic and intellectual expropriation that turn citizens-investors into human capital of financial firms.

Symptomatic receptions

Financialization can, however, be studied not only in the texture of the film, but also in its critical reception. In fact, a focus on the reviews of the film is a productive entry point into grasping *Boiler Room*'s rich ideological load. Analyzing *Boiler Room*'s reviews in the context of financialization is similar to solving a physics problem concerned with relative motion. Both film and its reception are part and parcel of a social process, and their relationship is comparable to that of two trains moving in the same direction at similar speeds. The difference between the common physics problem and the concerns of ideology critique is that the former focuses on difference while the latter on moments of sameness. The former asks students to calculate which train moves faster and at what speed, while the latter reflects on impressions of immobility, when, from a passengers' perspective, the observed train does not seem to move.

Applied to reception of film, this metaphor indicates that ideology critique is interested in moments when the sensibility of the film viewer translates into an experience of specular pleasure and cinematic realism. Consequently and in many ways, in order to understand the ideological horizon of *Boiler Room*, one needs to start, perhaps paradoxically, by investigating sequences of the film that are praised by critics as the most truthful to American economic realities. One should look for traces of the cultural impact of economic financialization exactly where critics praise *Boiler Room* for delivering a convincing and accurate (read ideologically undistorted) vision of financial business culture.

Even if for a present-day observer, *Boiler Room* looks in many ways ideologically staged, at the times of the release of the film, critics found it "humming-with-authenticity" (Ebert 2000). They commended its well-researched journalistic and ethnographic effort (Brooks 2000) and its convincing depiction of the passions and habits of the Darwinian ecosystem of trading floors, "fired by testosterone and greed" and "locked into its own secret language, mores and traditions" (Hunter 2000). Critics saw as most authentic the "adrenaline rush" of the business culture presented in the film (Taubin 2000), arguing that this rush reflected the transformation of the American business environment, which increasingly imagined companies as turbo-charged instruments of wealth production.

The same critics appreciated how the setup of the plot as initiation story served to match the speed of the train of the film viewers with that of the finance world (Gillespie 2000). The plot presents how an intelligent young man, passionate about getting rich, starts from scratch in such a turbo-charged stock-peddling firm called J. T. Marlin.[1] Seth Davis (Giovanni Ribisi), the protagonist, is the envoy of the film and of the audience into the secretive trading rooms of financial firms – a participant observer. He is twenty-one and determined, as he puts it, to "get in," to learn the trade, become a successful broker, and make a quick buck. To increase its ethnographic legitimacy the film provides its protagonist with a voiceover that enhances his investigation power. The voiceover records impressions, offers contextualization, post-factum reflections on decisions and experiences, and describes the functioning of the company.

From his first contact with the world of brokers, J. T. Marlin reveals to the participant observer its customs, norms, values, dynamics, hierarchies, and legends. He – and with him the audience – learns who are the firm's and finance's masters and servants, and winners and losers; how brokerage relates to the outside world, and how brokers spend their money. The observer soon finds out that J. T. Marlin drafts only young men with little knowledge of finance; that it trains them to become smart-talking money-hungry salespeople, and promises them accession to the elites of American society. "You will make your first million within three years!" they are told. In return, the company expects their total commitment and hard work in a hyper-competitive, boot-camp environment, populated by charismatic stock-jocks, who drive Ferraris, wear Armanis, think of themselves as masters of the universe, and speak the transgressive slang of Wall Street's trading desks (Levy 2000).

Another segment of the film, which the aforementioned critics valued as the most insightful, presents Seth's familiarization with the operations of the company. His work consists of making phone calls and persuading middle-class Americans to purchase the stock his company peddles. Several scenes in the film document his initiation into the aggressive sales practices of J. T. Marlin. Screen time is generously allocated to various transaction-related calls. Some are demos performed by senior brokers; others feature Seth and document the improvement of his salesmanship. *Boiler Room* also depicts how customers relate to these phone calls, and how easily they are lured into buying stock in the optimistic economic bubble-context of their time (the 1990s tech bubble). As one senior broker confesses in the film, "With the Dow where it is right now, everybody wants a piece of the market." He confidently concludes: "I can close anyone, anytime, anywhere. Just give me a phone number."

In addition to its descriptive work, which critics found so convincing, *Boiler Room* stages an investigation. Like most financial films, it depicts J. T. Marlin's culture with the purpose of explaining how unleashed greed became instrumental to moral degeneration.[2] As Seth grows more accustomed to his trade, he starts asking questions about the way in which his firm makes its money. Fast profits come with secrets, and Seth's role also becomes that of discovering them. His inquiries reveal how companies like J. T. Marlin defraud the American middle class by selling them equity of inexistent companies, manipulating stock prices and cooking its books. Cornered by FBI agents, Seth agrees to cooperate and thus become more than an ethnographer. He assumes the role of informer and helper of the victims of these predatory companies, and becomes an important actor in unraveling the scam ran by J. T. Marlin. The last scene of the film shows police troops raiding the headquarters of the company, suggesting that, with the help of Seth, some justice against financial predators can been done.

What critics did not notice was that Seth came through as a believable character not only because he is an insightful guide into the shady world of financial firms, but also because the American public of the era of the burst of the tech bubble shared his hope and disillusionment story with finance. From this perspective, Seth's initiation story was perceived as realistic not necessarily due to a certain narrative or stylistic aspect of the film, but because it reflected the desire of the American public of the 1980s and 1990s to become financially potent, which also led to disillusions when bubbles burst. A close analysis of one of the scenes critics appreciated the most brings to the fore how *Boiler Room* matched its representation of finance with the "speed" with which the American society of its time developed its passion for investing.[3]

The sequence marks the beginning of the second act of the film. In a dimly lit conference room with no windows, in a place that seems far away from the real

FIGURE 6.1 Jim Young producing company assets. Still from *Boiler Room*, 2000.

world, the latest J. T. Marlin recruits – with Seth among them – meet one of the senior brokers of the firm. The meeting has been announced as a "group interview," but it turns to be an exposure of the recruits to an incendiary motivational speech, which, as Seth recalls in his voiceover, "looked more like a Hitler Youth rally" than an interview. The speech is delivered by a trading floor alpha male named Jim Young (Ben Affleck). In his three-minute performance, Young circles the long conference table crowded with recruits like Seth and explains the work ethics, the drives, the hierarchies, and jungle power relations of the firm. He outlines the financial rewards for working for J. T. Marlin (the recruits will make a million dollars in three years), and gives his future trainees some info about their job, adorning it with mesmerizing stories about the lifestyles of brokers. Most importantly, his speech clarifies the necessary condition to success in finance: one has to undergo a radical inner transformation, and change the way he or she thinks and feels about people and money.

Critics talked at large about Young's (wild) "animal spirits,"[4] praised Affleck's performance ("the role may be the best thing Affleck has ever done" [Schickel 2000]), and suggested how it shed light on the moral and emotional transformation of Wall Street – that is, from Gordon Gekko's "greed is good" to an amoral industry "in which greed is simply axiomatic" (Scott 2000) and, one should add, disturbingly exciting.[5] Critics saw in Young's inflammatory and contagious sermon *Boiler Room*'s highest achievement in realistic reenactment of financial corporate culture. Young put on display the "adrenaline rush" and "raging testosterone" informing J. T. Marlin (Travers 2000), and by extension, the passions and emotions of the American economy of the times. Critics also noticed how Affleck's character turned the windowless meeting room into an ideological reactor. Young came through as a "devil in a blue suit" (Travers 2000) preaching "the seductive power of unadulterated capitalism" (Scott 2000), as a "headhunter who will do anything to lure his boys with promises of overnight success" (Levy 2000),[6] and as a "natty drill-sergeant guru" (Gleiberman 2000), who, following the path of Gordon Gekko, will make his apprentices break away from the values of industrial-era capitalism and embrace those of the financialized age.

Common-sense inter-human and economic relations, he sermons, no longer apply to the world of boiler rooms. Young tells recruits not to listen to what some people, who may be resistant to the transformed economic order of their time, say about their work. The film presents him in domineering low-angle shots from the perspective of the bedazzled newcomers, as he engages in a rant against all those who doubt the values of the finance-driven economy. His message is clear: don't listen to your friends, don't listen to your family and don't listen to anybody who is critical of stock trading and fast profits. He prescribes youth rebellion. "F… you, mom and dad!" is the winners' attitude. Parents' opinions will change once "you make their f…ing Lexus payments!" The new economy needs another type of subject, one who is driven by a single but strong passion: to become, in Young's words, "filthy rich." If friends or parents are critical of it, it is because they are envious, lazy, out of touch with the new economy, or, as he concludes, destined to teach third-grade public school.

Young stands in front of the recruits to serve as the embodiment of this transformation and to testify to its success. He is there to brag about his sports car, his house, and his liquidity, and demonstrate that the social narratives of expeditious moneymaking in the finance industry are real. The passions and emotions he arouses in his recruits indicate an economy and an economic system that imagine themselves as endowed with superpowers. As Gordon Gekko will later put it in *Wall Street II: Money Never Sleeps* (O. Stone, 2010), a new species of banking, injected with steroids, had developed while he was in prison during the 1990s. *Boiler Room* reflects it and its appeal. Thus even if, on a moral and legal level, the film criminalizes J. T. Marlin's activity, the critics' reactions show the persuasive potential of Young's teachings. His charisma and superhero effect on recruits reveals the Faustian temptation of a company like J. T. Marlin and of its "devils in blue suits" not only to banking freshmen, but also to American investors and participants in capitalist economies.[7]

Here one can notice how *Boiler Room* gestures toward social desires, as both the film and society are informed by similarly accelerated greed. One can also see how cinematic representation is misrecognized as realistic representation. Executive alpha male self-confidence, trading floor Darwinism, strict employee discipline, and veneration of hard work would excite depositors expecting solid profit returns. The capitalist categorical imperative of increasing shareholder value might even spur investors to secretly cheer for the "Hitler Youth" moneymaking fanaticism nurtured by the firm. Dictatorial hierarchies and CEO and senior broker personality cult pass as key ingredients of corporate efficiency and convincing populist collaterals for the kind of profitability imagined in the bubble era of the 1990s.

Based on the assumption that the reality-effect of entertainment products can sometimes be the result of congruence between film-viewing experience and ideology-informed misrecognitions of reality, I argue that it is the likeability of J. T. Marlin's emotional corporate profile that makes viewers perceive its representations as veridical. The passions of the cinematically represented trading floor come through as realistic because they meet with expectations regarding the "speed" of the other train, the train of the observer. They respond to social fantasies of economic activity informed by hopes of fast moneymaking and other social emotions that will be discussed below. Financial services and instruments present themselves as grand gleaners of global wealth for their users. As Young puts it in his speech, "the kessef" is there to be taken by any passenger of the turbo-charged ride of financialization, including college dropouts like Seth and all the people to whom he makes sales calls every day. The financialized economy opens the doors to speedy affluence – allegedly democratically – to anyone who has the means and the drive to experience the thrills of the investment ride.

Allegory of financialization

The impression of realism engendered by the film gestures toward the development, in the deregulation era, of the social emotion of financial entitlement. Financial entitlement expressed the claim of the population for a slice of the American investment pie, triggered by the eightfold growth in financial assets value between 1982 and 2000. It was deeply rooted in the middle-class consciousness of the time, since literature on it described it as a social or human right (Ackerman and Alstott 2000). In fact, it earned a name of its own, "silver rights," and advocates of financial emancipation of the time such as John Hope Bryant went as far as regarding the defense of these rights as important as the struggle for civil rights in the 1960s. They argued that, in the postindustrial age, the new idiom that everyone needed to understand was the "language of money."[8]

The consistent rise of stock values in the 1990s triggered not only private investors' overconfidence in the market, but also a shift in American economic identity. More middle-class Americans envisioned themselves as capitalists and less as manufacturers and employees (Akerlof and Shiller 2010, 131). Work itself became a less efficient economic activity as the financialized economy highlighted return on investment as a more important creator of wealth. This transformation triggered a shift in economic valuation from labor to output, which *Boiler Room* promptly recorded in its initial sequence: "Honor is in the dollar," Seth declares with assumed cynicism, emphasizing how "the bottom line" had become the supreme incentive of the new economy.

No surprise that, in the same opening scene, Seth quotes the ghetto rags-to-riches lyrics of the legendary Brooklyn rapper Notorious B.I.G. as best describing the mindset of the financialized economy. Rap music constitutes a significant part of the soundtrack of the film. B.I.G.'s songs eulogize fast avenues to affluence, and stress end result. They advertise the economic entitlement that drives Seth's story, suggesting that getting rich is just a matter of wanting it and fighting for it.[9] In the same opening monologue, Seth recounts, like a B.I.G. song, how he has been exposed to countless tales of fast financial success and how they have awakened his desire "to get in," as he puts it. He refers to the story of a Microsoft janitor posing next to his Ferrari, secretaries becoming millionaires by choosing options in their company stock instead of bonuses, and the latest lottery winner. "You see shit like that and it plants seeds," he reflects. They are the seeds of financial entitlement, making "you think it's possible, even easy," Seth concludes.

Seth's "it's possible, even easy" shows that entitlement runs in parallel with another powerful social emotion produced by financialization: financial empowerment. In the 1990s, silver rights came to be regarded as golden privileges. American investors' confidence in the market gradually turned into confidence in themselves, imagining that they are or can become smart players with little know-how. As Akerlof and Shiller put it, investing became the second job of many Americans. They "learned the vocabulary and habits of investors, [...] increasingly began subscribing to investment periodicals, and watched television shows about investing" (2010, 154). This apprenticeship made them feel empowered and believe that the system worked in their favor.

Seth's recollections also indicate that, in the era of financialization, one of the most influential apparatuses of fostering entitlement in the hearts of investors and a tool of their empowerment was the financial media (print, radio, television). Besides broadcasting Wall Street sagas – that is, the stories Seth recounts or the ones Young tells about himself – and sustaining trust in the financial system (corresponding to Young's persuasive power), the financial media of the time boosted the social emotion of economic empowerment by creating a climate of investment literacy among middle-class Americans (Pixley 2005, 44; Martin 2002, 194). Being knowledgeable and acting smart as individual investor became the enlightenment discourse of the last two decades of the twentieth century.

The financial media became the grand enlightening agency of the deregulation era, diversifying both supply and demand in information on investing. A *Los Angeles Times* article of the 1980s reflecting on the growth in number of financial information channels noticed that "through the roaring 1980s, business news was one of the fastest-growing formats in radio," catering to what promoters called an "insatiable public appetite for financial and economic news" (Lippman and Bernstein 1991). Soon afterwards, the "planting of seeds" migrated from print and radio to television. In 1985 FNN (Financial News Network) was delivering a 24-hour financial broadcast feed, only to be incorporated by CNBC in 1991 and then, in 1994, competed by Bloomberg.

The book industry also flourished. Michael Lewis, the author of the most influential Wall Street apprenticeship autobiography, *Liar's Poker*, recalls that books on bonds hardly existed until the 1980s, or they bore truculently specialized titles that scared laymen away (Lewis 2010, 41). But in the deregulation era things changed. Books on investing became best-sellers. Future finance TV guru Suze Orman's were among them. Her how-to literature featured enticing titles such as: *The 9 Steps to Financial Freedom* (1997) and *The Courage to be Rich* (1999). Her books and the hosts of similar others published in this era (and beyond) targeted the middle class, addressing it as an endangered species at the hand of speculators like J. T. Marlin. The books supported their liberating mission by including statistics indicating how millions of middle-class Americans had fallen into poverty at the hands of brokers, "perishing financially due to lack of financial education" (Kiyosaki 2011, 13). Without ever calling into question the exploitation inherent in the system and that the enlightenment that they claimed to herald created more losers than winners,[10] these books promised to liberate individual investors from the tyranny of the middle man, and regain and boost their economic and social status.

Exploitation

When Young addresses his recruits, he makes them the same promises these books make, only in a more incendiary way. What Young's speech does not address, but Seth's work at J. T. Marlin presents, is that at least until they learn the trade and cash their first million, junior brokers are the object of exploitation in the firm. None of the critics cited above remarked that, before giving birth to millionaires, firms like J. T. Marlin produce a finance proletariat. *Boiler Room* suggests that none of these recruits will ever make their million in the sector. Before any of them finishes their apprenticeship, the FBI raids the building. Seth and perhaps his entire cohort know that their career in finance is over, as financial firms will be reluctant to hire an ex-broker from a chop shop that blatantly cheated its clients.

J. T. Marlin exploits its brokers on two levels. It is important to analyze the functioning of this dispositif because it reflects the way financialization generates exploitation within the economic environment at large. The first is the traditional, industrial-age exploitation. It means abuse of unskilled labor. Junior brokers are poorly paid servants of their senior peers. They work long hours and perform the repetitive task of dialing hundreds of phone numbers a day reminiscent of assembly line labor. They even have to read a pre-prepared script, while the more creative salesmanship is performed by their bosses who also cash the big bonuses. The other form of exploitation, not so obvious, but more important for our times, is specific of post-Fordist economy and immaterial labor. Its victims are both junior and senior brokers, and, more importantly, the investing population at large.

This new form of exploitation pertains to collapsing the difference between human and fixed capital, production and reproduction of labor, and work and leisure (Hardt and Negri 2004, 111; Martin et al. 2008, 122, 124). In order to clarify it, let us revisit Young's speech.[11] One needs to regard it as a moment in which J. T. Marlin's workforce reproduces itself and, within this process, engenders exploitation. Exploitation through financialization means industrial and cultural transformation, and the production of "a way of knowing" and "a kind of being" (Martin et al. 2008, 122), which is of the financialized subject (Haiven 2014b, 5). Exploitation refers here to turning recruits into human fixed assets. By calling on their brokers to reject their anthropological landmarks outside the firm, Young becomes the grand agent of turning every aspect of their life into work for the company. *Boiler Room* shows how, with the exception of Seth, J. T. Marlin's employees have no life outside the firm. They are immersed in the trading floor mindset Young has drilled into them in the conference room with no windows. They don't seem to have a family, and spend their free time together with their work buddies, engaging in activities with dynamics similar to the ones at work. They gamble, compete, sell, antagonize the "other world," and the only time they do not wear their brokers' uniform – that is, their sometimes exaggeratedly flashy suits – is when, in Young's house, they watch *Wall Street* and perform Gordon Gekko karaokes.

Young's speech thus captures a moment of intellectual expropriation specific of the era of immaterial labor. It performs an operation of primitive accumulation. Hardt and Negri point out that political economists "should not be satisfied with accounts of neoliberalism that pose capitalist accumulation as merely or primarily the expropriation of existing [material] wealth" (2004, 139–140). In the initiation scene, the property that is accumulated (and the corresponding expropriation) is not material, but intellectual. Initiation speeches like Young's produce human capital that is appropriated as fixed. The minds of the brokers are turned into a 24/7 asset of J. T. Marlin, as it is expected of them to allow "work" to spread into every aspect of their life.

As allegory of financialization, *Boiler Room* suggests that what happens in the conference room is a reflection of a social process. On a broader scale, via

FIGURE 6.2 Greg (left) teaching Seth (right) to sell the investment dream. Still from *Boiler Room*, 2000.

financialization, company clients and society at large are appropriated as human capital of financial firms and turned into their part-time proletariat or assets. Slavoj Zizek has called exploitation at this broader social level appropriation of "general intellect" (Zizek 2009, 145–146). Finance produces frames that determine values, goals, and human actions. At a corporate level, through a discourse of shareholder maximization; it reduces concepts of profit and growth to a narrow understanding related to moneymaking and percentages, and engenders a bottom line hypercompetitive and short-termist culture (Ho 2009, 36). At a broader social level, it produces deceiving frameworks (intellects) of human empowerment, values, wealth, success, and happiness.

This process of intellect appropriation is revealed in a discussion Seth has with another senior broker of the firm, Greg (Nicky Katt). The purpose of the conversation is to make Seth understand "the nature of his job," as Greg puts it. They sit at a desk on the trading floor with a phone in front of them. The broker holds a box with leads in his hand. Leads are cards that include a name, a phone number and demographic information about a possible client, whom Seth is expected to call. The broker explains to Seth that he has to contact these people not to sell them stock, but only "the dream" of owning it. Seth has to make them interested in the ride. He has to inform them that there is a firm out there, called J. T. Marlin, who will get in touch with them in the future with an investment idea (like so many other investment firms do – only that J. T. Marlin's is better and its profit yields are higher).

What Greg explains to Seth is more than a marketing tactic of J. T. Marlin. Seth's phone call is one small contribution to a grand accumulation effort of the financial industry targeting the entire economic field. Seth's phone call is one operation in a broader process of rendering citizens cooperative with financial companies.

By making people curious about J. T. Marlin's upcoming investment idea, Seth reproduces Young's work in the conference room. He is not generating clients; he is recruiting participants in the grand ride of investment. Like Young, Seth indicates and appeals to his interlocutors' financial entitlement. As such he does not address them as future customers of the firm, but as co-workers, as human capital. He does not sell them stock, but the opportunity to work *with* J. T. Marlin, which, as we shall see, becomes work *for* the firm.

This operation is also worth emphasizing because, in the similar vein in which Adorno and Horkheimer gestured toward the dark face of the Enlightenment,[12] Seth's call sheds light on the exploitative aspects of the "silver rights movement" of financial literacy. Even if it informs, enlightens and empowers subjects, financial education also turns individuals into supporters and co-workers of the financial system (and eventually into its victims). This is the reason why critics of financial literacy like Arthur regard it as a grand operation of cultural appropriation that "mystifies the character and practice of the hyper-real financial economy and its relations to the real" (2012, xiv). So-called investors become the poorly paid, unpaid or more often paying collaborators of financial firms. They build a paradoxical proletariat, specific of the new forms of exploitation that go hand in hand with the spectacle of financial enlightenment. The paradox is that they are unskilled, but the social spectacle of financial literacy makes them envision themselves as skilled. They believe they are empowered, but are not, and financial companies exploit this misrecognition – which in banking language is called information asymmetry – by increasingly addressing them as "big boys," that is, as economic agents that are knowledgeable of the trade and its dangers; active, willing to assume risk, and consequently take responsibility for losses.[13] They are co-workers of financial firms because they self-exploit themselves under the banner of investment opportunity. They exploit their own private fortune for those who reap the actual profits of investment in the stock market.

From this point of view, Goldman Sachs's slogan "People are our greatest asset" gains uncanny connotations, as the slogan seems also to gesture toward the socializing labor of financialization and new modes of accumulation specific of the era of immaterial labor. Additionally, by turning society into a society of co-workers and big boy investors, the financial industry performs also a grand transfer of risk from company to population (Arthur 2012, xvii). By enlightening and involving the public, financial firms renegotiate in their favor industry ethics and professional responsibility. In these new terms, financial services limit their economic duty to providing its big boy clients with opportunities to invest, infrastructure, information, financial products, loans, and insurance. They can create markets, establish indexes, and manage exchanges, but increasingly, since many of these financial "instruments" can be exploitative and "toxic," financial firms withdraw from offering the binding fiduciary companionship that accompanied its services of the older, long-term greed Wall Street business model.

The disciplining aspect of financial literacy is best revealed by another important piece of advice Greg has for Seth: "Don't pitch the bitch." This infamous line, made popular by the film, refers to the company's commandment not to sell stock to women. This is also why brokers are advised not to let their customers talk to their wives before deciding to invest. According to J. T. Marlin's philosophy, "the bitch" is, however, not necessarily a gender category. Perhaps Greg refers only to women, but finance envisions this category as comprising a certain type of unreliable clients, both men and women, who are resistant to becoming co-workers of the firm. Real existing firms also include among "bitches" immigrants and Muslims (Faux 2013).

Thus in a broader sense and related to financialization, the "bitch" gestures toward an unreliability generated by being financially uneducated. It refers to players who do not know, do not respect or do not want to respect the rules of the investment game in the new economy. They are the financially illiterate who keep returning to the basic questions about investment and profit, some of them hard to answer by brokers. In other words, they voice the concerns of an economic group that has resisted being turned into human capital for financial firms. The many Young-style messages sent out to them by financial services were not able to appropriate their loyalty, as their uncouth cooperation disrupts the procedures of expropriation the finance industry has organized at a social level. They question the social emotions of trust (Pixley 2005), economic confidence (Akerlof and Shiller 2010), or their spectacle that supplant the investment ride.

In contrast, financial "masculinity" (the state of not "bitching" about the basics of the financial game) becomes tantamount to literacy. It assumes a participation in the investment sport that is observant of its allegedly incontestable rulebook. Seth notices this blind obedience to the commandments of finance game in his fellow-brokers at J. T. Marlin, who never bother inquiring about the way in which their company is generating its tremendous profits.[14] Critics of financial education like Arthur target precisely the role literacy plays in naturalizing respect for these rules. Literacy induces interest in and know-how about investment, but does not encourage asking questions, especially not fundamental ones. The shortcoming of contemporary financial education, Arthur argues, is that it engenders *consumer* financial literacy and not a *critical* one (2012, 31–32).[15]

Even Seth, whose voice reflects critically on the industry, finds out only by accident about the scam his company is operating. One night, returning to work, he sees the SEC supervisor shredding company documents. He admits that, perhaps, it would have been better for him not to learn J. T. Marlin's secret, and go on with his job like any other broker, including the senior ones. And even when he finds out, he does not quit. He is too money hungry and too seduced by being on the winning side of the game. As he tells his father, he has learned the sales trade, and enjoys being good at it. Only when the FBI puts pressure on him, he decides to step out and cooperate. His reflective, truly critical position, is articulated thus only in his voiceover – perhaps after he and his company have faced criminal charges in court. The film thus suggests that critical financial reflection takes shape only after he has professionally and economically lost everything in the investment game himself.

Coda: ghosts of J. T. Marlin

One of the objections to the anthropological relevance of *Boiler Room* for today's economy is that the era of the cold calls, salesmen brokers, high-pressure tactics, penny stock scams, traders with high school degrees, and visions of overnight profits has come to an end. The Internet, in particular online trading portals, and mass advertising have taken over most of the tasks of J. T. Marlin's workforce. Similar to online banking, which eliminated the teller and gave its clients direct access to their accounts, internet investment portals such as Plus500, The Telegraph Investor or FxPro replaced the broker and his phone calls with the click of the mouse. Due to computer and smartphone technology, investors can enter in direct contact with the market, allegedly without being exposed to the risk of dealing with the deceiving practices of a middleman like Seth. The only noticeable trace of the broker on these sites seems to be the free tips on investment the portals offer and a visibly posted phone number on the upper right side of the screen, which a consumer who doesn't feel financially enlightened can dial in order to receive investment services.

This objection to *Boiler Room*'s relevance is pertinent but not accurate. First, because boiler rooms are still up and running. An article in *Bloomberg Online* (Faux 2013) shows how one of them, named John Thomas, became quite profitable, and its CEO regarded as a respectable Wall Street businessman (even offered a cameo role in Oliver Stone's *Wall Street II: Money Never Sleeps*). John Thomas appropriated the structure, style, company ethos, and the aggressive sales tactics (including the golden rule of not pitching the unenlightened) of the boiler room presented in the film, making one even wonder if the company's name, John Thomas, was not inspired by the J. T. initials of its fictional homologue.

The other objection to this objection is that, even if spectral, the manipulative work of Seth, Greg and Young can be traced in the very spectacle of transparency and straightforwardness these sites entertain, and in their enlightening effort to disperse market mystique. As they deal with big boys only, they are perhaps the most important beneficiaries of the grand sale of the financial dream to the population in the deregulation era, which led to the rendering of the social field cooperative to financial services. Since it is in their interest, internet platforms both carry on the sale and exploit it. They become the new grand promoters of financial (pseudo) enlightenment and the enlargers of the pool of people who think they can "get in" – nowadays reaching out to blue-collar wealth and intellects, which, so far, have been exploited mainly by online sports betting.

Online trading portals continue to nurture, manipulatively, the same social emotions of entitlement and empowerment that made the dialers of numbers of yesteryear have people listen to them. Harking back to Seth's words, their marketing plan is to make clients think, like Seth, that trading has been democratized and that making a quick buck on one's phone is "possible" and even "easy" (as the Telegraph Investor slogan has it). In addition, online platforms empower. They offer leverage and smart technology. They stress that the investment decision rests solely with their big boy enlightened and empowered client. As FxPro's commercials have it, due to modern-day technology, the ordinary world citizen is finally equipped to "trade [Forex] like a pro."

The difference from the early deregulation days is that post-2008 entitlement is nourished mostly by accessibility of technology and not by the constant rise in the value of assets. The grand empowering incentive is the predicament that the gateway to the financial pie is located, in the shape of a smartphone, in an individual's pocket or just a few clicks away on their laptop. Financial competency, which used to be knowledge in the days of books, radio and television – that is, learning the trade, understanding or at least having the illusion of understanding spreads, transactions, etc. – has become, in the Web 2.0 era, the "intellect" and the speed of the interface tool (the phone and the app, or the computer). Additionally, the shift from confidence in the market to easiness and from savviness to speed is continued by a trend of discreetly associating successful investment with inspiration and good luck.

This shows how exploitation via accessible technology works. In spite of the platforms' emphasis on transparency, the deceit and manipulation earlier attributed to middlemen like Seth and his pals are inscribed in the marketing strategies of the platforms, in their alleged neutrality in delivering information and in their trading tools. The risk transfer process of financialization has transformed deceit into self-deceit (and self-manipulation), or, even worse, into addictive habits. The sales calls depicted in *Boiler Room* have become self-persuading dialogues about how and where to invest. They are often triggered by television or online commercials and take place in the big boy investor's mind or emerge as sales pitches made to family members or friends. Financial enlightenment has passed J. T. Marlin's "great idea" to customers. They are addressed as the empowered new Columbuses of the global securities oceans, discovering their grand opportunities and turning them into gold with the little and dangerously user-friendly navigation tool put at their disposal by the online trading companies.

One can even trace how online platforms have relocated to the homes of the platform users the windowless room where J. T. Marlin drilled its recruits to revolutionary finance intellect. Like online gambling, internet trading creates a windowless area around the computer screen. This space inspires clients to break away from their ordinary economic habits (and perhaps social ones as well). Endowed with leverage, smart data and some investment tips, they can imagine themselves as market superheroes and act accordingly. Online trading platforms allow them to practice their skills at any hour of the day and night, collapsing the distinction between leisure and work or expanding labor beyond the confines of the office into a 24/7 activity.

Last but not least, online platforms' commercials still pitch only men. The only difference from the world of *Boiler Room* is that, as more recent Plus500 commercials show, the marketing campaigns of online platforms have become more inclusive of women's presence and cooperation. If in 2013 ads, women still served only as rewards for investment success, latest commercials (of 2015 and later) integrate them into the ride, and present them as supporters of their partners' decisions (but not yet as helpers and even less as protagonists). The trend will probably

FIGURE 6.3 Plus500 commercial of 2015.
(Source: YouTube).

continue – and not because the finance world has become less stereotyping, but because the industry, as *Boiler Room* shows us, is more interested in capitalizing on the emotions and passions of its big boys and not on rational thinking. These passions and emotions comprise – not paradoxically – the ones that might be regarded, in the same stereotyping logic, as feminine. Among them are intuition, luck, and superstition, as in our era of increased illusory empowerment, online trading and online gambling (including sports betting) fight for the savings of the same social groups.

Notes

1 *Wall Street*, Oliver Stone's acclaimed finance film, is similarly structured. Several critics compared *Boiler Room* to *Wall Street* (e.g. A. O. Scott [2000]).
2 This is the typical morality play setup of the business and finance film of the 1980s and 1990s, such as *Wall Street* (O. Stone, 1987), *Tin Men* (B. Levinson, 1987), *The Bonfire of the Vanities* (B. De Palma, 1990), *Other People's Money* (N. Jewison, 1991), *Glengarry Glen Ross* (J. Foley, 1992), or *American Psycho* (M. Harron, 2000).
3 The public appreciated it as well, as it has millions of hits on YouTube.
4 Akerlof and Shiller define animal spirits as "an economic term, referring to a restless and inconsistent element in the economy. It refers to our peculiar relationship with ambiguity or uncertainty"(2010, 3). The authors give as examples "five different aspects of animal spirits and how they affect economic decisions – confidence, fairness, corruption and anti-social behavior, money illusion, and stories" (2010, 5).
5 Anticipating the later pronouncement of Gekko in *Wall Street II* that "greed is legal."
6 Critics regarded Affleck's monologues as memorable as the ones given by Alec Baldwin in *Glengarry Glen Ross* and Michael Douglas in *Wall Street* (A. O. Scott 2000).

7 Seth's father is an actual federal judge. Critics found the father-son conflict and the moralizing dimension of the film as its weakest points (Travers 2000). Like *Wall Street I* (1987), its better-known predecessor, *Boiler Room* is also a cautionary tale. Both films feature cooperation with the FBI and a moralizing father demanding redemption.
8 Under "The Silver Rights Movement" heading, Bryant described financial literacy as "the new civil rights issue in America and worldwide" (Arthur 2012, xii).
9 Notorious B.I.G.'s songs are set in McMansions, yachts, limousines, and scenes of endless and titillating leisure activities. They never show the rapper work, but only enjoy and sing about the good life after he has made his millions.
10 "When Finance Becomes You," the second chapter of Martin 2002 describes this phenomenon in detail.
11 *Boiler Room* includes three such conference room speeches, all within the same boot-camp emotional regime.
12 In their classic *The Dialectics of the Enlightenment.*
13 This is a trend Greg Smith identifies as both major and problematic for financial firms of the twenty-first century (2012, 73).
14 The skilled senior brokers are content with using the system without trying to understand how it works.
15 Arthur's thesis regarding the inefficiency of financial literacy is probably best confirmed by the 2007–2008 economic meltdown and the ensuing crisis.

References

Ackerman, Bruce A. and Anne Alstott. 2000. *The Stakeholder Society*. New Haven: Yale University Press.

Akerlof, George A. and Robert J. Shiller. 2010. *Animal Spirits: How Human Psychology Drives the Economy, and Why it Matters for Global Capitalism*. Princeton: Princeton University Press.

Arthur, Chris. 2012. *Financial Literacy Education: Neoliberalism, the Consumer and the Citizen*. Rotterdam: Sense Publishers.

Botos Katalin. 2014. "Financialisation or the Management Philosophy of Globalism." *Public Finance Quarterly*, (0031–496X) [serial online]. June 59(2): 258–271. Available from: Business Source Complete, Ipswich, MA.

Brooks, Xan. 2000. "*Boiler Room*." *The Guardian*. May 5. www.theguardian.com/film/News_Story/Critic_Review/Guardian_review/0,,217251,00.html

Davis, Stan and Christopher Meyer. 1998. *Blur: The Speed of Change in the Connected Economy*. New York: Basic Books.

Ebert, Roger. 2000 "*Boiler Room*." RogerEbert.com. February 18. www.rogerebert.com/reviews/boiler-room-2000

Faux, Zeke. 2013. "Red Bull-Fed Brokers Stand as John Thomas Draws Scrutiny." *Bloomberg Online*. February 25. www.bloomberg.com/news/articles/2013-02-28/john-thomas-financial-the-other-side-of-wall-street

Gillespie, Nick. 2000. "'*Boiler Room*' Boilerplate." *Reason.com*. May. http://reason.com/archives/2000/05/01/boiler-room-boilerplate

Gleiberman, Owen. 2000. "*Boiler Room*." *Entertainment*. February 18. www.ew.com/article/2000/02/18/boiler-room

Grossberg, Lawrence. 2010. *Cultural Studies in the Future Tense*. Durham: Duke University Press.

Hacker, Jacob S. 2006. *The Great Risk Shift*. Oxford: Oxford University Press.

Haiven, Max. 2013. "Walmart, Financialization and the Cultural Politics of Securitization." *Cultural Politics*, 9(3).

Haiven, Max. 2014a. *Crisis of Imagination, Crisis of Power: Capitalism, Creativity and the Commons*: London: Zed Books.

Haiven, Max. 2014b. *Cultures of Financialization: Fictitious Capital in Popular Culture and Everyday Life*. London: Palgrave MacMillan.

Hardt, Michael and Antonio Negri. 2004. *Multitude: War and Democracy in the Age of Empire*. New York: Penguin Press.

Ho, Karen. 2009. *Liquidated: An Ethnography of Wall Street*. Durham: Duke University Press.

Hunter, Stephen. 2000 "'Boiler Room': Hotter Than Blazes." *Washington Post*. February 18. www.washingtonpost.com/wp-srv/entertainment/movies/reviews/boilerroomhunter.htm

Kiyosaki, Robert. T. 2011. *Unfair Advantage. The Power of Financial Education*. New York: Plata Publishing.

La Berge, Leigh Claire. 2014. *Scandals and Abstraction: Financial Fiction of the Long 1980s*. Oxford: Oxford University Press.

Lazonick, William and Mary O'Sullivan. 2000. "Maximizing Shareholder Value: A New Ideology for Corporate Governance." *Economy and Society*, 29(1), 13–35.

Levy, Emanuel. 2000. "*Boiler Room*." *Variety*. February 6. http://variety.com/2000/film/reviews/boiler-room-1117778648/

Lewis, Michael. 2010. *Liar's Poker*. New York: W. W. Norton & Company.

Lippman, John and Sharon Bernstein. 1991. "Business Radio Picks Up Static." *Los Angeles Times*. September 15. http://articles.latimes.com/1991/sep/15

Lotz, Christian. 2014. "*The Capitalist Schema: Time, Money, and the Culture of Abstraction*." Lanham: Lexington Books.

Martin, Randy. 2002. *Financialization of Daily Life (Labor In Crisis)*. Philadelphia: Temple University Press.

Martin, Randy, Michael Rafferty and Dick Bryan. 2008. "Financialization, Risk and Labour." *Competition & Change*, 12(2).

McDaniel, Charles Jr. 2015. *Civil Society and the Reform of Finance: Taming Capital, Reclaiming Virtue*. London: Routledge.

Montgomerie, Johnna. 2009. "The Pursuit of (Past) Happiness? Middle-class Indebtedness and American Financialisation." *New Political Economy*, 14(1).

Olson, Erika S. 2010. *Zero-Sum Game: The Rise of the World's Largest Derivatives Exchange*. Malden: John Wiley & Sons.

Palley, Thomas I. 2007. "Financialization: What It Is and Why It Matters." *Economics Working Paper Archive*. Levy Economics Institute. www.levyinstitute.org/pubs/wp_525.pdf

Palley, Thomas I. 2013. *Financialization: The Economics of Finance Capital Domination*. London: Palgrave MacMillan.

Pixley, Jocelyn. 2005. *Emotions in Finance: Distrust and Uncertainty in Global Markets*. Cambridge: Cambridge University Press.

Sandel, Michael J. 2012. *What Money Can't Buy. The Moral Limits of Markets*. New York: Penguin.

Schickel, Robert. 2000. "It's All in the Selling." *Time*. October 9, 2000. http://content.time.com/time/world/article/0,8599,2047416,00.html

Scott, A. O. 2000. "*Boiler Room*." *The New York Times*. February 18. www.nytimes.com/movie/review?res=9E04E2DD1131F93BA25751C0A9669C8B63

Smith, Greg. 2012. *Why I Left Goldman Sachs*. New York: Grand Central Publishing.

Taubin, Amy. 2000. "Cashing In." *Village Voice*. February 15. www.villagevoice.com/2000-02-15/film/cashing-in/

Tiessen, Matthew. 2012. "High-Frequency Trading and the Centering of the (Financial) Periphery." Volume 32. volumeproject.org/2012/09/high-frequency-trading-and-the-centering-of-the-financial-periphery/

Travers, Peter. 2000. "*Boiler Room*." *Rolling Stone*. February 18. www.rollingstone.com/movies/reviews/boiler-room-20000218#ixzz3XT1QbnZO

Woodward, Kathleen. 2009. *Statistical Panic: Cultural Politics and Poetics of the Emotions*. Durham: Duke University Press.

Zizek, Slavoj. 2009. *First as Tragedy, Then as Farce*. New York: Verso.

7

MEDIATING THE CRISIS: REVISIONARY ECONOMICS IN OLIVER STONE'S WALL STREET FILMS

Scott Loren

> *. . . the esthetically sensitive man stands in the same relation to the reality of dreams as the philosopher does to the reality of existence; he is a close and willing observer, for these pictures afford him an interpretation of life, and it is by these processes that he trains himself for life.*
>
> *Friedrich Nietzsche,* The Birth of Tragedy

States of crises: representational economies and conjunctural contexts

In April 2012 the US Treasury Department estimated the total loss of household wealth resulting from the subprime mortgage crisis to be 19.2 trillion USD (Childress 2012). This figure does not account for a number of mid- and long-term effects, such as the impact on prior homeowners who became less socially mobile through the 2008 subprime crisis and whose future contribution to *the economy* would continue to be severely limited as a result. As a local estimate based on domestic losses, it also could not take into account the vastly larger picture of collateral damage across world markets and economies that ensued. Worldwide recession in the wake of the 2008 US subprime mortgage crisis was of such epic proportions, it seemed to herald the end of neoliberalism (Grantham and Miller 2010). And while the crisis generated a new wave of critical commentary on the hegemony of financialization in neoliberal economics, it also led individuals, organizations and institutions to question their own habits and worldviews; to consider how they might have contributed to the crisis; and to ask what might be done as a corrective measure (cf. Plehwe, Walpen and Neuenhöffer 2006). In the humanities and social sciences there has been growing consensus on the need to rethink neoliberal economics: not as a field of institutional power moving uniformly forward with intention, but one characterized by internal conflict, decentralization and imbrication in broadly diverse social institutions and cultural practices.

In "Interpreting the Crisis," Stuart Hall and Doreen Massey discuss a conjunctural approach as a way to understand and analytically frame current fiscal and social crises (i.e. in 2010). Conjunctural analysis entails a periodization of how "different social, political, economic and ideological contradictions that are at work in society come together to give it a specific and distinctive shape" (Hall and Massey 2010). According to Hall, "history moves from one conjuncture to another rather than being an evolutionary flow. And what drives it forward is usually a crisis, when the contradictions that are always at play in any historical moment are condensed, or, as Althusser said, 'fused in a ruptural unity'. Crises are moments of potential change, but the nature of their resolution is not given. It may be that society moves on to another version of the same thing…, or to a somewhat transformed version…; or relations can be radically transformed" (Hall and Massey 2010). As suggested by the title "Interpreting the Crisis," Hall and Massey's call for a conjunctural approach in 2010 references *Policing the Crisis: Mugging, the State, and Law and Order* – a seminal Cultural Studies text that employed conjunctural analysis contemporaneous to the rise of neoliberal policy in the late 1970s. *Policing the Crisis* considered a particular form of criminal activity (mugging) as a social phenomenon, contextualizing it with regard to national politics, legal reforms, medial representation and social reaction (in the form of moral panic) at the "precise historical conjuncture" (Hall et al. 1978) in which "the division between the 'traditional' and 'liberal' views [on crime] both *organized and formed the limits of* the public discussion on crime" at various levels of discourse (Hall et al. 1978). In the post-subprime moment of 2010, the conjunctural focus shifts from mugging and moral panic to hedging and moral hazard.

Considering the historical conjuncture in which neoliberal ethos falls into question due to its perceived effects forty years on, Hall and Massey's reference to *Policing the Crisis* is methodologically motivated in regard to conjunctural analysis as a still relevant and applicable approach, and historically motivated in its framing of the emergence and potential decline of neoliberalism. That is to say, the title of the 2010 interview semiotically performs the task of conjunctural analysis in small format: it marks a discursive field in relation to a historical event (critical interpretation of the post-subprime moment), encodes the event as a distinct point of rupture (the subprime crisis as conjuncture bookending an era shaped by neoliberal policy), situates it in reference to the moment of conjunctural rupture that appeared to mark the beginning of that era (the title's reference to the late 1970s as the moment in which neoliberal policy is formally implemented by the State), and sensitizes its readership to the very role of discourse and the *limits of public discussion* regarding the current conjuncture (*interpreting* the crisis).

Published the same year as Hall and Massey's "Interpreting the Crisis," Lawrence Grossberg's *Cultural Studies in the Future Tense* also articulates the necessity for reevaluation (disciplinary and otherwise) alongside a continued critique of neoliberalism, describing the ideological and practical application of Cultural Studies as "a radically contextual and conjuncturalist practice" (Grossberg 2010). Drawing on Grossberg's "Considering Value: Rescuing Economies from Economists" and Oliver Stone's Wall Street films (1987, 2010), this essay provides a reassessment of *economic perspective* through the lens of Media and Cultural Studies. Grossberg distinguishes three courses of action for "rescuing economies from economists":

- Stop thinking of *the economy* in monolithically singular terms and "see the complexity and multiplicity of economies."
- Recognize *the economic* and *economies* as a combination of discursive and material practices.
- Identify and examine the cultural and social contexts that the economic and economies are bound up in (Grossberg 2010).

As a project exploring what Cultural Studies can do to reform conventional notions of the economic where there is a need to break with popular or discipline-specific perspectives, Grossberg's rescue attempt is not without modesty. It neither seeks to put forth a new and improved economic theory, nor necessitates a claim of "new expertise in matters of economic policy" (Grossberg 2010). By producing "better conjunctural stories," one might engage "economic questions without falling back into forms of reductionism and essentialism" (ibid.). The task as Grossberg defines it is thus one of differentiation *through conjunctural and representational revision*: to multiply views on the economic in relation to and through a rich conjunction of historical, cultural and techno-social factors. By articulating scenes of conjuncture, one might "better understand 'economic' events, practices, relations, etc., by contextualizing them;" and with sensitivity to the multiple ways in which economies are inscribed into a larger social fabric, the contexts equally evince greater clarity in meaning (ibid.). Through attention to *economic plurality*, *techno-social constructivism* and *historical contingency*, perceptual conventions regarding the economy and, recalling Hall, the discursive limits of the current crisis might be renegotiated.

To further legitimate the assumption that specialist or *traditionalist* perspectives on economics might profit from a conjuncturalist approach, Grossberg's choice of these three focus areas can be contextualized in relation to Cultural Studies itself. To begin with, by calling for a reevaluation of *the economic* that prioritizes attention to economic plurality, social construction and cultural contextualization, Grossberg implies both that these three elements are of particular value and that they have been undervalued or partly neglected previously. Such assumptions are also reflected, either implicitly or explicitly, in the collection of essays here that seek to provide novel perspectives on the economic as plural in form, malleable in potential discursive production, and, viewed from diverse disciplinary points of view, subject to richly contingent contexts. In the natively hybrid discipline of Cultural Studies, pluralism, constructivism and contingency have a status of critical discourse super-categories. The intentionality of Grossberg's selection should therefore not be ascribed to areas of neglect in conventional perspectives on "the economy" alone, but from the happy coincidence that these areas of neglect happen to be central areas of concern in Cultural Studies more broadly. Like Hall and Massey's symbolic bookending of neoliberal conjunction, Grossberg's choice of focal points is also methodologically and historically motivated, with self-referential indexes to disciplinary theoretical concerns in relation to neoliberal contexts, and addresses states of crisis by ascribing to them problems of perception while prescribing for them solutions through representation (or as Grossberg suggests, by producing better conjunctural stories).

If the approach is to be an analysis of pluralism, constructivism and contingency in, and, or through film, a Cultural Studies conjunctural analysis is further suitable due to its theorization of representational practices and media technologies as modes and locations for the *per se production, mediation and maintenance of culture.*[1] My account of conjunctural intersections between cultural and technological discourse as represented in the filmic medium also draws on *media archeology* as "a conceptual and practical exercise in carving out the aesthetic, cultural and political singularities of media" (Parikka and Hertz 2010). Among the key features of media archeology are the *excavation of elements potentially neglected* in conventional media histories, the *identification of recurring themes*, and *analysis of resonances in the multiple connections* and modalities of media and medial objects. Petra Löffler has suggested that cinema-based media archeology seeks to "negotiate the agency of human observers as part of man-machine interactions or as part of viewing dispositifs" (Löffler 2012). In the following analysis, interactions can be conceptualized diversely across two areas of form-content imbrication. On the one hand there is the form-content of cinematic representation as a site of material-discursive praxis; on the other the form-content of economics as represented in the films considered. The man-machine interactions at stake here are individuals, groups and collectives that interact with technical economies as structures, techniques, systems. My analysis of cinematic content and/as representational form aims to make intelligible human-machine interactions as producing potential viewing dispositifs according to the task set out by Grossberg (to tell better conjunctural stories). Employing a theoretical framework that combines conjunctural analysis, representational praxis and media archeology, I want to foreground the following elements:

- imbrication of medial form and representational content;
- excavation of form/content elements conventionally or potentially neglected;
- analysis of resonances at various contextual layers, both in aesthetic expression and modalities of medium;
- identification of thematic repetition;
- departures in aesthetic techniques and thematic contents between alternate conjunctural contexts.

My aim is thus an exposition and application of Grossberg's injunction to conceptually pluralize and conjunctively contextualize notions of *the economic*, and thus counteract discursive practices that close down potential for critical reevaluation through reductionist or essentialist logics. In practical application, my method entails a comparative analysis of aesthetic economies that represent conceptually plural and historically contextualized notions of *the economic* in the opening scenes of Stone's *Wall Street* films. This comparative reading aims to make each of Grossberg's points graspable in novel but pragmatic ways. In a second step, I attempt to make more intelligible potential degrees to which inter-referential discursive meaning production can be plural and complex in symbolic (conceptual) and material (aesthetic) economies of filmic representation; and will do so in a close reading of *visual economies* in a key scene from Stone's second Wall Street film, *Money Never Sleeps*. While the comparative analysis of representational economies, each contentiously articulating historically specific conjunctures, has a higher level of theoretical correlation in conjunctural analysis, the close reading of plural and complex visual economies more explicitly employs media-archeological methods.

Wall Street: greed and good in the neoliberal moment

Directed by Oliver Stone and released in 1987, *Wall Street* opens with a hybrid-aesthetic economy in which layered media effects variously mark the space of narrative departure: first aurally with a drum beat that sets the tempo of a song about to begin, then visually with an image of New York City at dawn as the day begins. Having established the story setting and pace, the camera cuts to a crate of fresh fish packed in ice, opening a possible narrative trajectory in a substory of production, distribution and consumption: caught in the pre-dawn early morning, the fish begin their day's journey to a market where they will be displayed, procured and consumed at day's end. Six seconds into the film, the representational economy is plural in medial form and discursive signs indicating beginnings (of a song, of the film, of the day, of the fish's journey), has provided contexts of time and place, and produces the imaginary space of narrative discourse in relation to material practices of labor and consumption.[2]

The opening floating perspective quick-cut montage presents a plurality of locations, actions and agents, but gives priority of place to the blue-collar worker, both temporally at the opening of the day and of the film diegesis, materially as the first agents of action in the daily procedures of commerce capital New York, and spatially through the setting of subterranean work space. In this space, the atmosphere is of earthiness and corporeal embodiment: manual labor is to be understood as authentic *earthy* work whose value is tangible, as represented in the scene's haptic quality. Spatially, temporally and symbolically, labor workers subsist in value economies (commerce among them) at the foundation level. This form of representational prioritizing also foreshadows the ideological value inscribed into subsequent depictions of laborers as a valorized social group in the film narrative.

The opening scene's representational economy becomes more dense and complex when the off-screen sound of drums turns to song. With this subterranean earthy atmosphere, there is a touch of irony in the first words of the film soundtrack as Frank Sinatra sings *Fly Me to the Moon*.[3] On cue with the vocals and lyrical content, visual perspective moves from the subcutaneous space of industry underground to terrestrial surfaces and open space. A worker clinging to the back of a truck emerges into the daylight against a background of clear skies. In this brief scene of cinematic identification, the worker's immersion in the natural elements as the day begins functions as a double for the viewer's sensory immersion in the world of narrative cinema as the story begins. In an additional layer of cinematic doubling *Fly Me to the Moon* sets the mood of endless possibility, both for the fictional character of the worker, the potential real-world worker he represents, and the real-world viewer as it becomes immersed in the storyworld. For those with the capacity to be moved by music, and in particular those who had known the popular song in other contexts, its intention is undoubtedly to open a strong economy of emotions.

This dense staging of aesthetic, emotive and narrative economies sets the tone for the rest of the film's title sequence, and subsequently the rest of the film, which is very much about *movement* in and through various economies: of time, affect, commerce, labor, social relations, urban space, cultural value, and in particular movement in and through economies of mobility as representative of class mobility. In the title sequence, this is framed first with vertical movement upward and outward into open space, then as horizontal movement *inward* into the city through various modes of transport (by foot, boat, car, subway train). Once in the city, there is again movement from the subterranean, to ground level, and from ground level further *upward* into skyscrapers: the visual, audial and lyrical representational economies work in unison to impart the swinging sensation of freedom to move. Again on lyrical queue, as *fly me to the moon, let me play among the stars* becomes audible there is a visual cut to the World Trade Center as a conceptual key frame. The centrality of the World Trade Center sequence is marked through the superimposition of the director's name, which visually frames the towers by underlining (or underwriting) them. Accent is also given in the punctuated aesthetic shifts in music and camera motion, where the towers get a double perspective shot, shift in shot distance (switching from close-mid-range shot to slow-panning long shot), and receive more screen time than other city shots. In the title sequence's symbolic economy of meaning, if one wants to play among the stars, this is what it is about (neoliberal commerce) and where it is going to happen (commerce capital NYC).

Fly Me to the Moon is a love song about *feelings* of astral wonderment experienced when falling in love. However, the explicit love object in *Wall Street* is not a person. The object of love represented in upward motion toward the stars into the celestial spheres of financial trade is monetary wealth. The accent on mobility in the opening sequence functions metaphorically in reference to class mobility through financial empowerment. Symbolic and topographic movement upward as we follow protagonist Bud Fox (Charlie Sheen) in the direction of the stars is plotted in the opening sequence's temporal and spatial economies of narrative progression in the following order: from the subway to ground level, from ground level to a view of the sky, through the masses of pedestrian and vehicle traffic (both depicted as troublesome to Bud's practical economy of upward motion), finally into a more excusive space of elite labor in the financial sector, where there is a more refined yet no less troublesome throng of foes who, like Bud, audaciously attempt to move upward and play among the stars. Roughly two and a half minutes into the film, the viewer arrives with Bud at the top and, as if to clarify the symbolic economy in which arrival among the stars correlates to arrival in the upper echelons of world trade, the music stops. Through the aesthetic economy of sensorial input, in the realm of the audial and visual, there are two ruptures in motion: a halt in the melodic flow of music orchestrated in unison with a halt in Bud's upward movement as he arrives at the offices of Jackson Steinem & Co. This double aesthetic halt functions as a framing mechanism for the notion of arrival, but also for the first diegetic verbal exchange that directly follows: a secretary at Jackson Steinem asks the protagonist, "How you doing Buddy?" To which Bud Fox replies, "Great Carol. If I were doing any better it would be a sin." With its relatively complex plural aesthetic and symbolic representational economies, this exchange closes the title sequence.[4]

A hallmark of narratively significant title sequences is the efficient and effective presentation of concepts that will be relevant to the film's plot as the story progresses. If you can imagine the title sequence of *Wall Street* as punctuated[5] with a collection of *economy* concepts (and you should), the movement upward and arrival at the brokerage that represents arrival into an exclusive social space is the *penultimate* economy concept presented thus far in the film. In terms of both narrative progression and symbolic import, the *ultimate* economy concept punctuating the opening sequence as its closing notation is to be found in Bud's reply: *if I were doing any better it would be a sin*. By the end of the film, and at various points along the way, it becomes evident that among the economy concepts presented in the film diegesis, the one inscribed with maximum value is a *moral economy*. In navigating the class-mobility ladder upward, the primary economies to be negotiated by the protagonist are presented in the conventional notion of *the economy* as a space of potential financial gain, the less conventional notion of *libidinal economy* as the management of personal desire, and finally the a sense of moral obligation as an *economy of feelings* (discursively constructed and culturally contingent). Conflict that organizes action and plots progression in the film's narrative economy is presented in the form of moral dilemma: how to *move up* in the world without betraying one's family and one's social values, without losing one's sense of moral integrity? The dilemma is articulated in a variety of ways throughout. Recalling Gordon Gekko's (Michael Douglas) infamous (and purposefully ambiguous) claim that *greed is good*, one might note how well it aligns with the initial framing of moral economies *vis-à-vis* monetary economies as the film's central *agon* at the opening.

In the 1987 neoliberal moment, *Wall Street* presents a conjunctural story of social conditions and cultural contexts inscribed within and inscribing itself into *the economic*. Emerging from the 1970s economic recession, the "New Economy" is a time of relative prosperity characterized by the displacement of industrial and agricultural economies through financialization, which had become broadly institutionalized and taken on the appearance of natural selection in the techno-social order of things.[6] Indeed, this is the quasi-essentialist meaning inscribed in the claim "greed is good." If you want to *move up* in the world, then take note of how the film's protagonist leaves his blue-collar family heritage behind for a bright white-collar future. Whether demonized or fetishized, movement beyond the drudgery of manual labor and throng of the masses into the refined realms of financial trade becomes an ideational *Gestalt* prominent in the cultural imaginary of the 1980s neoliberal moment. In accord with the techno-social conjunctions, material conditions and discursive productions of its time, it is unsurprising that the film's aesthetic economy represents the troublesome bind between upward mobility and moral hazard with regard to class divisions, gender differences and racial distinctions. Two decades later, the material and discursive limits of neoliberal economics have some remarkably different characteristics.

Money Never Sleeps: debt and accountability in the post-neoliberal moment

Greed was good in 1987 – it could get you to higher places, even if the path upward was not without treachery. The atmosphere of Stone's 1987 film reflected well the cultural climate in which a ticklish sense of possibility is intermingled with latent skepticism and moral ambiguity around class mobility in the New Economy. Following the 2008 subprime mortgage crisis that led to global recession, the moral universe of *Wall Street* in 2010 is far less ambiguous.[7] Like the 1987 film, the title sequence of *Money Never Sleeps* is set against the backdrop of New York City and employs an aesthetic economy of time, space, motion and emotion (the fundamental aesthetic economy of narrative cinema) to achieve its multiple layers of symbolic meaning. A (simulated) fixed camera position watches as the *new* New York skyline pans steadily across the screen. Movement is mechanically lifeless, the glass and metal surfaces of the cityscape flat, and machine-like tones of David Byrne and Brian Eno's "Home" add the finishing touches to the suggestion that in this brave new world of surveillance and silicon technologies (i.e. of control and artifice), things may not be what they seem. Entry into a *through the looking glass* symbolic logic (a favorite trope of Stone's) denotes that although the setting is the same old Big Apple, it is no longer the Apple it used to be. Both title sequences are concerned with the effects of techno-social change regarding the "interdependence between financial market and everyday social life" (Pelzer 2015); but the 2010 film explicitly punctuates the passage of time around a set of social changes wrought by financial, digital and political technologies. Before the title sequence of *Money Never Sleeps*, a prologue negotiates temporal shift in correlation to techno-social change. Its representational economies index change in extremely broad categorical framings of temporal, social, technological and epistemic (meta-) economies. It is in fact the prologue that offers a more resonant comparison to the 1987 film's title sequence.

When the film opens, sound and vision coincide: a stack of legal documents slams down on a surface and fills the screen. Where priority of place was given to manual labor in the first film, in the post-subprime moment, aesthetic and thematic priority of place is given to *bad paper*.[8] A police clerk (real-life ex-convict Richard Stratton) reads off a catalogue of Gekko's personal possessions: silk handkerchief and necktie, gold watch, gold ring, gold money clip "with no money in it, and one mobile phone." The mobile phone is the first blunt accentuation of the relation between time, space and techno-social change. Looking like a small piece of Samsonite luggage, the late 1980s cellular phone was *the* media fetish object of its time, indicating social status, combined technological and business savvy, and upward social mobility – with the mobile telephone, symbolically as literally, you were *going places*. In this scene, it is a relict of the world where greed was good. Now the mobile phone is a commonplace object weak in symbolic value due to its ubiquity in presence and function; more a technological meta-medium than a telephone. Following this touch of irony, (thirty seconds in) emotive music is introduced. Low-toned, slow-paced, mundanely dramatic, it accompanies Gekko's release from prison. As he stands at the counter collecting what remains of his material possessions, the camera cuts to front-page news. It is October 22, 2001 – one month and 11 days after September 11 (9/11–10/22). The camera pans in close-up over the cover page to show the headline: "Grim recovery at Ground Zero." The discharging officer lays a US Treasury check on top of the newspaper for $1,086.62 – "50 cents a day, minus what you spent on the inside. And a train ticket to the Big Apple." If this is what greed gets you, the prologue to the 2010 film should also be read as an epilogue to the 1987 film.

A white-collar criminal with a three-day beard, Gekko exits the prison gates in the company of a migrant-worker-styled Mexican-American who gets into a taxi and gangster-rap-styled African-American for whom a stretch limousine arrives. Music blares from the limousine as the door opens to let the young man in. It's a thug life, right? Yes and no. The scene turns our attention toward race, class and gender discourses as in the opening of the 1987 film (where Bud as rising Anglo-American money man is also contextualized by social otherness in literal economies of mobility and transportation), but does so in ways that suggest the tables of privilege may have turned – it *is* a thug life.[9] However, what is finally prioritized regarding the distribution of privilege among the proverbial *haves* and *have-nots* is not a question of social status through monetary wealth as in the first film; though it is a social institution at stake in both films – that of family. A reverse shot from the Latino's perspective shows his wife and child smiling as they walk toward the camera. When the door of the limousine opens a small girl can be seen waiting and heard calling "daddy" above the music. The foci are on shifting economies of gains and losses that have taken place since Gekko's incarceration. According to the prologue's symbolic economy, more significant than Gekko's monetary losses are his non-monetary losses. With no limo or driver, no family awaiting his return, and alone in the world – for Gekko, it is decidedly *not* a thug life.

As the viewer pieces together the implicit moral tale of the prologue through the film's visual economy, an extra-diegetic voiceover (Shia LaBeouf) explains how such radical change comes about:

> "You wanna know what the mother of all bubbles was? It came out of nowhere; by chance. They called it the 'Cambrian Explosion'. Happened around five-hundred and thirty million years ago. For the next seventy eight

> million years, the rate of evolution accelerated so fast, *we* came along: the human race. They still can't explain how it happened, except that it happened. Some people say it was by chance; others design. But who really knows?"

Fade to black, intertitle inscription "Seven Years Later," Byrne and Eno's "Home" keys the entrance to the title sequence.[10] With the prolepsis from October 2001 to October 2008, context shifts from the post-9/11 moment to the post-subprime-crisis moment; each adding rich subtexts of symbolic meaning interwoven with the symbolic economy of Gekko's character and story. There are three prominent possible *bubbles* addressed through the prologue voiceover in relation to this historico-temporal economic frame: with the bad papers, the jump to 2008 and "Home" on the soundtrack, one first assumes it is the subprime mortgage crisis. Then the voiceover informs us it is the Cambrian explosion. In addition to these, and recalling the newspaper title story, the chosen terminology (an *explosion* that seemed to come *out of nowhere*, instantaneously changing everything) gestures toward the 9/11 attacks on the World Trade Center (material explosions that generate financial, cultural and political crises; thus radically shifting the conjunctural state of affairs). Beyond the subprime, World Trade and Cambrian bubbles, there is the exploded bubble of Gekko's personal affairs as he represents a kind of everyman-ideal neoliberal *homo economicus* five-hundred and thirty million years after the Cambrian explosion. Though Gekko is ambivalently framed as an anti-hero/villain hybrid, he is unambiguously coded as an agent of neoliberal corruption. And still, he appears to have suffered losses like everyone else. In the style of a proper Greek prologue, it is suddenly the question of society itself that is at stake regardless of race or class, and represented through the institution of family as the microcosm of society.

Nevertheless, as meaning-rich discursive nodes representing social economies of difference, race and class cannot be disregarded. In the prologue's symbolic economy, perhaps one is to understand that the very element of privilege – so often co-determined through economies of class, race and gender in preaching the goodness of greed – encourages people to lose sight of non-monetary economies and forms of wealth or wellbeing. The point returns us to Grossberg's critique and the task at hand: the representation of economic *plurality*, recognition of complex economic construction through material and discursive practices, and the conjunctural analysis of how these are situated. If the economic moment of 1987 could be symbolically characterized by flight into celestial spheres, the post-9/11 moment and post-subprime crisis are well represented through plummeting back down to earth in a series of historic bubbles, explosions, crashes and crises that significantly renegotiate the dynamic interplay of economies, discourses and cultural conventions.

Conjunctural difference: representing the techno-social moment

As for plurality, many of the economies noted are present in both films: extra-diegetically, there is the whole range of representational aesthetic economies characteristic of narrative cinema, as well as the generic conventions associated with Hollywood fiction film. A broad range of financial- and monetary-based economies is present in both: financial institutions and their household organization, stock market trading, information exchange, value creation, production, and consumption, interaction between corporate and state policy, New Economy consumer-capitalist habits as ideologically or ethically constitutive, etc. While the 2010 film makes explicit references to the 1987 film through aesthetico-symbolic similitude, more culturally and ideologically significant are the conscientious differences in economic types and states framed through its multilayered and complex representational economy. At the level of broad organizational categories, both films prominently depict imbrications of financial and social organization by technological means (whether institutional or mechanical). In the portrayal of financial systems as social technologies or in the capacity of socio-technological hegemony, *technical* and *technological* elements are foregrounded. Both films are characterized by techno-fetishism; but while the 1987 film depicts technology *qua* novel social fetish-objects and in terms of novel technological innovation boosting trade markets capacities (reflecting the techno-social cultural dynamic of its time), the 2010 film makes an effort to depict technology (in particular digital information and communication technologies, ICTs) as quasi-naturalized in the conjunctural condition of information flows that have rearranged the techno-social landscape in its very topography and in regimes of practice.

However, the film does not portray techno-social change as statically engrained in (and co-determining) novel ways of being. Rather, dynamic techno-social transition should be understood in terms of continual flows of change and their material effects that generate possibility – not for a select few as in the 1987 film's class mobility, but in the Hardt and Negri vision of digitally democratic grass-roots action that has the capacity to cut through conventionally restrictive access to hegemonic power.[11] If the broad dissemination and naturalization of digital technologies have opened the way for new nodes of power, the way has also been opened for new modes of distributing and negotiating power. The 2010 film prominently takes other techno-social changes into account; framing less machine-*technical* (e.g. the interaction of computer and financial technologies) and more social-technique oriented (i.e. discursive, aesthetic, symbolic) shifts in culturally situated identity discourses. In taking cultural contexts as frameworks for meaning in 2010, key discourse areas overlap, as seen with race-class-gender difference relative to social power. Though as noted above, this is also done with a view to distinguishing how power dynamics have changed in accord with shifting sensibilities equally engendered through discursive and material practices. The tangible material changes between 1987 and 2010 are accompanied by less tangible, though no less significant, changes in social order. In the 2010 film, elements such as empowerment and entitlement, access and exclusion, hierarchy and equanimity are represented in a way so as to rearrange the techno-social order of things in contrast to the race-class-gender social dynamism associated with the 1987 neoliberal moment.

In 1987, the self-willed son navigates new flows of techno-social possibility in relation to biological father (played by non-fictional father Martin Sheen) and symbolic replacement father (Gekko). In 2010, the self-willed daughter is centralized as an index for non-monetary value, social empowerment and, in her categorical disenfranchisement of the father, anti-paternalism. Though the symbolic son (Shia LaBeouf) has an ambivalent role, Winnie Gekko (Carey Mulligan) represents progress along economic flows with completely different sets of ideological prescriptives for action from the ones Bud or Gekko had in 1987, and distinct from those her partner or father have in 2010. Winnie's more humane economism is not based on the logic of the one where *greed is good*, but of the many: if in reference to the moral economy of Western civilization prior to the neoliberal moment – *altruism is good*. One might recall the way Hall and Massey symbolically bookend an era of neoliberalism by using a title ("Interpreting the Crisis") that makes reference to concerns at the beginning of that era, and suggesting it is time for a change yet again. *Money Never Sleeps* provides a conjunctural framing of neoliberalism that is similar insofar as it symbolically bookends an era of social order whose particular moral economy has exhausted itself. In the post-subprime crisis moment, risk society's culture of debt and catastrophic breaches in liability are represented alongside the notion of one's debt to society. Not only is greed *not* good; altruism has become a necessity.

While *Money Never Sleeps* presents many of the same economy types seen in the 1987 film (technological, economic, cultural, social-hierarchical, emotional, libidinal, institutional, etc.) significant conjunctural distinctions are made with regard to crisis, debt and liability. These constitute nodes of impacted meaning and heightened antagonism for the historical moment (or moments) the film is concerned with (recall here Hall's claim that crises drive history forward from one conjunctural period to another). Though the concept of indebtedness plays an important role in the 1987 film, from narrative and symbolic points of view it is primarily coupled with *feelings* of moral obligation relative to familial and social behavioral norms: to what extent is Bud Fox morally obliged to act in accord with his biological father's expectations and values? To what extent should he act in accord with feelings of indebtedness toward Gekko as his symbolic father? How is he to remain true to himself, so to speak? Where senses of moral obligation come into focus for this film, they are presented as indications for correct behavior, and as such have a *guiding* organizational function. They do not *necessitate* a course of action so much as they have a *co-determining* organizational function for individual (and cultural) identity. One is not socially *obliged* to act in accord with moral feelings, though one may choose to do so as a question of individual integrity. Thus, the economy of indebtedness is local and reflexive: you are liable to your sense of self (i.e. an economy of character). This particular economy is given priority in the film's symbolic meanings, particularly in relation to other prominent economy ideas: the conventional notion of *the economy* as monetary, financial wealth, material accumulation, social empowerment, etc. The question posed is: how to maximize profit in the one without dramatically compromising the other?

Money Never Sleeps portrays a world more experienced in the ways of debt. On the one hand, there is less of a touchy-feely atmosphere regarding moral obligation: where it is common practice to have a former partner orchestrate one's execution, moral obligation is represented in manners ranging from pragmatic (green energies = good, but the idea is expressed in flat non-moralizing tones) to a general sense of callousness. The economic moment of post-subprime crisis is characterized as less naïve when it comes to *feeling* indebted. Even Gekko's desire to reunite with his daughter is colored with ambivalence; and when it is not, his character does not display any sense of *feeling* morally obliged. Unlike Bud, Gekko's actions are not presented as *guided by moral feelings*. Rather, when he seeks contact with his daughter in non-monetary contexts, his compulsion to do so is characterized through an atmosphere of desperate necessity: he *needs* to see her because she is *all he has got* (you can read this emotionally, socially or financially). The dynamic conjunction of socially inflected senses of indebtedness in 2010 significantly departs from the guidelines of moral register in 1987: indebtedness (if this is the proper term) becomes a pragmatically determining factor for social action, not a grey area of feeling that may influence you to act one way or another. At stake is the future of humanity; represented in reference to the Cambrian explosion from the film's prologue and later in the film through Winnie's unborn child. This is not the only (nor perhaps the most significant) way in which the dynamics of debt have taken a pragmatic turn.

Second chances: bad paper and deep-debt-economy aesthetics

If indebtedness as an abstract sense of moral obligation constituted an economy of feeling in 1987, in the meantime *debt* as a concrete technical object has become a financial resource *per se*. Between 2001 and 2008, debt as a financial tool and product has become so prominent that it is the determining factor of some particularly large financial economies. You can accrue debt, buy debt, trade debt, capitalize on debt or lose all in debt. No longer one element among many factors of household organization, there are now rich economies of debt. In economies of debt, there are winners and losers; and at the end of the day someone always has to pay. One particular scene from *Money Never Sleeps* portrays the conjunctural shift from emotive moral economies to an organizational pragmatics of debt economies. The following analysis of *visual* economies is presented as an alternative economic model (i.e. visual economies of semiotic value as alternative to commercial economies and monetary value). The combined media-archeological and conjunctural analysis approach should achieve two things. First, in accord with the task set out by Grossberg at the beginning of this chapter and with a focus on formal aesthetic process, it aims to *emphasize the notion of economic plurality through richly inter-referential representational economies per se*. Next, by rendering visible the dynamic interplay of media-specific representational economies as they meaningfully interact with the political and commercial economic discourses on which the film focuses, one might obtain a clearer impression of the organizational complexity through which the film re-presents and comments on a "precise historical conjuncture" and potential subsequent (indeed inevitable) change.

The scene of interest portrays Bretton James's (Josh Brolin) demise. Head of big bank Churchill Schwartz, James is a young god among the Titans of finance. His character should evoke antipathy: he is scrupulous without compunction, has youth without illusion, is naturally condescending, takes pleasure in the pain of others, exercises belligerent power with calm reserve, and has an air of preternatural entitlement. At the historical conjuncture of post-subprime mortgage crisis, he represents the institution of finance and banking as a systemically corrupt entity that will devour those who feed it. The viewers' antipathy is focalized and given poignancy through Jacob Moore's (LaBeouf) antagonistic relation to him.[12] Moore holds James *accountable* for the death of his father-figure mentor. James's agonist position is further substantiated via Gekko, who holds James accountable for his imprisonment. The film's narrative logic thus positions James's downfall as a necessary payment of debt on the diegetic level through Moore, Gekko Churchill Schwarz, and others, as well as extra-diegetically insofar as James is portrayed as a holy goat whose slaughter will ease the sense of injury for all those looking on (we, the viewers). The scene of his demise constitutes a peripatetic moment of recognition and reversal. Among the many indexes marking the scene's centrality, it opens with a pan-in close-up of an article draft titled "BRETTON JAMES, CHURCHILL SCHWARTZ AND THE FALL OF AMERICAN CAPITALISM," and is aesthetically punctuated by hand-written text in red exclaiming "YOU NEED TO READ THIS!" A match-cut media shift from paper to digital displays a news flash: "Trader at Churchill Schwartz Accuses Bretton James of Illegal Trades and Causing Suicide of Louis Zabel…SEC asked to investigate 'the greatest heist that never was.' There's an old saying…'Steal a little and they throw you in jail…steal a lot and they make you a king.'" The application of this logic in James's case stands in symbolically for prominent cultural sentiment following the 2008 State bailout. The conventions of mainstream American melodrama require a scene of reversal, recognition Churchill Schwarz, and retribution; and the greater the crime, the more dramatic the retribution: the king must fall!

FIGURE 7.1 Second Chances. Still from *Wall Street: Money Never Sleeps*, 2010.

Following a cliché of market panic psychology, the rumor's rapid spread has the function of judge, jury Churchill Schwarz, and trial: James is guilty according to the courts of new narrowcast social media and old broadcast news media. Cutting from the montage sequence to James's office, one sees James plead to the bank CEO (a father-figure mentor) for a second chance. The near-perspective shot conspicuously frames James against the backdrop of a large painting showing a woman in nurse's uniform, her eyes gazing coyly out above the facemask. Discernable in the grey cloud floating above her head are three words: SECOND CHANCE NURSE (see Figure 7.1). The attendant symbolic discourses are medical and ecclesiastical: with her mask on, the imaginary scene the nurse witnesses involves surgical incision. The useful associative idiom here in accord with viewer expectations is that James will be (sacrificially) disemboweled. As he shifts slightly to his right, James replaces the nurse in the cinematic frame, which is now split between the painted text on the left and James on the right. With the text mirroring James's gesture of repentance seeking absolution, Second Chance Nurse becomes Second Chance James.

Second Chance Nurse is prominent throughout the scene's visual economy of gazes, objects and actions in which iconic figures look down on a dramatic scene of recognition and reversal as if in a position of both knowing, determining and mimetically symbolizing. It is a work from Richard Prince's *Nurse* series. The subject matter, medium and technique relevant in Prince's *Nurse* paintings are meaningful for the film scene's construction of a symbolic economy via a pictorial-iconic economy that is part of its more generally rich visual economy. First, the *Nurse* paintings are not paintings in the conventional sense. They are painted over printouts of photographic montages taken from photographs or images previously in circulation. Prince refers to the technique of appropriating photographic content for reuse as *rephotography*. In 2008, the year bad papers that had turned gold now definitively turn bad again, Prince's *Overseas Nurse* sold for a record $8,452,000 at a London Sotheby's auction (cf. Jovanovic 2014). The source for image appropriation is a collection of pulp fiction novellas written by Adele Maritano under the pen name Jane Converse, and published through the 1960s and 1970s. In the painting from *Money Never Sleeps*, one can see clear aesthetic correlations to the covers of Converse's *Dr. Holland's Nurse* and *Nurse in Hollywood*.[13] With its reference to pulp fiction and medial appropriation, Prince's *Nurse* series opens discourses on the production, consumption and facile satisfaction of cheap pleasures and disposable media in throw-away society that are relevant to the film's staging of the conjunctural moment.

For the scene's conjunctural and media-archeological deliberation on bad paper, there are a few points on pulp to consider regarding form, content and technique. Pulp fiction books were printed on cheap paper, sold for small change (between 25 and 45 cents), and were already on the way to the dustbin right off the press. In financial economies of scale, pulp fiction is co-determined by coupling reduced material quality (low-grade pulp) with cheap mass production and sales in a manner that seeks to multiply marginal profit per item into a total of significant returns. A distinguishing feature of economies of scale is that at the micro-level of considering an individual product-item in terms of its cost-value dynamic, there is no apparent potential for gain intrinsic to the individual product-item. Rather, it is the technique of production (and distribution) that constitutes the real resource. As with debt, value does not reside in the symbolic or material content of a thing, but in the economic techniques through which the thing is constituted and circulated. The term *pulp fiction* has an element of poetic resonance due to the way narrative content mirrors material form. It is thought to be cheap on both accounts: cheap products for cheap pleasures that amount to nearly nothing (or even to loss) individually, but have considerable potential impact in larger economies of scale (financially amassing margin profits; and socially constituting popular culture).

The reference to *pulp fiction* via Prince's *Second Chance Nurse* links to the notion of *bad paper* represented in the film's subject matter (the banking sector as a corrupt institution) and temporal conjunction (the 2008 subprime crisis) alongside other bad papers: default mortgage-backed securities (MBSs), collateralized mortgage obligations (CMOs) and collateralized debt obligations (CDOs). The irony generated through this plural economy of signs achieves fullness through parallel notions of turning garbage into gold: where Prince's rephotographic appropriation transforms worthless mass pulp into million-dollar works of art, Churchill Schwartz's (and the real financial institutions it represents) bundling and trading of MBSs, CMOs and CDOs turns mass debt into a financial-products resource the scale of which was previously unimaginable. In debt economy aesthetics, junk (bonds), debt and bad paper are turned into profit through new techniques of production, packaging, repackaging and reuse; subsequently introducing novel discourses on ownership, rights and wrongs through constructs of proprietorship and appropriation. All of this is conjuncturally situated with regard to specific technological, social and financial economies in the post-subprime moment.

Seeing meaning: the techno-epistemic bind

As the CEOs leave James's office, pictures on the walls continue to play an important role, positioning James both through their geometric aesthetic of spatial arrangement, through the economy of looks and gazes they construct, and through their symbolic intertexts – in particular the presence of Francisco Goya's *Saturno devorando a un hijo* (see Figure 7.2). It depicts Saturn eating his children after the oracle's claim that he would be overthrown by one of them. In the film, once the door shuts and James is alone, the camera pans from Second Chance Nurse to *Saturno* in a deliberate manner that moves from left to right, consistent with the camera movement used in the scene till now. Then the camera stops for a static over-the-shoulder shot.

The significance of over-the-shoulder shots is to provide the viewer access to the diegetic focalizor's perspective (in this case James) while keeping the focalizor in the frame. Unlike an eye-line match perspective shot – a technique for cultivating identification with the focalizor by putting the viewer in her or his position – an over-the-shoulder shot allows the viewer to see what the focalizor sees and at the same time see the focalizor in the very act of seeing. In its framing of the act of seeing, *it foregrounds recognition*. At this moment in the scene's visual economy, the

FIGURE 7.2 Look Away. Still from *Wall Street: Money Never Sleeps*, 2010.

viewer witnesses James's recognition that his own symbolic position is doubled in the visual economy he is witness to. The viewer sees James see Goya's *Saturno* and, in witnessing this act of seeing, witnesses James's recognition of himself in the painting as the child being devoured by his Titan father. The shot (more precisely, the dynamic signification of the shot's inter-referential visual economy) establishes a moment of dramatic reversal and recognition; but like Oedipus who at the moment of recognition blots out any further possibility of signification via an economy of vision, James revolts against the meaning of the signs around him. Where the camera had consistently panned to the right in accord with James's perspective previously, it suddenly changes direction and swirls to the left in a circular motion. The change in camera direction and speed mimics two familiar aesthetics. It gestures toward an aesthetic of reverse motion in the style of a rewind, which should be recognized as also reversing the movement of diegetic time; thus undoing what has already been done.[14] It also mimics the aesthetic of violently shaking one's head in negation and a gesture of looking away. The double gesture of turning back time in negation and looking away in negation is doubled yet again in the extra-diegetic aesthetic of the soundtrack. As James tears the painting from the wall and smashes it over a chair, Byrne sings, "look away, look away, look away, oh yeah."

In the film's conjunctural story of criminal activity as a social phenomenon contextualized with regard to cultural politics, legal reforms, media practices and social interaction in the post-subprime moment, divisions between traditional and liberal views (on financial services and debt-based economy; or in a broader context on personal entitlement and social indebtedness) continue to organize and form the limits of public discourse on institutionalized crime. A good conjunctural story will pose the following question: approaching these limits, what is a society's capacity to recognize and begin to think beyond them? In moments of crisis and potential change, will society move "on to another version of the same thing," or might relations "be radically transformed" (cf. Hall above)? In early 2017, it seems that desire for the former may lead to the latter. The question remains as to how and what viewers choose to see or not to see in the current conjunctural crises.

Notes

1 In the relatively brief history of Cultural Studies as a discipline, combinations of the three focus areas noted above, representational praxes and media presence can be found in some variation in seminal texts such as Williams's *Keywords* (1958) and *Television* (1974), or Hall et al.'s *Policing the Crisis* (1978) and *Representation* (2013). The five exceptional keywords in Williams's *Keywords* (intro p. 13) – industry, democracy, class, art, culture – are also still a valid reflection of what is at stake here: with finance as industry, democracy as plural voices and collective choices, class and culture as power and context to read out contingencies, and art as representational praxis with the partial objective of analysis.

2 I am not suggesting that this type of aesthetic hybrid density is unusual or particular to the films analyzed here. One of the things my analysis should emphasize is the rather common presence of complex representational economies, and the common condition of engaging in such economies even if one does not generally think of them as such (i.e. to emphasize the presence of and our engagement in a plurality of economies).

3 Recorded in 1964 with the Count Basie Orchestra, Sonny Payne on drums.

4 It is also worth noting that *material and discursive construction of these economies* are poignantly and purposefully accentuated, yet care is taken not to break, and thus make intelligible, the imaginary fourth wall. A convention of dramatic visual story-telling, the fourth wall provides the viewer with a sense of anonymity, enabling access to voyeuristic pleasures under pretenses of non-voyeurism in cinema's co-organization of material and conceptual space. Management of this material and conceptual space constitutes yet another complex layer of organizational economy present and functional in the title sequence of *Wall Street*.

5 I borrow the notion of *punctuation* as an aesthetic technique in narrative cinema from Thomas Elsaesser. Cf. "Tales of Sound and Fury: The Family Melodrama."

6 Cf. for example the cover story of *Time* magazine, May 30, 1973: "The New Economy."

7 Cf. the opening statistic from the US Treasury Department on estimated loss of household wealth.

8 A correlative framing of *bad paper* in the post-subprime moment can be found in Scorsese's *Wolf of Wall Street*, where both dollars and pink sheets are contextualized through corruption early in the film.

9 Born Carlos Irwin Estévez and raised in Los Angeles, Charlie Sheen's ethnic ancestry is Galician-Irish.

10 It is as little a coincidence that the track accompanying the temporal shift to the post-subprime crisis moment of October 2008 is titled "Home," as it is a coincidence that Byrne and Eno were contracted to work on the soundtrack (production label Todo Mundo) – designed as it is to mark elements of digitized techno-social change and characteristics of the film's cultural context. As the lead singer of *Talking Heads*, Byrne helped pioneer the new wave genre in the 1970s and '80s. A prolific composer, performer, producer, and inventor, Brian Eno pioneered the ambient music genre and is widely recognized as a founding figure of electronic music. He is less known as the author of his most famous composition to date: the "Microsoft Sound" that accompanies the Windows 95 system start-up (cf. www.minyanville.com/businessmarkets/articles/intel-microsoft-research-in-motion-apple/5/25/2010/id/28465?refresh=1).

11 Cf. part 4 of *Empire*.

12 Within the referential contexts of Titans and Gods, patriarchs and children, a relevant intertext might be found in Moore's given name: etymology of the biblical name Jacob is sometimes interpreted to mean *struggles with God* (cf. David Jeffrey (ed.) *A Dictionary of Biblical Tradition in English Literature*; 1992, p. 852).

13 Both published by Signet and sold for 40 cents per copy.
14 Cf. Michael Haneke's *Funny Games* (1997, 2007).

References

Byrne, David and Brian Eno. 2008. "Home." *Everything That Happens Will Happen Today*. [Audio] Todo Mundo.

Childress, Sarah. 2012. "How Much Did the Financial Crisis Cost?" *PBS Frontline* [online]. Available at: www.pbs.org/wgbh/frontline/article/how-much-did-the-financial-crisis-cost/ [accessed September 29, 2016].

Elsaesser, Thomas. 1972. "Tales of Sound and Fury: The Family Melodrama." *Monogram*, 4, pp. 2–15.

Grantham, Bill and Toby Miller. 2010. "The End of Neoliberalism." *Popular Communication*, 8(3), pp. 174–177.

Grossberg, Lawrence. 2010. *Cultural Studies in the Future Tense*. Durham and London: Duke UP, pp. 3, 101, 201.

Hall, Stuart. 1997. Representation: Cultural Representations and Signifying Practices. London: Sage.

Hall, Stuart, Chas Critcher, Tony Jefferson, John Clarke and Brian Roberts. 1978. *Policing the Crisis: Mugging, the State, and Law and Order*. London: Macmillan, pp. vii, 139.

Hall, Stuart and Doreen Massey. 2010. "Interpreting the Crisis." *Soundings*, 44, pp. 57–71.

Hardt, Michael and Antonio Negri. 2000. *Empire*. Harvard: Harvard UP.

Jovanovic, Rozalia. 2014. "artnet News' Top 10 Most Expensive Living American Artists." *artnet news* [online]. Available at: https://news.artnet.com/market/artnet-news-top-10-most-expensive-living-american-artists-11863 [accessed September 29, 2016].

Löffler, Petra. "Towards a New Media Archaeology? A Report on Some Books and Tendencies." *NECSUS European Journal of Media Studies* [online]. Available at: www.necsus-ejms.org/towards-a-new-media-archaeology-a-report-on-some-books-and-tendencies/#_edn2 [accessed September 29, 2016].

Nietzsche, Friedrich. 1995. *The Birth of Tragedy*. New York: Dover.

Parikka, Jussi and Garnet Hertz. 2010. "Archaeologies of Media Art: Jussi Parikka in Conversation with Garnet Hertz." *CTheory Interview* [online]. Available at: www.ctheory.net/articles.aspx?id=631 [accessed September 29, 2016].

Pelzer, Anja. 2015. "No Guns, No Rules, Just Pure Capitalism! Hollywood's Portraits of Wall Street." In G. Murdock and J. Gripsrud (eds.). *Money Talks: Media, Markets, Crisis*. Bristol: Intellect, pp. 151–168.

Plehwe, Dieter, Bernhard Walpen and Gisela Neuenhöffer (eds.). 2006. *Neoliberal Hegemony: A Global Critique*. Abingdon: Routledge.

Sinatra, Frank and William Allen Basie. 1964. "Fly Me to the Moon." *It Might as Well Be Swing*. [Audio] Los Angeles: Reprise Records.

Wall Street. (1987). [film] Oliver Stone.

Wall Street: Money Never Sleeps. (2010). [film] Oliver Stone.

8

NO ETHICS, NO HEROES

How immorality flattens Wall Street characters

Ignacio Ferrero, Marta Rocchi and Robert E. McNulty

> "There are three ways to make a living in this business: be first, be smarter, or cheat".
>
> Margin Call – *John Tuld*

Introduction

Since the 2008 financial crisis, ethics has been in the spotlight for all seeking to understand what went wrong with the economy: according to many analysts, the crisis resulted in large part from the lack of moral integrity of financial operators (Santoro and Strauss 2012). The post-crisis analysis can be parsed according to two different paths: a technical analysis in terms of failures at the institutional level (e.g. Financial Crisis Inquiry Commission USA 2011; Fox 2013; Lewis 2011; Reinhart and Rogoff 2009; and many others), or legal and ethical failures on the personal level. Documentaries like *Inside Job* (C. Ferguson 2010) show the usefulness – and at the same time the narrowness – of focusing only on both economic and legal theories to clarify what really happened and who was responsible for it. However, it is insufficient to study personal responsibilities only from a legal and institutional point of view. Rather, if unethical behavior played a role in the crisis, there is a need to reflect on the causes among the financial agents involved.

To explore these social phenomena, the narrative capacities of film provide a vivid vehicle for conveying some of the factual and technical elements that would be found in newspaper articles, while also communicating the unwritten emotional side of human beings. And by substituting words on a page with actors on a screen, the inflections of their voices, facial expressions, and many other cues, we get a glimpse into the deeper human motivations, projects, desires, and ideals that drive events (Smith 2003; Tan 1995). Moreover, movies express not just a situation, but they are the spokesmen of a culture (Griffiths 2002). For this reason, employing Wall Street characters in movies is highly representative of a genre of personal behaviors enmeshed in the dynamic situation of the era in which the implications of those behaviors are played out.

This chapter aims to reflect on the representation of the moral character of financial managers in the cinematic narrative, arguing that the lack of personal and institutional ethics has generated a loss of thickness in the represented characters. Plots are built on one-dimensional characters, whose actions follow from the view that the protection of personal wealth and positions of power constitute the ultimate horizon. *Margin Call* (J. C. Chandor 2011) serves as a dramatic parable for illustrating the values and character of Wall Street leaders over a tense 12-hour period during which an investment bank discovers that its financial holdings are essentially worthless because it has become highly overexposed in the risky trading of mortgage-backed securities the entire market of which is set to implode. Under these circumstances the characters must make decisions that will pit self-interest against that of their company's stakeholders and financial markets globally.

Classic dramas depict moral conflicts in which heroes embody virtues that are tested as characters are thrown by circumstances into struggles great and small. If they fail, we witness tragedy, but when they succeed, we are inspired by their triumphs. However, whether they succeed or fail such drama helps instruct the audience in the value of virtues and the costs of heroism. In this chapter, however, we consider a film full of drama, pathos, and high-stakes struggle, while entirely bereft of moral heroism. Situated within the social norms of a mythic Wall Street, the gentility of virtue has been supplanted by the logic of a dog-eat-dog Darwinian capitalism. We see here a drama comparable in intensity to the classics from Euripides to Chekhov, with one major difference: the story unfolds all within a domain that not only lacks moral heroism, but where heroism seems not to even be an option. The viewer witnesses the calculated triumph of the protagonists unfold in a seemingly moral-free zone in which the drama results from events that are disturbingly realistic and forebodingly dystopian.

The two key protagonists of this movie are John Tuld (played by Jeremy Irons), the hardnosed CEO of the investment bank, and his colleague Sam Rogers (Kevin Spacey), head of the trading floor. The character of John Tuld seems to be based on the real John Thain and Dick Fuld, the former heads of Merrill Lynch and Lehman Brothers. The assonance between Tuld and Fuld is notable. Tuld's main job is to mobilize the firm around a strategy to unload the toxic assets to a market completely unaware of the catastrophe that is about to explode. It is noteworthy that while the characters of Tuld and Rogers are forced to make decisions of a momentous nature, they do so as if no moral reflection were needed. Our thesis is that *Margin Call* presents a scenario in which it appears as if financiers are able to pursue their aims in the absence of traditional models of fictional and social heroism, and while they are clearly violating conventional moral norms, by the logic of Wall Street, they seem to have no other alternatives.

By setting the film within the 2008 economic crisis, the characters are stereotypical Wall Street anti-heroes who embrace the creed of profit maximization and carry it to its logical end irrespective of the costs to society at large. In so interpreting the crisis, the financial industry and the film's protagonists are portrayed as absolved of individual responsibility for their decisions, as remedial interventions appear as pointless as fighting the movements of ocean tides. This narrative, however, begs to be challenged, and to assist us we refer to Fournout's *Hero-Leader Matrix* (Fournout 2017), as well as a significant body of scholarship that uses film as a teaching tool on the impact of financial firms on society (Champoux 1999; Hosmer and Steneck 1989; Huczynski 2004) and more specifically, on the global financial sector (Belden 1992, on *Wall Street*; Biktimirov and Cyr 2013, on *Inside Job*; Chan et al. 1995, on *Other's People Money*; Cox et al. 2009, on *Enron: The Smartest Guys in the Room*; Van Es 2003, on *The Insider*; and Werner 2014, on *Margin Call*).[1] Such contributions are useful for teaching business ethics or integrating ethical reflection into the teaching of finance (Dobson 2008) as they dramatize the kinds of ethical dilemmas that can arise in the conduct of business. As stated by McAdams and Koppensteiner (1992, 627), studying fiction "is useful in strengthening the manager's ability to resolve specific ethical dilemmas" because it "offers a challenging and personally compelling method for managers (and management students) to improve their moral sensitivity and strengthen the decision-making skills used in addressing the ethical ambiguities of business practice." Moreover, according to Crossan et al. (2013), movies help to develop an awareness about strengths and character, and they afford the spectator the conditions to vicariously participate in the experience of virtues and vices.

This work is structured as follows: section 1 summarizes the plot and principal characters. Section 2 analyzes the decision-making process employed by the firm's executives. In light of Fournout's *Hero-Leader Matrix*, section 3 explores the film's representation of morality as illustrated by the moral thinness and absence of moral heroism among the characters. We then offer a brief reflection on the potential role of education in the formation of the moral character of future financial professionals. We conclude by reflecting on some of the chapter's key takeaways.

1. *Margin Call*: exploring plot and technical issues

The film begins one morning when the investment bank is firing many of its employees, among them the chief of the risk department, Eric Dale (played by Stanley Tucci). On his way out, Eric gives Peter Sullivan (Zachary Quinto) – a young former aerospace engineer who is now working as a risk analyst – a document he had been working on. As the tumultuous day is drawing to a close, Peter takes a look at Eric's work and discovers that, based on the analysis and given the changes in the market, the bank's proprietary portfolio has become dangerously overexposed. Although not stated, it is implied that banks around the world are similarly exposed. With this, Peter calls his immediate supervisor, Will Emerson (Paul Bettany), making him aware of the imminent financial catastrophe revealed through Dale's model.

From there, the senior executives – Sam Rogers, who heads the trading floor, Sarah Robertson (played by Demi Moore), the chief risk management officer, and Jared Cohen (Simon Baker), the investment division head – are convened for a meeting. Each of the main characters faces a crisis and responds somewhat differently. That night, the situation triggers an emergency meeting of the executive committee, presided over by John Tuld, the company's CEO.

Just before the meeting, the atmosphere is dark, with artificial light, reinforcing the severity of the situation, characterized by a fearful waiting, given the urgency of the situation. There is no music: the steps of the people gathering in the meeting room give the rhythm of the scene. The tension is accentuated by the presence of a woman, coldly addressing the participants of the meeting at the entrance of the meeting room alerting them that "he" is already arrived. The spectator does not know the identity of the person they are about to meet, although it is evident that it is the same person who just came by helicopter few scenes before. Everything contributes to highlight a sudden notable arrival.

Finally, John Tuld enters into the scene. The role of CEO is usually crucial for protecting the moral tone and character of a company, accepting responsibility where appropriate, and seeking to keep violations to stakeholder interests to a minimum, and when problems arise, deciding on steps to take to provide remediation and to mitigate the chance of recurrence of similar events in the future (Seeger and Ulmer 2001). Therefore, with Tuld's arrival, a momentous point in the film has occurred. The camera follows his walk up to the moment he sits at the head of the table. All the main characters of the film are silently seated at the table. Tuld is clearly the dominant character of this scene, his red tie distinguishes him from the others, and the way he addresses each of the participants at the meeting attests to his power.

Tuld begins by remarking on the gravely extraordinary event that has brought them together and issues the call to action: "This matter has to be handled urgently." He looks for information to understand the present situation and asks to speak directly with the person who wrote the report. The focus turns to a hesitant Peter Sullivan.

Seeking a clear explanation, Tuld feigns ignorance about the matter saying: "Please speak as you might to a young child or a golden retriever." Peter Sullivan explicates his model's projection regarding what will happen to the investment bank, concluding that even a moderate decrease in the market value of mortgage-backed securities (MBS) would result in a loss greater than the total capitalization of the company.

Sullivan provides a concise summary of the situation: "Over the last 36 to 40 months the firm has begun packaging new MBS products that combine several different tranches of rating classification in one tradable security. This has been enormously profitable as I imagine you noticed."

"The key factor here," continues Peter, "is these essentially are just mortgages, so that has allowed us to push the leverage considerably beyond what you might be willing, or allowed to do in any other circumstance, thereby pushing the risk profile without raising any red flags." Peter's model suggests that a moderate decrease of the value of MBS will lead the bank into bankruptcy. The unavoidable conclusion that the executive committee has to draw from Peter's analysis is that, given the exposure to these toxic assets, the bank is now on the brink of collapse.

2. The decision-making process

"Music is about to stop," dramatically announces John Tuld, once he realizes the importance of the situation, "and we are going to be left holding the biggest bag of odorous excrement ever assembled in the history of capitalism."

The first five minutes of this crucial meeting were dedicated to understanding the context and gathering data. Now a decision needs to be made. The Committee now has the needed elements to deliberate and exercise their judgment. John Tuld stands up and goes to a window that looks out on the panorama of the city. He then concludes the deliberative process, calling on his key lieutenants. His strategic framework is simple. "There are three ways to make a living in this business: be first, be smarter, or cheat. Now, I don't cheat, and although I like to think we have some pretty smart people in this building, it sure is a hell of a lot easier to just be first." In this way, Tuld has shown himself to be the Socrates of the school of Wall Street profit maximizers. He has set up his dialog so perfectly that the outcome is self-evident, and he leaves it to his interlocutors to then draw the ineluctable conclusion. And that is where he turns to Jared Cohen, head of the bank's investment division. Cohen succinctly translates Tuld's precept into logical concrete action: "Sell it all today..."

Tuld then turns to Sam Rogers on whom he will rely to operationalize this strategy. He asks Sam to enumerate the pros and cons of immediately selling the bank's entire portfolio of MBS. Sam appears existentially distressed by these prospects because they all know that what they would be selling is worthless, and doing so would be knowingly putting many of their buyers out of business. Not only would the bank be inflicting financial damage, doing so would destroy the trust that is foundational to the relations between traders and their clients. Everybody in the room knows that even if legal, their fire sale violates the ethos of the trade, and will trigger the intervention of the regulatory agencies. Here is where the distinction between ethics and compliance is stated in blunt terms. Anticipating such intervention, Ramesh Shah (played by Aasif Mandvi), the compliance officer, indicates how compliance with law provides all the cover the company needs: "They can slow you down, they can't stop you."

With the meeting over, the characters move to the next phase, which is execution, knowing full well the practical implications thereof.

3. The representation of morality and the need for heroes: ethics, dramatic tension, and dilemmas

This section is divided into four parts: section 3.1 sketches the ethical issues associated with the response of the bank to the situation they face; section 3.2 examines the place of ethics in the personal and social narrative of some of the key characters. It is here that the idea of "heroism" is most relevant. We examine how the characters react – or not – when faced with significant ethical challenges. Section 3.3 concludes by comparing some of the characteristics of a *Hero-Leader* according to the Fournout's matrix (Fournout 2017) and the virtue ethics approach and how they may apply to the *Margin Call* characters. The final section looks ahead to the education of future moral heroes.

3.1 Presenting the dilemma: "you are selling something that you know has no value"

When asked about the moral consequences of selling the company's portfolio of MBS, Chandor, the screenwriter and director of the movie, affirms that the characters act as "pure capitalists." He adds: "The moral question to me was never going to be...very long that they debated" (Benardello 2011). Moral deliberation requires that the actors consider their interiority and the broader context of their actions: the antecedents, the relevant circumstances, and the foreseen consequences. In this sense, Sam seems to be the only one recognizing the moral complexities associated with selling.

The moral thinking of Tuld and Rogers is expressed through their dialogue during the executive committee meeting and in the private meeting they held afterwards. In this latter conversation, during the last dark hours of the night before the new day starts, they are both looking outside. The contrast of two of the lead characters is revealing. They are both skillful and clever professionals. Sam knows how to technically realize Tuld's strategy, above all through his ability to mobilize his troops and lead them into battle. To succeed, the bank has to sell its portfolio before the market realizes the real value or risk of these products, which will lead to a collapse in price. This plan can be assessed on at least two basic levels: technical (and legal) and ethical.

Technically, one needs to ask what is at stake in selling highly risky or even valueless products. According to the United States Security and Exchange Act, "It shall be unlawful for any person, directly or indirectly...(a) To employ any device, scheme, or artifice to defraud; (b) To make any untrue statement of a material fact or to omit to state a material fact necessary in order to make the statements made, in the light of the circumstances under which they were made, not misleading; or (c) To engage in any act, practice, or course of business which operates or would operate as a fraud or deceit upon any person; in connection with the purchase or sale of any security" (US Securities and Exchange Commission 1934, 10b-5). Based on these rules and on its Standard of Practice, the CFA Institute speaks about the integrity of capital markets citing a particular category of violation of market integrity, which is the "material nonpublic information" (CFA Institute 2014, Standard II-A). Information is "material" if "its disclosure would probably have an impact on the price of a security or if reasonable investors would want to know the information before making an investment decision. In other words, information is material if it would significantly alter the total mix of information currently available about a security in such a way that the price of the security would be affected" (CFA Institute 2014, 59). Information is "nonpublic" until "it has been disseminated or is available to the marketplace in general (as opposed to a select group of investors)" (CFA Institute 2014, 61). The Standard on material nonpublic information states that "Members and Candidates who possess material nonpublic information that could affect the value of an investment must not act or cause others to act on the information" (2014, 6). The CFA Standard of Practice Handbook also states that "serving the best interests of the investing clients and employers lies at the heart of what collectively must be done to ensure a sense of trust and integrity in the financial markets" (2014, 1).

In *Margin Call*, the decision of the executive committee opens different levels of moral evaluation. First, the decision demonstrates a deliberate willingness to sell valueless or highly risky products probably using nonpublic material information. Does this violate SEC rules? Judges would need to decide the legality, but the ethics is a lot clearer.

Second, the consequences of the bank's actions on clients and traders have to be considered. Clients will be damaged buying worthless products without being appropriately informed of the risk they will incur; and traders will ruin their professional reputation by engaging in destructive actions, since their trades will have direct and dire consequences on the lives of many others, and yet, they are being carried out without regard for what is "right." This is evidenced by the fact that clients begin the day buying shares at over $90 apiece and by day's end, the shares are selling at less than a dollar.

Except for Sam, none of *Margin Call*'s characters reflect on these considerations. Their moral character has been stymied – they care for themselves and their financial future, without any sense of involvement in a broader community or history, without guilt, and without sacrificing anything for the interests of others. Chandor confirms this perspective: "Every character is looking in towards the center of the building. As a result, they're only worrying about what's happening on that exact floor and their exact lives. You have the city, and as a metaphor, the world is over their shoulders in a lot of the shots…I always wanted the outside world there, reminding the audience what these people in the foreground are going to do is going to echo out" (Benardello 2011).

Margin Call's characters have no horizon other than themselves. However, their decisions will have an enormous impact not only on their clients, but on markets around the globe. And yet, the characters play out their roles with no stopping to assess their decisions in light of the storm they are unleashing; they are operating in a guilt-free zone because they have permitted their conscience to be coopted by an ethic of profit maximization above all else. If the characters of *Margin Call* feel any qualms, it is out of concern for their personal job prospects and their personal fortunes.

3.2 How does ethics make a difference? Wall Street's new "heroism"

In order to find out whether the film provides any opportunities for the characters to redeem themselves as heroes, it is important to clarify what we mean by the term "hero." We use the term "hero" to refer to persons who, in their everyday practice, summon the courage to retain their moral integrity in the face of temptation and adversity and apply that moral integrity to the projects of their lives, whether it be running a business, raising a family, offering a helping hand to those in need, or acting responsibly within the broader context of society. The everyday moral hero recognizes that as members of communities, our responsibilities extend beyond our narrow self-interests, and he or she accepts this as part of the social contract. This notion of hero can be framed in terms of *virtue ethics*, which situates ethics in terms of personal happiness that is thoroughly connected with the social flourishing of the community in which one lives. From the perspective of virtue ethics, a hero is someone who tries to live a virtuous life.

Virtue ethics focuses on the role of virtues in the life of the human beings and their decision-making process. Virtues are those habitual dispositions oriented to the good that a person needs to cultivate in order to obtain happiness (Aristotle 2000). Virtue ethics also links the actions an agent performs with the person the agent becomes. Virtue, then, can be defined as a freely acquired habitual disposition or character trait that enables one to perceive, experience emotions, deliberate, decide, and act in a proper way; it is also the controlling factor for *eudaimonía* (human flourishing) (Ferrero and Sison 2014, 386). Virtue ethics has three relevant features: it is about free actions; personal behavior, which is linked to personal identity; and a teleological structure, with happiness as the end of personal ethics, and the common good as the ultimate horizon of social ethics. Moreover, in line with the virtue ethics perspective, we share Seger's idea that in the cinematic narrative, heroes are characters who can "encourage us, motivate us, or push us into new behaviors or new understandings" (Seger 1990, 85).

This ethical framework leads to articulate three features of a hero from a virtue ethics perspective. A hero has: (a) personal courage and integrity to choose what is good even when facing temptations or adversity; (b) a project, as this is essential to a teleological orientation to personal and social good; and (c) ideals, which are needed if a hero is to motivate and inspire him or herself as well as others.

Let us now apply these concepts to analyze the decisions and actions of *Margin Call*'s characters, Sam Rogers and John Tuld. As we see it, in its effort to represent the anomie of Wall Street corporate culture, *Margin Call* depicts the characters as essentially lacking in interiority, and as a result, there is an absence of the moral engagements that afford ordinary people the opportunity for moral heroism. Here, we find it helpful to introduce Fournout's *Hero-Leader Matrix* as a tool for analyzing the ethics of both movie heroes and real-life decision-making economic actors (managers), relying on Fournout's hypothesis that "cinema heroes and efficient managers… actually share a certain number of behavioral traits" (Fournout 2017, 30).

Based on a research involving 200 movies and 50 books on management, Fournout, formulates six features that can be recognized in the character of the *hero-leader* in business and cinema (Fournout 2017, 34). These six features are paired in dialectical tension:

- Features centered on the *hero-leader*'s self: ROL (*Role*) and INT (*Interiority*); *Role* designates the social identity the *hero-leader* assumes; this could be aligned with his deep personal identity and beliefs, or it could be a mask the *hero-leader* wears. *Role* is intended to be in tension with *Interiority*, which represents the personal beliefs, emotions, and opinions of the *hero-leader*. This pair represent the tension lived by the *hero-leader*, especially when his or her social or professional roles conflict with his or her personal beliefs and lifestyle.
- Features centered on the *hero-leader*'s position within his group: MIS (*Mission*) and DIV (*Divergent*); *Mission* represents the purpose the *hero-leader* is supposed to fulfill, while *Divergent* is the way the *hero-leader* chooses to fulfill that mission. Depending on the degree of creativity or unorthodoxy (in general, of divergence), *hero-leaders* choose the conventional or expected path to fulfill their mission, or they may act divergently, in a creative manner, finding alternative and unexpected solutions. The creativity in solving problematic situations may conflict with the mission when it seems to be fixed or imposed and, therefore, does not allow different path as may be needed.
- Features centered on the *hero-leader*'s relationships with others in general: NEG (*Negotiator*) and SPW (*Superpowered*); *Negotiator* shows the ability of the *hero-leader* to be open and available to dialogue with others (the others could be the members of a team, or a family, or a group sharing an interest – wherever a hero-leader acts and lives); on the contrary, *Superpowered* expresses the attitude of the *hero-leader* to use his personal access to power to achieve ends. *Superpowered* is in tension with the capability of negotiating when the *hero-leader* chooses to use his authority instead of seeking common ground through discussion and coordinated action with others.

Although Fournout's features are presented as pairs in tension, they are not necessarily mutually exclusive. Indeed, Fournout presents the six features in different movies and he highlights how they can be traced simultaneously in different characters.

3.3 Margin Call *and the lack of heroes*

In this section we draw on both the ideas of Fournout and the virtue ethics to highlight at least three features of a moral hero already mentioned in the previous section: (a) integrity and a virtuous way of living; (b) a project; and (c) ideals.

3.3.1 Heroes choose with integrity: tension between Role *and* Interiority

During the executive committee meeting the group assents to Tuld's precept of the three methods for success (i.e. be first, be smarter, or cheat) and accept that "being first" is the option to choose. Indeed, Tuld and his bank could rationalize their actions by saying that it is only a matter of time before someone else discovers the problem they have now recognized and, since someone necessarily must be first, it might as well be them.

Chandor explains the group's logic as follows: "The interesting thing is that there really isn't any decision. If these guys don't do this, the firm goes out of business, and someone else is going to do it if they find out" (Benardello 2011). If Chandor's assertion that the characters had no choice was the case, the situation would not be a moral matter. But as we will discuss later, what makes this movie interesting is that *Margin Call* is a modern-day morality play that challenges us to either accept that when engaged in business, even leaders are stripped of their capacity to choose, or to the contrary, the characters made the moral choice to succumb to the logic of selfishness and greed and the film simply unwinds the implications of that moral perspective.

True to the logic of profit maximization, Tuld has put to the side the morality of everyday life and migrates to the alternate reality of life as market, in which the narrow immediate interests of the firm trump the common good. From this perspective, the reasoning is expressed with crystal clarity when Tuld says to Rogers: "When did you start feeling so sorry for yourself? It's unbearable...What, so you think we might have put a few people out of business today, and that it's all just for naught. Well you've been doing that every day for almost forty years Sam. [...] It's just money, it's made up, pieces of paper with pictures on it so we don't have to kill each other just to get something to eat. It's not wrong and it's certainly not different today than it's ever been."

This captures the bleak world of the Wall Street anti-hero, engaging in manipulations designed to extract some personal gain from the never-ending tidal waves of impersonal market forces, and "role" prevails over "interiority" (ROL over INT). The hero, by contrast, is someone who when facing a dilemma chooses to exercise his or her moral imagination with the aim of engineering outcomes that work for the broader social good and decides accordingly. The hero and anti-hero may find themselves in identical situations, but their way of responding will follow from entirely different perspectives on morality and notions of personhood.

We find no moral doubt in John Tuld. He seems to be the same before and after the critical event. He complies with accepted norms when they serve his purpose, but will neutralize those moral positions to support his aim and shield himself behind regulatory compliance (Werner 2014). The last scene is emblematic: after the end of the tragic trading day in which the bank has been selling all the valueless assets present on its books, Tuld is peacefully eating at the highest floor of the building, reading a newspaper in a silent atmosphere now free from any stress or strain.

By contrast, Sam Rogers is wracked by doubts about the actions the bank took. He is trying to salvage some vestiges of his conscience that have not been consumed by the logic of Wall Street. In Sam's character the *interiority* has weight, but Sam is not strong enough to lead himself or anyone else to another side. He lets his role prevail over his personal judgment. He knows that something is foul, but he lives with the cognitive dissonance and sees no other way forward. He is the most alone of characters. He is not with Tuld, but he lacks the imagination or power to create alternatives. He is too weak to withstand the logic of Wall Street that has a hold on the conscience of all present. In the dialogue between Tuld and Sam the substitution of what is good with what is effective (Horvath 1995) is evident. Sam perceives that there is a lack of goodness in their decision, but he is in need of money, and at the end he accepts the effectiveness of Tuld's strategy, and therefore, he resigns himself to accept his role in piloting the firm on the miserable course it has chosen.

Capitulation to the logic of a savage form of capitalism was on display through the film, but Sam's angst serves as the foil that shows that even within Wall Street's heart of darkness, he retains awareness of the moral corruption. Thus, he dares to pose the crucial question to Tuld to make him aware of the risks and wider implications of their actions: "Who are we selling this to?" Tuld replies that they are going to sell to the same buyers as always. "If you do this, you will kill the market for years, it's over. You are selling something that you know has no value. [...] You will never sell anything to any of those people ever again." Sam may be mistaken in terms of the firm's business, but it is realistic in terms of the standards of trust that undergird healthily functioning markets. And yet, this exchange between Tuld and Sam allows the viewer to gain a deeper insight into the full significance of the actions that are taking place and the nuances within the ethical framework within which they operate. Sam demonstrates a deeper moral awareness and sensitivity (he possesses a deeper tension between his *Role* and *Interiority*). He has conscience, but a conscience that is not strong enough to withstand the morality of Wall Street in a time of serious trial.

Sam Rogers is powerfully portrayed in two of the final scenes. In the first of these, he rallies the traders: he honestly confronts his traders telling them that he knows the clients are going to lose money and the traders are going to lose their reputation, the essential stock-in-trade in the financial market. However, succumbing to the logic of Wall Street, he assures them their way forward is the only way to survive. Speaking as the captain of a sinking ship, he offers generous bonuses if the crew can complete the final leg of their voyage. By day's end, the traders have done their best and, having achieved their goal, Sam – exhausted and contemptuous of the role he has played in Tuld's game – informs Tuld of his decision to leave the firm. Tuld, however, values Sam's talents and asks him to stay two years more. Professing a need for the money, Sam bitterly accepts. Clearly Sam's actions belie his explanation. Having navigated the firm through a catastrophic tempest, surely he should have earned enough to walk away with adequate financial security. However, even though he clearly sees the corruption of what has just transpired, he lacks the slenderest thread of heroism needed to walk away and in so doing afford himself some possibility of a life redeemed. Freedom and integrity may sound alluring, but Sam chooses to remain with Tuld and company within the golden cage they have constructed.

The other scene is the lonely closing of the movie, in which Sam is seen in the act of burying his dead dog in front of his ex-wife's house. It is a mournfully significant scene. He is a man alone at night burying what he cherishes on the property of what had previously been his family. He may have won a battle at work, but everything of personal meaning to him is lost.

3.3.2 Heroes have projects: tension between Mission *and* Divergent

In various ways, most people can be said to have projects. Through our projects, we define what is important to us. Sometimes, our projects will test our moral mettle. John Tuld is a profit maximizer; this is his *mission* (MIS). He does not want to personally lose, and therefore he is not concerned with what is good for the market or other people. Nor does he demonstrate any awareness of having broader social responsibilities. Tuld embodies the archetype of the ruthless businessman for whom notions of "win-win" and the greater good are social niceties that will not be allowed to get in the way of market conquests.

We said above that CEOs are usually expected to project the moral tone of a company, accept responsibility where appropriate, seek to limit violations to stakeholder interests, decide steps to take to provide appropriate compensation, and takes measures to prevent the recurrence of negative events in the future. They are expected to exercise creativity in problem-solving. A brief analysis of Tuld's behavior shows him as eschewing the characteristics of moral leadership. The first thing he does is to look for someone who can be saddled with responsibility for the situation as a scapegoat before the investors and shareholders: he chooses Sarah Robertson, the only female character in the senior ranks of the firm. He undercuts the moral reputation of the company by forcing traders to sell what he knows to be valueless to preserve the survival of the company. Lastly, he is not only thinking about how to save the company, but how to profit from the crisis he is about to trigger. With these decisions, Tuld decisively tips the scale on the "mission" rather than on the discovery of potential different "divergent" path (DIV).

Some of Tuld's colleagues, like Eric and Sam among others, see the shallowness and destructive nature of Tuld's project, but they go along because they lack the strength of character and moral imagination to stand up for alternatives (again, no "divergent" solutions). Within the framework of profit maximization, Tuld's project is neat, simple, and logically consistent. He does not complicate things by inserting moral reflection. According to this framework, one has to choose between being a person or a banker, and the two are starkly separated. He prefers being a moral loser to being a material loser. Tuld tells Sam: "We are selling to willing buyers at the current fair market price, so that *we* may survive, Sam." He follows the precepts of instrumental rationality – his how – and his actions are motivated by the axiom of "material acquisitiveness" – his why (Dobson 1997, 5). Aristotle informs us that the way one behaves not only changes the course of events, but it changes oneself (Aristotle 2000; Hartman 2006). The tragedy of Tuld may be that despite the wreckage he has initiated, he preserves the outward trappings of success. He is a troubling reminder that the burdens of moral corruption are not always justly apportioned.

Heroes are always faced with challenges. It is in the crucible of crisis that they demonstrate their character (Bennis and Thomas 2002). If Tuld were a hero he would assess the situation with a goal of minimizing harm and maximizing social wellbeing. His priorities, such that material goods might be regarded as important, but subordinated to the higher good of social wellbeing. His locus of concern would have to be not just the survival of the firm, but managing a crisis with global implications. By ruthlessly pursuing his "being first" philosophy, he is knowingly triggering a global financial tsunami. Had Tuld instead simply been guided by the universally recognized moral principle, the Golden Rule, "Do unto others as you would have them do unto you," his concern would have been how to manage the crisis so as to minimize its destructive force. He could have sought the most creative and constructive strategies to respond to the crisis that respected the interests of his firm without sabotaging his neighbors in the business community. As the anti-hero, however, moral concerns were of no concern to Tuld. His actions follow predictably from the profit-maximizing project that defines his leadership.

3.3.3 Heroes inspire and motivate: tension between Negotiator *and* Superpower

Someone who chooses to act with integrity when facing a dilemma, and whose projects advance the greater good, is someone who tends to inspire and motivate others, and to involve them, as does, for example, a good negotiator or a positively charismatic leader. We are thinking, for example, about the paradigm of "inspirational leaders." Waldman, Balthazard and Peterson summarizing the literature on inspirational leaders, state that "outstanding leaders go beyond simple performance-versus-reward transactions and have a deep impact on their followers and their organizations, including their potential to be a major force in realizing new visions and change" (Waldman et al. 2011, 61). They add: "inspiration rests at the core of what these theories propose in terms of consummate excellence in the leadership role" (Waldman et al. 2011, 61). Inspiration could be considered a "superpower" (SPW), in a positive meaning, as directly opposed to "superpower" in the sense of exercise of authority with no space for negotiation.

In *Margin* Call, the most-representative scene of a leader motivating his team is the speech Sam delivers to his traders at the beginning of the last trading day, following the hard night of meetings and decisions. He gives each trader a packet, containing instructions and targets. He offers them huge bonuses if the target is reached by the end of the day, and extra compensation if everyone reaches it.

Sam is preparing his traders to fight a hard battle and offering them money for sacrificing their reputation and to assuage their consciences. Sam is a loser-leader, who is aware of the consequences of what he is asking to his team: "I'm sure it

TABLE 8.1 Analysis of the two main characters of *Margin Call* in light of Fournout's Hero-Leader Matrix.

Features of a hero in the virtue ethics perspectives	Personal integrity and virtue	Project, teleological structure	Ideals, desire of imitation	Is this character a hero?
Features of Fournout's Hero-Leader Matrix	ROL (Role) INT (Interiority)	MIS (Mission) DIV (Divergent)	NEG (Negotiator) SPW (Superpower)	
John Tuld	Prevalence of ROL over INT. No personal integrity.	Prevalence of MIS over DIV.	Prevalence of SPW over NEG.	Tuld exhibits no dramatic tension. He is the archetype of Wall Street anti-hero.
Sam Rogers	Prevalence of ROL over INT. Interior dilemma but lack of strength to make it prevail.	Prevalence of MIS over DIV.	Prevailing of SPW over NEG.	Sam is the archetype of the skilled Wall Street journeyman. Although he has a personal conscience, he lacks the moral fortitude to follow it.

hasn't taken you long to understand the implications of this sale, on your relationships with your counter parties and as a result...on your careers." The traders are going to the battlefield of an incredibly intense trading day, while Sam is going to spend the trading day in his office, thinking about his dissatisfaction and his silenced dilemma. There is no negotiation or empathy. Sam is exercising the last piece of his authority.

From this scene, we notice the prevailing feature of the SPW (superpower) over the NEG, the capability of a negotiator. In this scene if there is any superpower to exert its influence, it is the power of the desire for money on employees, not by Sam Rogers himself, who exhibits the demeanor of one conquered by the success he himself has orchestrated.

This last section of our analysis addresses the issue of desire and imitation. The person one wants to become is the person one wants to imitate and follow. "The virtuous person, acting on his or her own character, is often held as a model of appropriateness, credibility, suitability, and character. Because the virtuous serve as role models, those in leadership positions, including CEOs, can be expected to exemplify admirable and laudable traits" (Seeger and Ulmer 2001, 371). Sam was followed by his traders for the sake of money, not because they are inspired by him. The lack of empathy shows a mere professional relationship.

3.3.4 Sam Rogers, John Tuld, and the Hero-Leader Matrix*: summing up*

Table 8.1 sums up the analysis of the two main characters of *Margin Call* in light of Fournout's Hero-Leader Matrix.

3.4 Future heroes: educating moral character in finance through the Margin Call *tragedy*

Earlier it was stated that *Margin Call* is a contemporary tragedy in which none of the protagonist rises above their status as anti-heroes. It is important to recognize, however, that the tragedy does not lie in the economic disaster that is being set in motion in the bank's boardroom. The tragedy can be traced to Tuld's framing the pathways to success as limited to three options: being first, being smarter, or cheating. The entire movie constitutes a response that unfolds within this framework and no one bothers to ask, "Is that true?" The characters and perhaps even the audience are swept up in this limited logic, and in so doing we permit ourselves to passively relinquish our moral integrity. By what law of nature are they limited only to three options? If *Margin Call* lacks heroes, it is because no one ever questions their strategy and no one even suggests that there might be alternative options – we have already shown that Sam tried to raise the doubt and open to potential alternative solution, but in the end his role prevailed on his interiority. The bank's plan could be cast as a struggle for survival, but the price of their brutal strategy will be countless casualties blindsided by catastrophe they will unleash.

What should have been obvious is that Tuld's trilemma is utterly false and designed to provide no escape. It quashes moral imagination when it is most needed and when the characters are most vulnerable due to the urgency of the situation they face. First, it goes without protest that the goal should be optimal financial outcome for the firm rather than the good of society. Second, it goes without discussion that there were only three options: being first, being smarter, or cheating. For example, could the bank not have quietly shared the information with governmental leaders and sought to engineer a soft landing before the market imploded? Could the bank not have put the customers' interests first and chosen a way forward that might have opted to minimize the damage even if it had to share in the negative consequences, especially given that the bank is entrusted to serve as the custodian of its customers' money? There might have been other options, but Tuld and his team acted as if being first was the only one. It is here that we should remember that moral heroism often involves personal sacrifice. Tuld and his colleagues execute a strategy designed to avoid any sacrifice and instead to externalize it to countless unsuspecting victims.

4. Conclusions

Margin Call is a powerful drama that strikes close to the truth of the economic crisis that struck the global economy in 2008. It is a dark reminder of how easily characters can be drawn into an ethically corrupt downward spiral. It is a true tragedy in that no one escapes from the twisted logic in which all actions are aimed at extracting wealth wherever possible, and no characters have the moral or physical capabilities to positively transform the situation. The executive committee shows itself to be incapable of responding to the crisis with dignity, and, hence, the only plan they can conceive is one in which societal carnage is the price paid so that a few can benefit from following Tuld's precept of being first.

This chapter shows how the two main characters (John Tuld and Sam Rogers) are locked in their personal small-minded perspective: the lack of the three features of a hero from the virtue ethics perspective – personal courage and integrity; a good project; and ideals – make them morally "thin" in their dramatic reflection in which fast and cold decision-making takes place in a vacuum isolated from the ethical dilemmas that ought to be associated with the pain their actions are going to inflict on others.

In addition to the two main characters, John Tuld and Sam Rogers, the movie narrative involves many other characters each of whom support a common narrative, which is that on Wall Street, there is no place for the ethics of ordinary life – an ethic that calls all people to the everyday heroism of leading a good life. Instead, the world is reduced to winners who are rich and losers who are not. And in this world the idea of moral heroism is meaningless.

This Wall Street story may not be factual history, but it is so compelling that it serves as a rich pedagogical tool for investigating the status of ethics in finance. It may be that such discussions serve to help develop more ethical financial leaders than those we have seen in recent decades, and if so it should have a secure place in the repertoire of educational resources in today's business schools.

Reflecting on the reality of the financial meltdown of 2008, the *Economist* magazine makes the following observation:

> Most of the people at the heart of the crisis – from Dick Fuld at Lehman Brothers to John Thain at Merrill Lynch to Andy Hornby at HBOS – had MBAs after their name (Mr. Hornby graduated top of his class at HBS [i.e. Harvard Business School]). In recent years about 40% of the graduates of America's best business schools ended up on Wall Street, where they assiduously applied the techniques that they had spent a small fortune learning. You cannot both claim that your mission is "to educate leaders who make a difference in the world," as HBS does, and then wash your hands of your alumni when the difference they make is malign.
>
> *(Schumpeter 2009)*

This quotation assigns to business schools and universities responsibility in the ethical education of future business leaders. Business schools are best equipped to systematically educate those who want to have a career in business and, as in the case of the film *Margin Call*, finance. However, where the educational system has failed is in giving students robust technical skills, without the corresponding guidance in the development of sound critical judgment. As teaching tools, movies have the special value that can help compensate for that pedagogical shortfall. It would be a violation of the spirit and purpose of university education if we train our students in the technical skills of business and finance without giving adequate attention to the formation of moral character. This can be achieved in part by providing students with dramatic simulations through films that offer scenarios for exercising judgment of someone's decisions, actions, and character. This effort in the education of individuals is crucial to pursue a change in the broader context of Wall Street culture. In this regard, there is a constructive proposal by Crossan et al. (2013) on how to encourage the development of moral leadership among students enrolled in university business education programs. According to these authors, just as "it takes a village" to raise a child, the same holds true when universities seek to educate a future business leader. In other words, we need to see consistent and strong ethical messaging across the business school community, rather than a few lone voices among a few business school professors.

From this perspective, business schools should be seen as having a higher and broader purpose beyond instructions on the techniques of business management – its aim ought to be to teach students how to serve society as a whole, and not only their companies. Teaching ethics in business schools is not enough to shape the moral character of students, but it may be an important part of creating the educational village, to use the Crossan et al.'s metaphor (2013). Drawing on the language of cinema helps students to better grasp moral problems by vicariously identifying with the exercise of their professional roles through the characters they encounter in films. Film serves as a simulation in which students can realistically confront ethical challenges without having to put their personal resources, reputation, and values on the line. As such, film is a powerful resource that business professors, and especially business ethics professors, can draw on to cultivate critical thinking and moral awareness, as well as to encourage in their students a desire to become good people who embrace the challenge of being moral heroes.

Note

1 See also Ferrero and Rocchi (2016) for a didactic-oriented reflection on this topic.

References

Aristotle. 2000. *Nicomachean Ethics*. Cambridge Texts in the History of Philosophy. Cambridge, UK; New York: Cambridge University Press.

Belden, Susan. 1992. "A Comment on 'Wall Street': A Case in Ethics." *Financial Practice and Education*, 2(1), 53–54.

Benardello, Karen. 2011. "Exclusive Interview With J. C. Chandor On Margin Call." *We Got This Covered*. http://wegotthiscovered.com/movies/interview-jc-chandor-margin-call/. Available online. Accessed: September 15, 2016.

Bennis, Warren G., and Thomas, Robert J. (2002). "Crucibles of Leadership." *Harvard Business Review*, 80(9).

Biktimirov, Ernest N., and Don, Cyr. 2013. "Using Inside Job to Teach Business Ethics." *Journal of Business Ethics*, 117(1), 209–219. doi:10.1007/s10551-012-1516-y.

CFA Institute. 2014. "Standards of Practice Handbook." www.cfapubs.org/doi/pdf/10.2469/ccb.v2014.n4.1. Available online. Accessed: September 15, 2016.

Champoux, Joseph E. 1999. "Film as a Teaching Resource." *Journal of Management Inquiry*, 8(2), 206–217. doi:10.1177/105649269982016.

Chan, Kam, Marsha Weber, and Michelle Johnson. 1995. "Using Other People's Money in the Classroom." *Financial Practice and Education*, No. Spring/Summer, 123–127.

Cox, Pamela, Barry Friedman, and Ann-Loraine Edwards. 2009. "Enron: The Smartest Guys in the Room – Using the Enron Film to Examine Student Attitudes towards Business Ethics." *Institute of Behavioral and Applied Management*.

Crossan, Mary, Daina Mazutis, Gerard Seijts, and Jeffrey Gandz. 2013. "Developing Leadership Character in Business Programs." *Academy of Management Learning & Education*, 12(2), 285–305. doi:10.5465/amle.2011.0024A.

Dobson, John. 1997. *Finance Ethics: The Rationality of Virtue*. Lanham, Md.: Rowman & Littlefield Publishers.

Dobson, John. 2008. "Introducing Ethics into the Finance Curriculum: A Simple Three-Level Guide." *Journal of Financial Education*, No. Spring.

Ferrero, Ignacio, and Marta Rocchi. 2016. "Teaching Ethics in Finance Curricula: Personal and Institutional Virtues in Financial Markets." In *Teaching Ethics Across the Management Curriculum. Contributing to a Global Paradigm Shift*, edited by Kemi Ogunyemi, Vol. III, 133–156. USA: Business Expert Press.

Ferrero, Ignacio, and Alejo José G. Sison. 2014. "A Quantitative Analysis of Authors, Schools and Themes in Virtue Ethics Articles in Business Ethics and Management Journals (1980–2011)." *Business Ethics: A European Review*, 23(4), 375–400. doi:10.1111/beer.12057.

Financial Crisis Inquiry Commission USA. 2011. "The Financial Crisis Inquiry Report: Final Report of the National Commission on the Causes of the Financial and Economic Crisis in the United States." Official Government Edition. www.gpo.gov/fdsys/pkg/GPO-FCIC/pdf/GPO-FCIC.pdf.

Fournout, Olivier. 2017. "The Hero-Leader Matrix in Business and Cinema." *Journal of Business Ethics*, 141(1), 27–46. doi:10.1007/s10551-016-3063-4.

Fox, Justin. 2013. "What We've Learned from the Financial Crisis – Five Years Later, How Has Theory Adjusted?" *Harvard Business Review*, 91(11), 94–101.

Griffiths, Alison. 2002. *Wondrous Difference: Cinema, Anthropology, and Turn-of-the-Century Visual Culture*. New York: Columbia University Press.

Hartman, Edwin. 2006. "Can We Teach Character? An Aristotelian Answer." *Academy of Management Learning & Education*, 5(1), 68–81.

Horvath, Charles M. 1995. "Excellence V. Effectiveness: Macintyre's Critique of Business." *Business Ethics Quarterly*, 5(3), 499–532. doi:10.2307/3857396.

Hosmer, LaRue, and Nicholas H. Steneck. 1989. "Teaching Business Ethics: The Use of Films and Videota." *Journal of Business Ethics*, 8, 929–936.

Huczynski, Andrzej. 2004. "Theory from Fiction: A Narrative Process Perspective on the Pedagogical Use of Feature Film." *Journal of Management Education*, 28(6), 707–726. doi:10.1177/1052562903262163.

Lewis, Michael. 2011. *The Big Short: Inside the Doomsday Machine*. New York: W.W. Norton.

McAdams, Tony, and Roswitha Koppensteiner. 1992. "The Manager Seeking Virtue: Lessons from Literature." *Journal of Business Ethics*, 11, 627–634.

Reinhart, Carmen M., and Kenneth S. Rogoff. 2009. *This Time Is Different: Eight Centuries of Financial Folly*. Princeton: Princeton University Press.

Santoro, Michael A., and Ronald J. Strauss. 2012. *Wall Street Values: Business Ethics and the Global Financial Crisis*. Cambridge; New York: Cambridge University Press.

Schumpeter. 2009. "The Pedagogy of the Priviledged." *The Economist*, online edition, September. www.economist.com/node/14493183.

Seger, Linda. 1990. *Creating Unforgettable Characters*. 1st edition. New York: H. Holt.

Seeger, Matthew W., and Robert R. Ulmer. 2001. "Virtuous Responses to Organizational Crisis: Aaron Feuerstein and Milt Cole." *Journal of Business Ethics*, 31, 369–376.

Smith, Greg M. 2003. *Film Structure and the Emotion System*. Cambridge; New York: Cambridge University Press.

Tan, Ed S. 1995. *Emotion and the Structure of Narrative Film: Film as an Emotion Machine*. LEA'S Communication Series. Mahwah, N.J.: Routledge, Taylor & Francis Group.

U.S. Securities and Exchange Commission. 1934. "Securities Exchange Act of 1934." www.sec.gov/about/laws/sea34.pdf.

Van Es, Robert. 2003. "Inside and Outside The Insider: A Film Workshop in Practical Ethics." *Journal of Business Ethics*, 48, 89–97.

Waldman, David A., Pierre A. Balthazard, and Suzanne J. Peterson. 2011. "Leadership and Neuroscience: Can We Revolutionize the Way That Inspirational Leaders Are Identified and Developed?" *Academy of Management Perspectives*, 25(1), 60–74. doi:10.5465/AMP.2011.59198450.

Werner, Andrea. 2014. "'Margin Call': Using Film to Explore Behavioural Aspects of the Financial Crisis." *Journal of Business Ethics*, 122(4), 643–654.

SECTION 3

Screening crisis and recessions

9

DOCUMENTARY TREATMENTS AND CULTURAL HIERARCHIES

The 2008 financial crash in American documentaries

Daniel Marcus

Documentary film and television has inspired several levels of cultural attention and respect over its history. Generally, documentaries have enjoyed cultural cachet imbued with airs of moral seriousness, social relevance, and brave truth-telling. As documentary has enjoyed a resurgence of interest in the last thirty years, production has expanded in quantity and creators have introduced new technologies and distribution strategies to the field. With this expansion, non-fiction film narratives have experienced a concomitant dispersal of attitudes toward their positions in cultural hierarchies of authority and veracity. With more people making and viewing documentaries, the field has attracted a greater range of reactions and attempts to define their proper aims, forms, and techniques.

The 2008 global financial crisis elicited significant attempts to understand and illustrate associated economic and political issues by many types of documentary producers. This chapter examines four documentaries to sketch the range of methods used to describe the American roots of the global crisis, and the cultural hierarchies in which the filmmakers positioned their work. Their placement and activity within these hierarchies can help to elucidate the shape of the discursive field that has been organized around issues of the economy, political power, and inequality in contemporary America. By looking at the distributional strategies and reach of these films, their methods and appearance, and the bases for their knowledge, we can trace the varied placements of documentary in contemporary cultural hierarchies. In addition, we can examine how they function in the current epistemological struggles in American and global media and politics.

The four films to be discussed are *Inside Job* by Charles Ferguson (2010), *Park Avenue: Money, Power and the American Dream* by Alex Gibney (2012), *Capitalism: A Love Story* by Michael Moore (2009), and *Zeitgeist: The Movie* (2007) by Peter Joseph. Their cultural positions are constituted by the reputations of the filmmakers in the field, their links to media institutions, and the films' textual approaches and investigative epistemologies. The sober, rationalist *Inside Job* gets its information from elite, well-placed experts, repeating Ferguson's method from his investigation of Bush administration missteps in Iraq, *No End in Sight* (2007). The films of Gibney and Moore adopt more populist tones and approaches, but still operate within the realm of accepted documentary practice, especially as defined since Moore's breakthrough debut *Roger & Me* (1989). Gibney, one of the most prolific documentary makers in recent decades, holds to a more conventional documentary posture than the roguish Moore. They share, however, a disgust for financial inequality in the name of a more wholesome modesty of economic ambition presented as a traditional American value. Peter Joseph's *Zeitgeist: The Movie* came out before the crash but gained popularity after the debacle, as it epitomizes a conspiracy-minded approach to the entire banking system. Wholesale criticisms and suspicions of the Federal Reserve System gained greater credence as conventional explanations and defenses of the system seemed inadequate to explain the catastrophic loss of value in stock portfolios, citizens losing their homes, and the federal government channeling hundreds of billions of bailout dollars to financial institutions. *Zeitgeist* has been a major YouTube hit, circulating outside of the previously established systems of commercial and public television exhibition. *Zeitgeist* is amateurish and, while posing as a serious study, operates in more of a post-truth fashion of obliterating skepticism of established thought, and has succeeded by word of mouth while being ignored initially by critics.

Fictional film treatments of the economy

Until the 2000s, American documentary producers rarely took the financial sector as the subject of their work. Most of the practical activities of financial deal making are not well-suited to visual presentation, and firms working with confidential information are usually reluctant to let filmmakers enter their sanctums. Left-leaning documentary makers may have felt more comfortable following the travails of working-class union members facing the exigencies of life under capitalism, as in Barbara Kopple's *Harlan County USA* (1976) and *American Dream* (1990), than trying to gain the trust of Wall Street money managers. Ronald Reagan's election to the Presidency in 1980 spurred cultural interest in the stock market and other wealth-producing institutions, as did financial innovations such as junk bonds and the rises and falls of celebrity tycoons. The documentary field was slow to respond to this interest, and it was left to feature filmmakers to represent Reaganomic elites on screen, most notably in Oliver Stone's *Wall Street* (1987) (Arsenault 1998), and to finance-focused cable television channels such as CNBC (Clark et al. 2004). With the end of the Reagan administration, Hollywood lost most of its interest in examining Wall Street's machinations, with a few notable exceptions, such as HBO's *Barbarians at the Gate* (G. Jordan, 1993), which used docudrama to portray the denouement of the junk bond era.

The ensuing build-up of the financial sector during the Clinton years was closely associated with the rise of high-technology start-ups, and Silicon Valley superseded

Wall Street in cultural attention. While the rise in stock prices and the hope for making a killing with the latest technological whiz kid was the subject of avid social conversation, this optimistic scenario did not attract much attention from mediamakers. Three noteworthy productions did predate the Great Recession. Chris Hegedus and Jehane Noujaim's *Startup.com* examined the hopes and failures of young entrepreneurs who could not financially survive the crash of the technology sector at the turn of the millennium. The low-budget feature *Boiler Room* (B. Younger, 2000) was based on straightforwardly fraudulent stock schemes (the same schemes which were later the bases for Martin Scorcese's *The Wolf of Wall Street* [2013] [Peltzer 2015]). The documentary *Enron: The Smartest Guys in the Room* (2005), by Alex Gibney, dived into the byzantine financial structures of an energy giant that marauded across the American landscape for a few years before collapsing, taking huge swaths of worker pensions with it. Enron's manipulation of offshore shadow companies and impossibly complicated derivatives based on energy futures foreshadowed the use of mortgage-based derivatives that fueled the 2007–2008 crash.

The 2008 financial crash inspired a spate of feature and television films that have addressed the mechanics and values of high (and low) finance, such as the Oliver Stone sequel *Wall Street: Money Never Sleeps* (2010), *Margin Call* (J. C. Chandor, 2011), HBO's *Too Big to Fail* (C. Hanson, 2011), *Arbitrage* (N. Jarecki, 2012), *The Wolf of Wall Street* (2013), *The Big Short* (A. McKay, 2015), *Equity* (M. Menon, 2016), ABC's mini-series *Madoff* (R. De Felitta, 2016), and a feature on Bernie Madoff, Barry Levinson's *Wizard of Lies* (2017). Many of these productions were based on actual events, and borrowed from docudrama traditions to assert their relevance and insight into the murky doings of derivative trading, financial leveraging, and boardroom power plays. Only *The Wolf of Wall Street* and *The Big Short* enjoyed significant commercial success. Each film focused on outsiders in the financial realm – blatantly fraudulent stock peddlers in the former, and in the latter, a small group of doubters who prospered by disbelieving that the derivatives market was viable. Dramatizations focused on the type of firms most responsible for the crisis have not found a large audience in the post-crash era.

Many of the fictionalized feature productions use the frame of personal choices to explain the crisis, often equating disastrously excessive financial risk-taking with excesses in sexuality and conspicuous consumption. The political resolution to financial crisis, Marieke de Goede has stated,

> always depends on a particular definition of an *excess* in the system. The excess is understood as a mode of behaviour that is not properly part of the markets, but that has crossed a certain line of normality, morality, or rationality, causing the system to spin out of control (2009, 299).

This behavioral excess can be expressed in natural terms, as a flood, or as a bubble that will inevitably pop (de Goede 2009, 304). These sorts of metaphors point to both the wide-ranging impacts that the crisis has within society, and to their impersonal nature, seemingly out of human control. It is the system itself that has careened out of control, after the suspension of normal governance. Just as humans must endure the disasters of nature but also can clean up after them, the comparison to nature points not only to the inevitability of financial crisis but also to the possibility of recovery if proper procedures are followed. As de Goede argues, another set of metaphors to explain crisis is heavily gendered, in which the speculative temptations that lead to disaster are equated with female hysteria, fickleness, and madness (de Goede 2009, 303). Early writers on capitalism personified new debt mechanisms as Lady Credit, who could bestow her charms on the judicious businessman, making his work productive and fecund. But Lady Credit could also tempt honest men to ruin, her Siren-like charms overwhelming their rational deliberation with the promise of easy wealth and luxury. In this construction, the problems of the system are more human than impersonal, the result of human frailty and irrationality. The crisis should be within human power to not just repair, but to avoid in the first place, by vigilance against individual misconduct and wayward behavior.

The recent entertainment productions on the crisis display the tensions between these explanations. A few productions, such as *Margin Call* and *The Big Short*, hold out the prospect of more systemic critique, depicting an entire economic sector as careening out of control with no one able to stop it, no matter how virtuous. The depiction of excessive risk-taking is also related to the question of who has access to participate in the financial markets as key players. In several of the fiction films on the subject, working-class characters are particularly prone to excessive risk-taking in order to break into the exclusive ranks of the rich. They let the intoxicating effects of new wealth cloud their judgment, so ambitious strivers are especially prone to engage in behavior that makes the system careen out of control.

Documentary's status and the crash

While documentary producers by and large ignored Wall Street before the crash, the severity of the crisis and its relationship to the growing economic inequality in the country did inspire new productions to address the financial system. The Occupy Wall Street movement kept public attention on the doings of the financial sector beyond the original shock and controversial government bailout that followed. (For an on-site depiction of Occupy, see *99%: The Occupy Wall Street Collaborative Film* [A. Aites, A. Ewell, N. Krstic, and L. Read, 2013].) Documentary methods could seem well suited to unraveling the legal and institutional complexities of crisis, creating audiovisual counterparts to the spate of non-fiction books that reported on the machinations of the industry. These methods constitute documentary's contribution to the "discourses of sobriety," as conceptualized by Bill Nichols; such discourses are characterized by speaking directly to social reality, used by institutions such as legal, medical, and educational systems to define the world in which we live (Nichols 2010, 36–38). They seek to provide concrete information upon which to base our actions, and bear the moral heft connected to inspiring action in the real world. Documentary's placement within the discourses of sobriety can give productions credence as authoritative inquiries into a global crisis with real effects on people's lives. Producers sought to untangle the jumbled combinations of business strategy, economic theory, legal wrangling, and political history that marked discussions of the issues. Documentary's sustained inquiry, in terms of both pre-production research and screen time, can surpass fragmented news reporting in treating complex problems. Its claims to moral seriousness provide a foundation upon which a critique of a devastating crisis can be discursively built and calls to corrective action sustained.

While documentary can claim greater credibility in presenting the facts of the crisis than fictionalized stories, it shares some of the techniques of fiction films in holding audience interest and drawing them deeply into its presentation as a visual medium. The historic use of close-ups, dialogue, and a limited number of leading characters at the center of narratives in American film make audiences prone to identifying protagonists and antagonists as individuals in documentary as well as fiction films. The crisis's origins within a relatively small number of companies and executives in banking, brokering, insurance, and real estate play into film's strengths at individuation and personalization. Producers can point to specific individuals, representing particular companies accused of malfeasance and failure, in explaining a social phenomenon with global ramifications. With New York City as the epicenter of the crash, and Washington D.C. as an ancillary, contributing nexus of power, producers can also construct manageable production schedules and visual fields to tell their stories.

Inside Job

The film on the crisis that most clearly stakes its claim to the discursive power of sobriety is Charles Ferguson's *Inside Job*. Ferguson's qualifications for producing an authoritative inquiry include a doctorate in political science from the Massachusetts Institute of Technology (MIT), entrepreneurial success in the high-tech boom, and a stint in the Clinton White House as a technology adviser, which gave him experience in the ways of elite policy-making. Ferguson's career in documentary began with *No End in Sight*, his investigation of the American invasion of Iraq by George W. Bush and his administration. Ferguson understood that losers of elite policy battles are often happy to share stories of how debacles occurred because their advice and recommendations were ignored or defeated during the decision-making process. In *No End in Sight*, Ferguson offered a chance for former high-ranking government officials to detail the multitude of policy mistakes made by Bush, Dick Cheney, Donald Rumsfeld, and other architects of the war.

Inside Job continues Ferguson's method, as he seeks to understand the causes of the financial implosion of major Wall Street firms in 2008, and how that triggered the global economic crisis. He identifies several foundational problems and policy mistakes that plagued the system, and places them in the historical context of a political offensive by business interests in recent decades to assert their primacy in determining the course of the economy. This effort was supported by intellectual elites who helped to sell deregulation to the government, media, and the public. Ferguson and his interlocutors focus on an array of factors in the crash: the federal deregulation of banking in the 1990s, the lack of significant regulation of derivatives, especially credit default swaps (bets on whether companies would fail) and collateralized debt obligations (the bundling and selling of multiple financial instruments like mortgages), and failed monitoring by credit ratings agencies (which failed to alert investors to the fragility of major companies and their investment offerings). These failings explosively multiplied the economic effects of a decline in the residential real estate market. Ferguson relies on former Chair of the House of Representatives Financial Services Committee Barney Frank, former Federal Reserve System Chair Paul Volcker, and professors from Harvard University and MIT to provide detailed recountings of policy decisions and regulatory failures. Narrated by the noted actor Matt Damon, the film provides an almost miraculously comprehensible explanation of how everything went wrong in the financial sector through deregulation, fraud, and undue influence on governmental policy by corporate elites. *Inside Job* constructs a closed loop of governmental and business elites, against whom reformers have been largely powerless. Ferguson's status as Beltway insider likely gave him access to those contributors to the crisis who agreed to be interviewed. Conversations with pro-deregulation economists are a persistent highlight, as they clearly expected a fellow policy wonk to be sympathetic to their work, only to be confronted by Ferguson's scathing exposure of their mendacity and conflicts of interests.

Ferguson clearly wants to provide a systemic critique, but cannot help himself from detouring into a cocaine-and-hookers section on the mindset and personal lifestyles of financial professionals at the height of the bubble. In this way, *Inside Job* aligns itself with the scenarios of feature films such as *Arbitrage* and *The Wolf of Wall Street*, which center on individual figures in possession of active agency whose unethical business behavior is mirrored by their scandalous hedonism in personal relationships. In her analysis of the financial film genre, Kate Maclean flips the gendering of risk, focusing on the predatory Alpha Male as the bearer of the values and dangers of risk, rather than the man weakened by feminized lures of easy money (Maclean 2015). The coding of the risk-taking inherent in capitalism and its mechanisms of investment as masculine marginalizes women within the industry and its representations. The only female executive of note in the first wave of fiction films is Demi Moore's character in *Margin Call*, who is literally in charge of risk management at her Lehman Brothers-type firm. She doubly fails in her responsibilities, stifling the prerogative of a lower-ranked man who wants to warn the company of its incipient crisis, while not being sufficiently forceful with the upper echelon male executives to live up to her assigned role. In *Inside Job*, Brooksley Born of the Commodity Futures Exchange Commission and Sheila Bair of the Federal Deposit Insurance Corporation are two of the only women discussed in its depiction of financial institutions. They are among the small numbers of regulators who are alert to the growing dangers of the deregulatory age. They may be unimpressed by the hyperconfident men who dominate high finance, but are also unable to win the policy battles that marked the build-up of the crisis. In American politics, Elizabeth Warren has taken on a leading role as Wall Street critic, based on her work in financial reform and regulation before being elected to the Senate. Fictional narratives, documentary investigations, and electoral politics mix to create gendered notions of risk and caution, and the conflicting dynamics of seizing opportunity and enforcing responsibility.

Ferguson does not identify working-class intrusions into high finance as a source of dangerous risk; the personal excesses presented seem to stem from hubris, greed, and arrogance. *Inside Job* displays a keen aesthetic sense to convey the world of wealth and power of Wall Street titans. The film looks better – and more expensive – than many feature films. The visual field of the film depicts a dazzling lower Manhattan world of luxury, carried across by beautiful aerial shots of the towers and lights of financial capital. Its visual mastery evokes both the power of its subjects and the assurance of its well-informed and -articulated critique. The film combines the sheen of premium Hollywood entertainment and the high-toned seriousness of legal investigation. *Inside Job*'s occupation of the heights of documentary production was confirmed by the very positive reviews it received in the media, its screening at the Cannes film festival, and its winning the Academy Award for best long-form documentary.

Inside Job's forays into multiple aspects of the crisis, and its personalization of the decision-making processes involved, create a feeling that the problems originate with a fairly small number of people. They manage to convert the entire banking and securities system to serve their own ends, to the point where only systemic remedies are worth considering. The film posits a fall from a stable post-1929 era in which government regulation kept the securities system honest and modest in its scope and ambition, even as it was a key mechanism of American corporate capitalism's domination of the global economy (Froese 2011, 59–60). In classic narrative film structure, a stable status quo is disrupted by new desires among characters that create a chain of events that lead to escalating conflict and crisis. In Ferguson's analysis, a liberal, statist regulatory environment is upended by business-elite calls for deregulation. The reduction in government oversight contributes to the increased financialization of the economy, with Wall Street firms taking large shares of corporate profits, which exacerbates the increases in economic inequality throughout the nation. Ultimately, it leads to wildly risky speculation, conflicts of interest, and widespread fraud. Articulating a position that can appeal to both the leftist and moderate wings of the Democratic Party, Ferguson calls for a return to sober and egalitarian values as necessary to restore balance and constrain the greed of financial elites. His film, with its careful explication of complex machinations within the industry, and willingness to call men in positions of power and influence to account, exemplifies these values. In doing so, the production relies on Ferguson's financial resources and connection to elite policy circles to gain access to interview subjects and depict the world they describe with appropriate visual splendor. While decrying the ultimate irrationality of the financial cycle that proceeded from great accumulations of wealth to a global meltdown, Ferguson positions his film as finely honed in both rational argument and production values. *Inside Job* attests to documentary's authoritative status as bearer of truth and its director's care and expertise in shaping the material.

Park Avenue: money, power and the American dream

Alex Gibney has been one of the most prolific documentary makers of recent decades, and has covered the conjunction of financial and political scandals in several films, including *Enron* and *Casino Jack and the United States of Money* (2010), about master lobbyist and felon Jack Abramoff. In *Park Avenue*, the Academy Award-winning Gibney looks at the lifestyles of investment bankers and hedge fund managers to illustrate their abuse of the financial system, rigging of American politics, and pursuit of policies that increase inequality in the United States. The film focuses on an apartment building at 740 Park Avenue on the Upper East Side of Manhattan, which houses the most billionaires of any residence in the country. The building was famous for housing oil company executives until they were largely surpassed by financial sector elites, including John Thain (CEO of Merrill Lynch) and Stephen Schwarzman (one of the most outspoken private equity managers, best known for comparing a proposed tax increase on high incomes with Hitler's invasion of Poland). David Koch continues the tradition of extraction industries represented in the building, and has become one of the highest-profile donors to Republican and conservative causes in the last decade.

The building functions as a mild rhetorical device in the film; Gibney does not attempt to pull the building into the kind of stunts for which Moore is famous. Instead, Gibney contrasts the luxury of 740 Park Avenue and power of its residents to the South Bronx, an impoverished neighborhood that shares the street – one of the most famous in the United States as a symbol of wealth and power – a few miles north of the building. Gibney does not provide a detailed portrayal of South Bronx residents, but acknowledges the extremes of wealth and poverty more dramatically than Ferguson. The United States used to pride itself on its upward mobility, but changes in public policies, the political power of the wealthy, and the cost of education have now rigged the game. The top 1 percent of wealth holders now hoards the gains from increased productivity, while the minimum wage has descended to poverty levels. Gibney shares in the declension narrative of Ferguson, though he does not dwell on the strengths of the old system. His focus is on how a system that had already favored the wealthy (those Rockefeller executives living on Park Avenue during the previous century) has grown significantly more unequal through graft, greed, and the growth of libertarian ideologies that celebrate individual achievement over the public good. This critique is in keeping with the Occupy Wall Street movement and the Presidential candidacy of democratic socialist Senator Bernie Sanders in 2016.

Gibney's tone of righteous indignation is measured, and his documentary practice subscribes to conventional notions of credibility and argument. He interviews a range of economists and reporters to establish his points, and supplies statistics and info-graphics to prove his arguments about income inequality. A denunciation of greed based on moral terms is met by an analysis about power in the political system. Gibney illustrates the extremes of wealth and poverty that exist just a few miles apart in the country's financial capital. This comparison appeals to basic senses of equity and shared community – people who live in such close proximity and belong to the same political and economic system should not experience such great differences in outcomes. The chasm in results is self-maintaining – the wealthy keep their position by using their riches to unduly influence the political system into supporting inequality. Gibney's combination of moral arguments and political diagnosis of the nation's ills corresponds to widely held ideas among progressives on growing economic inequality and the corruption of Congress. The style and look of his films are not as refined as Ferguson's, and his access to elite policy-makers is much more limited, but Gibney has become one of the most prominent documentary producers in this era of increased visibility and support for the genre. His status as a respected filmmaker who follows standard precepts of evidence-gathering and expert witnessing, while organizing his material in service of progressive populist goals, provides him a comfortable place within the documentary scene, despite occasional controversies when he takes on powerful subjects.

He attracts funding from well-known supporters of cultural work in the US. *Park Avenue* was paid for in part by the Independent Television Service (ITVS), which channels politically charged work to the Public Broadcasting System (PBS); *Park Avenue* aired on *Independent Lens*, one of the primary conduits for documentary on public television beyond its many science and nature productions. Gibney's film engendered controversy and reaction because of the political and financial elites' relationships with PBS, which is heavily dependent on private donations and also receives funding from federal and state governments. The airing of the film on WNET, the flagship PBS station in New York City, was followed by televised opposing statements by two of the targets of criticism in the film, including Koch, who was on the board of directors of the station at the time. Koch apparently refused to make a large contribution to the station that he had been considering, and soon left the WNET Board, while ITVS cancelled its planned support for a documentary specifically investigating the effects of his political activities, *Citizen Koch* (C. Deal and T. Lessin, 2013) (Mayer 2013). *Park Avenue* also was included in the international series *Why Poverty*, supported by a large number of European television systems and cultural organizations, and which attracted significant audiences around the world (Bondebjerg 2016, 179–181).

Capitalism: A Love Story

The best-known political provocateur in American documentary remains Michael Moore, who gained renown for his investigation of General Motors' effect on his hometown of Flint, Michigan in *Roger & Me*. Moore returned to the consequences of corporate strategies in *Capitalism: A Love Story*, produced in the midst of the 2008 crisis and completed after the election of Barack Obama to the Presidency.

The film continues the mix of elements that made Moore famous. It includes a pointed examination of public policy in the United States from a progressive point of view and a satirical tone that cheekily upends documentary conventions to invoke popular culture tropes as a way of communicating his points.

Moore signals his unconcern with documentary sobriety from the first; the film opens with fellow Michigander Iggy Pop singing the 1960s garage classic "Louie Louie" on the soundtrack, as surveillance camera footage of armed bank robberies constitute the visual field, foreshadowing Moore's criticism of the banking industry as robbing middle-class Americans with its manipulations and fraud. The production offers a compendium, alternately whimsical and scathing, of old movie scenes, hokey educational-film snippets, sarcastic commentary, home video of foreclosures, and interviews with participants in objectionable industry practices. Moore offers few explanations for the housing crisis or crash, beyond following the downward path of foreclosed families abetted by generalized statistics on economic trends. Rather, he presents outrageous anecdotal examples of corporate trends in greed and soullessness. One typical example reveals that companies take out life insurance policies on average employees without their knowledge, so that the companies will profit from their deaths – policies known in the trade as "Dead Peasant" contracts.

These investigations of discrete aspects of corporate malfeasance are accompanied by Moore's comic stunts along the lines of *Roger & Me*. In *Capitalism*, they include bringing an armored truck to Wall Street and using a bullhorn to ask for the public's money back from brokerage houses, trying to gain access to executive suites to place firm leaders under citizen's arrest, and perhaps most effectively, surrounding corporate headquarters with crime scene tape. Most of the stunts seem more tired than inspired by this point in Moore's career, and do little to illustrate the polemics that energize the film. They are meant to dramatize the insularity of Wall Street executives from the lives of the people they are robbing and destroying. For Moore, the problem of Wall Street is not so much excess as it is distance – distance from the social world where people actually build things and contribute productively to the world, and lose their houses when they do not read the fine print on their mortgages (Corner 2015, 173). Charles Ferguson, as stealth traitor to the policy-making class, was able to obtain access to the financial elite's technocratic assistants who provided ideological cover and regulatory laxity to untrammeled financial manipulation; Alex Gibney relied on shots of billionaires' residences to create a sense of investigatory proximity to them. Moore's stunts serve as metaphors for the inaccessibility of the elites to questioning by him and accountability to the public.

Moore's status as avatar of the industrial working class provides a folksy feel to his exposition. All three of the films are expository, but Gibney remains measured and faceless in his presentation and Ferguson only reveals himself in his pointed exposure of mendacious interview subjects. Moore's presentation is more personal, mixing his family history with the shtick with which he is heavily identified, in addition to on-site, informal interviews with victims of financial and corporate malfeasance. As John Corner argues, it is only in Moore's work that viewers get a real sense of the consequences of the capture of the government regulatory apparatus by those responsible for the global downturn (Corner 2015, 173).

As Kendall R. Phillips points out, a nostalgic narrative threads through the film, as Moore uses home movies of his childhood in Flint to illustrate American industrial capitalism at its height (Phillips 2015). The wholesome scenes of the young Moore contrast with the home videos of families having their possessions thrown out onto the street in contemporary America. The industrial might that built a middle class and provided job security and good benefits has been replaced with financial shenanigans as the source of elite wealth, to the dispossession of the rest of society. Moore pays tribute to his father's capacity as a blue-collar single-earner provider for his family, part of an invocation of a line of father figures from Franklin Roosevelt onward that to Moore represent the best, most humane side of capitalism. Phillips faults Moore for ignoring the sexist and racist constraints of the post-World War II era in his attempt to contrast a New Deal-structured, regulated capitalism to contemporary neoliberalist, deregulated business practices. Moore ignores the backlash against organized labor and the social safety net by corporations in the 1970s to lay blame on present trends on the energy crisis of the 1970s and resulting political triumph of Reagan in 1980. Under Reagan, even as productivity continued to rise, wages stagnated, deindustrialization and bankruptcies increased, and the prison population grew. The culmination of Reaganomics was George W. Bush's response to the 2008 crash, which Moore sees as a manufactured crisis that served as a pretext for a financial coup d'état by Wall Street to bilk the US Treasury out of hundreds of billions of dollars in emergency bailouts.

Capitalism's presentation does not always follow the patriarchal, racially unnuanced declension narrative that moves from Roosevelt's concern for the public good to Bush's service to the ultra-rich. Moore brings in a family priest to assert that all of capitalism is at its heart a sin, and the director argues for the importance of workplace democracy as an alternative to hierarchal relations built into corporate capitalism. He spends time with strikers at a factory in Chicago, a racially and ethnically mixed group whose most articulate spokesperson is a female union organizer. In showing people actually struggling against corporate power, Moore acknowledges the diversity of the working class today. While Ferguson and Gibney appear wishful in their appeals to reform the system, Moore shows responsive activism uniting disparate populations. The film ends in early 2009, as Obama supports the Bush bailout but also inspires a new wave of hope and progressive activism by his election. (The film ends before both the Tea Party backlash against his stimulus package and health care reforms, and the Occupy Wall Street movement's raising of the politics of economic inequality to new heights of public visibility.)

In the wake of Donald Trump taking office in 2017, Moore's hopeful summation in 2009 now seems bitterly ironic:

> Just two years earlier, had anyone predicted this moment, they would have been considered crazy. But that's how fast things changed. It was, in an instant, a farewell to the old America.

The old America, an alliance of white working- and middle-class small-town and rural voters and Republican financial elites, put an Administration and Congress in place in 2016 who plan to far outstrip their conservative and neoliberal predecessors in deregulatory zeal. They have done so in the name of a new, reindustrializing nationalist project that claims to be able to bring back the factories of which Moore mourns the loss, to bring back the sense of American mastery that Moore identifies with the post-World War II era.

Capitalism: A Love Story is often considered as one of Moore's less successful films, finished quickly to respond to the 2008 crash and bringing in a fraction of the viewers that made *Roger & Me* and *Fahrenheit 9/11* (2004) significant interventions in public debate and documentary economics. Yet Moore's celebrity and unwieldy mix of news reporting, popular culture, and historical analysis took in over 12 million dollars in domestic theatrical box office receipts, three times what *Inside Job* earned (www.boxofficemojo.com, accessed March 2, 2017). (*Park Avenue* was released to television and the Internet without theatrical exhibition.) Beyond any other contemporary filmmaker, Moore has challenged conventional documentary practice in commercially successful ways, broadening the techniques available to politically minded producers and making documentary polemics relevant to public debate. He has brought political documentary into the realm of popular culture, earning concomitant criticism of his accuracy, taste, and credibility. He has deposed public policy documentary investigation from the apex of cultural respectability, resituating it within the realm of entertainment, celebrity culture, and reality television. In doing so, he has maintained public interest in even his more minor productions.

Zeitgeist: The Movie

The extent to which the field of documentary has grown in recent decades through the diffusion of production technologies and expansion of distribution outlets available to non-traditional producers can be seen by the success of the *Zeitgeist* series of films. The films were made by Peter Joseph, a musician who is a follower of a utopian movement called the Venus Project. The original *Zeitgeist* production was a multimedia performance, which Joseph adapted into a compilation film with his own expository narrative, chiefly distributed via YouTube and his own website (www.zeitgeistmovie.com). Joseph claims that the film and its two sequels have been viewed 200 million times; at the very least, the original film has registered over 2.4 million hits on YouTube; the first sequel garnered over 4 million hits, and the most recent film has had 800,000 views.

Bjorn Sorenssen has identified *Zeitgeist: The Movie* as belonging to what Michael Barkun has called the "superconspiracy genre," in which a vast system of conspiracy is held responsible for huge swaths of human experience – a network of conspiracies rather than a single phenomenon of secret power-mongering (Sorenssen 2014, 203; Barkun 2003, 6). *Zeitgeist* addresses three concerns: (1) the establishment of religion, particularly Christianity, as a form of social control; (2) the 9/11 attacks on the World Trade Center and the Pentagon as having been perpetrated by the Bush administration as an excuse to start wars and weaken domestic civil liberties in the United States; and (3) the establishment of the Federal Reserve System, the American central bank and currency system, as a means of financial and social control by a cabal of international bankers (Chapman 2009, 172). The film links these three threads – already existing as ideas separately circulating in American society – into a warning about dominant powers nationally and globally, and their plans for a repressive global government. The film's relevance to this study is in its treatment of the financial system – *Zeitgeist* was released in 2007 but attracted attention in the wake of the 2008 crash, as viewers searched for explanations for the calamity and the government bailout. Joseph argues that the nation's troubles stem from the completely private and undemocratic nature of the Federal Reserve (which is actually a hybrid of public and private institutions, with a governing board appointed by the President). The Federal Reserve is portrayed as controlled by a small number of families, including the Rockefellers and the Rothschilds, who dominate the world economy, reap obscene profits, and have initiated American involvement in all of the major wars since World War I.

Sorenssen sees Joseph as attempting to create the film in the tradition of fact-based, empirically provable documentary, regardless of its functioning as an agit-prop production of the sort delegitimized by Nazi propaganda efforts during World War II (Sorenssen 2014, 203–204). Joseph assembles quotes from historical figures and visuals of newspapers and other documents recounting important events and legislation. He includes a few interviews with figures of former middling authority, such as ex-Internal Revenue Service agents who argue that the entire system of income taxation in the US is illegal. Faced with criticism that the film is widely marked with historical inaccuracies and sloppy reasoning, Joseph compiled a lengthy "Companion Source Guide" to show his research, available on his website (www.zeitgeistmovie.com/Zeitgeist, The Movie-Companion Guide PDF.pdf). He also revised the original film to remove apocryphal quotes and statements that veered between inaccurate assertions and fear-mongering predictions, such as that the United States, Canada, and Mexico had already legally and secretly merged into one political entity that was about to replace the US dollar with a new currency.

Although Joseph made claims to the film's status within the discourse of documentary sobriety, its overall affect is more of a jeremiad than a thorough recitation of facts. Ominous music underscores rhetorical points, and Joseph mixes visual sources in a rush of photographs, news footage, feature film scenes, and iconic abstract gestures from unidentified sources. The result is akin to watching a Ken Burns documentary in a fever dream, a narrative in keeping with the fears of a "post-truth" era inspired by the mendacious practices of the Bush administration (Alterman 2005, 305). With American politics increasingly filled with conspiracy theories ranging from United Nations plots to invade the US to assigning Barack Obama an African birth, skepticism of official versions of truth often shade into the creation of alternative sets of beliefs stubbornly resistant to rational refutation. Some of the claims of the film are actually true or legitimately debatable – the Gulf of Tonkin incident that was used to justify the full invasion of Vietnam was indeed manufactured by the US, the Bush administration did trample some traditional civil liberties in the wake of 9/11, and a more democratic system of managing the currency could have been created by the government a hundred years ago. These points, however, are put to use in a narrative that borrows heavily from anti-Semitic theories about Jewish world domination, even if Joseph scrupulously avoids any explicit mention of that particular angle. The absence of overt anti-Semitism both lessens the tendentious nature of the presentation and increases its respectability in the American context by cleansing the narrative of some of its pernicious origins.

Zeitgeist suffers from a reductionist love for the gold standard favored by right-leaning libertarians, and betrays fatal misunderstandings of how bank financing actually works. The film's discursive threads can be traced to a dizzying array of contradictory sources, from socialists and left-wing populists to Ron Paul libertarians and cultish authoritarians such as Lyndon LaRouche. An expository author is usually viewed as an authoritative figure whose value stems from their ability to foster heightened coherence of the film's argument. Joseph functions more as a curator of a variety of viewpoints and obsessions, a connoisseur of stigmatized knowledges and pseudo-expertise forced to share a single voice. He invokes George Orwell, critical thinking skills, and media literacy, but displays a penchant for creating a postmodern miasma that puts into question all matters of fact regarding the economic and political system. This radical disbelief is in keeping with the disillusion felt across the American political system, but sits uneasily with his insistence that he can disclose the key secrets that viewers need to understand modern society.

In the sequels to the original, Joseph dives further into the problems with currency, eventually advocating the abolishment of money altogether, in keeping with Venus Project orthodoxy. The films' relationship to the Project and its leader Jacque Fresco becomes more open in the later films, as Fresco appears onscreen to espouse his philosophy. The Venus Project is spiritual but skeptical of religion, against consumer culture, and pro-environment. By the third film, Joseph has moved away from the strongly expository mode of the original, relying more heavily on expert interviews, visualizing the panoply of discourses that his project attempts to synthesize. The films and the accompanying website also move from vague suggestions at the end of the first film urging social change to more specific recommendations and invitations to join a movement to pursue its agenda. Whereas Ferguson and Gibney clearly hope for momentous change in the American financial system, their urgings remain vague and muted, in keeping with high-culture documentary's eschewal of agitprop devices. Moore and Joseph, in keeping with their populist positioning, celebrate specific movements as worthwhile responses to widespread social wrong.

The *Zeitgeist* series has been seen by millions, and has been gaining attention from film festivals and documentary scholars. The films' initial success in internet distribution has led to more prestigious exhibitors; the latter two films are available as of this writing on the Netflix streaming service. *Zeitgeist* demonstrates the loosening of barriers to mainstream distribution resources for culturally and politically marginal material, in the wake of YouTube's success. Internet popularity can lead to more respectability for films with low cultural cachet. The original outlaw status of the films, however, is illustrated by the incident that led to its first major mention in mainstream media – when it was cited as a favorite film of and inspiration for the notorious, likely schizophrenic, would-be assassin of Congressional Representative Gabby Giffords (Walker 2011). Whatever the truth of that claim, the sense that the films feed the political extremes of American life, akin to Donald Trump favorite Alex Jones and his InfoWars conspiracy-theory apparatus, points to a conjunction of political and media trends. The disillusion with whatever one might consider the Establishment, whether it be neoliberals, internationalist hawks, or liberal cultural elitists, has combined with a new media ecology open to incursions by previously marginalized voices across the political spectrum.

Conclusion

Agitprop productions with mass reach used to be the domain of national governments that had the resources to produce feature films or continuing series. Today, individual producers and small organizations can flout documentary convention and create audiovisual manifestos with global reach, from Jihadists to Fourth World indigenous rights groups. A range of documentary producers has tried to explain the financial crisis of recent years, from established, award-winning purveyors of measured explanations to satirical, indignant celebrities invoking populist principles, to hawkers of dark conspiracy theories about the true structures of power that govern the world. A crisis of such scale, significance, and complexity is ripe for responses that embody the variety of sources, styles, and epistemological approaches that have come to the fore during a fecund period of documentary production. Audiences for documentary have proliferated in both size and means of exposure, and documentary occupies multiple places in systems of cultural authority, respect, and appeal. The films connect to larger threads of social critique and antipathy toward financial elites, ranging from democratic socialism and reform-minded liberalism to conservative populism, anti-government libertarianism, and ethnonationalism. Political discourse in the United States has entered a period of heightened contention, antagonism, and skepticism, and documentary's roles in its creation and circulation offer a concomitant range of explanation, accusation, and solidarity to its varied audiences.

References

Alterman, Eric. 2004. *When Presidents Lie: A History of Official Deception and Its Consequences*. New York: Viking.

Arsenault, Raymond. 1998. "Wall Street (1987): The Stockbroker's Son and the Decade of Greed." *Film & History* 28: 16–27.

Barkun, Michael. 2003. *A Culture of Conspiracy: Apocalyptic Visions in Contemporary America*. Berkeley: University of California Press.

Bondebjerg, Ib. 2016. "Documentary, Multi-Platform Production, and Cosmopolitan Dialogues." In *Contemporary Documentary*, edited by Daniel Marcus and Selmin Kara, 171–186. London: Routledge.

Clark, Gordon L., Nigel Thrift and Adam Tickell. 2004. "Performing Finance: The Industry, the Media and its Image." *Review of International Political Economy* 11:2, 289–310.

Corner, John. 2015. "System Down! Three Documentary Accounts of Crisis." In *Money Talks: Media, Markets, Crisis*, edited by Graham Murdock and Jostein Gripsrud, 171–185. Bristol: Intellect.

De Goede, Marieke. 2009. "Finance and the Excess: The Politics of Visibility in the Credit Crisis." *Journal of International Relations* 16:2.

Froese, Robert. 2011. "The Limits of *Inside Job*: Crisis, Ideology, and the Burden of Capitalism." *Studies in Political Economy* Autumn: 59–76.

Joseph, Peter. n.d. (www.zeitgeistmovie.com/Zeitgeist, The Movie-Companion Guide PDF. pdf).

Maclean, Kate. 2015. "Gender, Risk, and the Wall Street Alpha Male." *Journal of Gender Studies* 25:4, 427–444.

Mayer, Jane. 2013. "A Word from Our Sponsor." *The New Yorker*. (May 27) www.newyorker.com/magazine/2013/05/27/a-word-from-our-sponsor.

Nichols, Bill. 2010. *Introduction to Documentary*. 2nd ed. Bloomington: Indiana University Press.

Peltzer, Anja. 2015. "No Guns, No Rules, Just Pure Capitalism! Hollywood's Portraits of Wall Street." In *Money Talks: Media, Markets, Crisis*, edited by Graham Murdock and Jostein Gripsrud, 153–168. Bristol: Intellect.

Phillips, Kendall R. 2015. "'I'm Sorry to See It Go': Nostalgic Rhetoric in Michael Moore's *Capitalism: A Love Story*." In *Michael Moore and the Rhetoric of Documentary*, edited by Thomas W. Benson and Brian J. Snee, 170–192. Carbondale: Southern Illinois University Press.

Sorenssen, Bjorn. 2014. "Digital Diffusion of Delusions: A World Wide Web of Conspiracy Documentaries." In *New Documentary Ecologies: Emerging Platforms, Practices and Discourses*, edited by Kate Nash, Craig Hight and Catherine Summerhays, 201–218. New York: Palgrave Macmillan.

Walker, Jesse. 2011. "Unpacking Jared Loughner." *Reason* 42:11, http://reason.com/archives/2011/02/17/unpacking-jared-lee-loughner. Accessed March 3, 2017.

www.boxofficemojo.com, accessed March 2, 2017.

10

GLOBAL FINANCIAL CRISIS IN LOCAL FILMIC SCENARIOS

Transnational cinema of the Great Recession[1]

Elena Oliete-Aldea

Even though signs of economic trouble with the default of subprime mortgage payments could already be identified in 2006–2007, the enormous impact of the fall of Lehman Brothers in September 2008 confirmed that the US economy was facing an unprecedented crisis which could only be compared with the Crash of 1929. Needless to say, the financial meltdown in Wall Street immediately spread across global markets, giving way to a financial crisis of a global scope and a subsequent period of economic decline or recession, the longest since World War II.[2] The causes and effects of this crisis were covered by the media at a global scale and, interestingly enough, for the first time in history, a major economic crisis and recession was reported by the Internet and new media, such as blogs and social networks. This phenomenon gave way to a wide variety of responses which soon went beyond strictly economic debates, as the effects of the new status of the world economy had a clear impact on social matters such as "marriage and divorce rates, social and political attitudes, lifestyle and consumption practices, and much more" (Grusky et al. 2011, 9). As a consequence, the terminology to refer to this period of economic downturn has been quite varied: "financial/economic crash," "credit crunch," "mortgage crisis," "meltdown," "great financial/economic/capitalist crisis," and "great recession," among others.

The etymology of the word "crisis" refers to a *moment* of change or transition which requires judgment and measurement of a situation followed by a definitive, irrevocable decision (Koselleck 2002; Bauman and Bordoni 2014). Considering the Greek origins of the word, I will restrict the use of this term to the moment of the market crash in September 2008. Because of its scope and specific financial dimension within the context of the economy of late capitalism, I will refer to this "moment of change" as "Global Financial Crisis."[3] For the subsequent years of economic decline and lack of growth worldwide, I will use "Great Recession," yet in a wider sense than economists do and closer to what Zygmunt Bauman and Carlo

Bordoni call "State of Crisis," namely a "sign of profound change that involves the whole economic and social system and will have long lasting effects" (2014, vii). In their own words, it is "a permanent status, endemic, in the liquid world [...]. So just as we live in an insecure society, where uncertainty prevails, we also live in a perpetual state of crisis, dominated by repeated attempts at adjustment and adaptation, which are continually challenged" (2014, 59). Therefore, I will not limit this period to concrete years, but will apply it to describe the cultural products and practices that have emanated from the otherwise called "post-boom era" (Boyle and Mrozowski 2013), "age of austerity" and "recessionary culture" (Negra and Tasker 2014) during the last decade.[4]

The current conjuncture brought about by the Great Recession reflects the changes propelled by the processes of globalization which David Harvey describes as a temporal and spatial re-organization of deeply interconnected socio-economic structures at a global scale. As Harvey also states, globalization is understood as an "uneven temporal and geographical development" (2003, 60), therefore, both the 2008 Global Financial Crisis and Great Recession should also be analyzed in terms of their local specificities. A common factor in this globalized scenario corresponds to the growing inequalities between a "transnational overclass"[5] and the increasingly precarious "99 percent." This situation has propelled interconnected forms of protest to express the unfairness of the social, political and economic system, with movements such as the Spanish *indignados* (indignants) and the "Occupy" movement in the United States (Bauman 2008; Chomsky 2012).

Against this background, competing discourses on "crisis" and "recession" have been voiced in the fragmented yet intrinsically connected mosaic of social groups which have been affected by the connectivity of this global recessionary process. Such discourses have flourished in a wide variety of cultural products such as literature, film and television. Cinema has soon echoed these recessionary discourses through a cycle of "Financial Crisis Films" and, indirectly, in a wide variety of cinematic productions which could be included under the label of "Great Recession Cinema." The distinction between Global Financial Crisis and Great Recession and its reflection in distinct cinematic productions is also paralleled to the description offered by Bauman and Bordoni: "This crisis is characterized by the simultaneous combination of an economic gamble on an international level (the causes) and the measures taken locally to deal with it (the effects)" (2014, 3). They also argue that "[t]he present crisis differs from its historical precedents in as far as it is lived through in the situation of a *divorce between power and politics*" (12; italics in original), which has resulted in an absence of agency. The current crisis, therefore, instead of spurring change, is prompting a state of paralysis which may only be solved with a remarriage of power and politics. The main problem is the global interdependence of the causes and effects of the crisis, which makes it impossible for local governments to solve global problems.

Such dialectics between the global and the local, between power and politics is reflected in the transnational connections of Financial Crisis and Great Recession films, which generally offer a harsh criticism of the causes and consequences of the recessionary context in the local scenarios where the films are set. This transnational cycle of films, though, is also imbued with the pessimistic sense of paralysis that hinders their narratives from offering any kind of solution to ameliorate the precarious situations depicted on the screens. The global dimension of this "state of crisis" represented in these cinematic productions entails a sense of powerlessness and lack of hope for the future which is shared by most recessionary narratives in both American and European cinemas. It is important to notice, though, that the fact that different cinematographies have coincided in portraying a common experience of vulnerability, precarity and suffering helps connect recessionary cultures at a transnational level, which can also be interpreted as an adamant sign of refusal to accept the apparently unavoidable permanence of the current state of crisis.

Following the distinction between Global Financial Crisis and Great Recession, the first group includes films that stage the "moment of change" when the crisis hit the global financial centers, mainly of Wall Street and the City of London. Apart from many documentaries such as *Capitalism: A Love Story* (M. Moore, 2009), *Inside Job* (C. Ferguson, 2010), *Overdose: A Film about the Next Financial Crisis* (J. Norberg, 2010), *Debtocracy* (A. Hatzistefanou, K. Kitidi, 2011) and *The Flaw* (D. Sington, 2011), fiction films in this category are corporate dramas such as *The Last Days of Lehman Brothers* (M. Samuels, 2009, BBC), *Wall Street II: Money Never Sleeps* (O. Stone, 2010), *Too Big to Fail* (C. Hanson, 2011, HBO), *Capital* (Le capital, C. Costa-Gavras, 2012), *Margin Call* (J. C. Chandor, 2011), *The Guarantee* (I. Power, 2014), and *The Big Short* (A. McKay, 2015).

The second group refers to films in which the Great Recession plays an important part in the plot and is crucial for the development of the narrative with US dramas – e.g. *99 Homes* (R. Bahrani, 2014) and *Money Monster* (J. Foster, 2016) – but also other European productions which crudely criticize the outcomes of the culture of precarity such as *Dogtooth* (Kynodontas, Y. Lanthimos, 2010), *Yesterday Never Ends* (Ayer no termina nunca, I. Coixet, 2012), *Human Capital* (Il capitale umano, P. Virzi, 2014), and *I, Daniel Blake* (K. Loach, 2016), among others. This heterogeneous group of films also embraces cinematic productions that use other generic conventions like the horror movies *Drag Me to Hell* (S. Raimi, 2009) and *Fired* (S. Warrier, 2010); comedies such as *Horrible Bosses* (S. Gordon, 2011) and *The Internship* (S. Levy, 2013); action films, for instance *Assault on Wall Street* (U. Boll, 2013); and science-fiction films, *In Time* (A. Niccol, 2011) and *Elysium* (N. Blomkamp, 2013) are some of the most conspicuous examples.

Taking into account the transnational dimension of Financial Crisis and Great Recession films, it could therefore be affirmed that cultural representations of the so-called "recessionary culture" have created new cultures of connectivity between different social groups in countries deeply affected by the crisis. In the case of cinema, recessionary cultures seem to be connected by similar discourses with distinct yet related modes of filmic representation. From a cultural and film studies methodological approach, I propose to compare three representative films which deal with the Global Financial Crisis and Great Recession in three different contexts: *Margin Call* (J. C. Chandor, 2011) in the United States, *Freefall* (D. Savage,

2009) in the United Kingdom and *Justice&Co* (Justi&Cia, I. Estaregui, 2014) in Spain. I will show how different film cultures have offered varied yet connected responses to the new recessionary context, all of them engaging in the dialectics of the disembedding mechanisms of global finance – as portrayed in Financial Crisis films – and re-embedding local responses by marginal and vulnerable groups as shown in Great Recession productions.

Set in the premises of an investment bank in Wall Street, Chandor's Financial Crisis film *Margin Call* depicts the moment when the top management of the firm realize that a failure in their trading algorithms have led them to the edge of bankruptcy. The top executives, together with the CEO, spend the night discussing the possibilities the firm has for survival. They finally decide to dump their toxic assets and thus maintain their top positions of power and wealth in spite of the fact that their actions may cause great damage to both the firm and society at large. Presenting the office as a suffocating, claustrophobic dark place, the film accurately portrays the tense decision-making process the characters undergo; it shows how differently each of them reacts when realizing that their own excessive ambition has driven the firm into bankruptcy and that greed will also be the force that leads them to survive even at the expense of others.

Although the film offers exclusively the perspective of the financial executives, it indirectly hints at the impact the financial crash is going to cause on society, more specifically on so-called "normal people" by the bankers in the film. Several scenes include secondary characters playing the role of cleaning staff in the office. Although they never speak, their presence symbolically makes reference to the role the precariat will take as "cleaners" of the toxic assets that the financial executives will dump on society. When the Federal Reserve decided to bail out large investment banks in order to prevent a financial catastrophe worldwide, many American taxpayers who had to face unemployment and evictions were not backed by public money, nor protected by the State. As Diane Negra and Yvonne Tasker put it, risk was transferred from the financial elites to those with the lowest incomes in society (2014).

This marginal appearance of the precariat in *Margin Call* becomes the center of the narrative in Ignacio Estaregui's Great Recession film *Justice&Co*. Making indirect reference to the Global Financial Crisis, Estaregui's film focuses on the precarious lives of two Spaniards deeply affected by the austerity measures implemented by their government. The film's protagonists decide to reveal the numerous political and corporate cases of corruption in the country. They kidnap politicians and businessmen and make them publicly confess that they have taken advantage of the crisis and increased their profits while the Spanish population was suffering the consequences of dramatic cuts in health, education and labor rights. The film thus aims to denounce the unethical accumulation of wealth on the part of the overclass even at a time when the country was experiencing unprecedented cases of foreclosures and evictions as well as the highest rates of unemployment in the last decades.

A conspicuous British cinematic response to the economic crash is *Freefall*, a BBC TV movie that focuses on the impact of the financial crisis on both investment banks in the City of London and working-class families failing to pay the fluctuating interest rates of their subprime mortgages. By combining the perspective of both the financial overclass and the vicissitudes of the precariat, and by trying to portray the global causes of the crisis and its local consequences in Britain, *Freefall* stands in between Financial Crisis and Great Recession films. Even though their plot and filmic styles are apparently completely different, *Margin Call*, *Justice&Co* and *Freefall* are connected by the common purpose of depicting on screen the origins of the financial crash, its global dimension and local responses.

According to David Harvey, the effects of the crisis with the first wave of foreclosures in the United States already started in 2006 and 2007. The Global Financial Crisis, however, was not officially accepted until it hit the financial centers of Wall Street and the City of London. It seemed that, while the crisis affected low-income people, single-parent families and mostly non-white minorities, the media did not seem to care much about those first signs which were already hinting at a flaw in the system (Harvey 2010). The collapse of "too big to fail" investment banks in 2008 was often portrayed in the media by means of apocalyptic news of an economic catastrophe at a global scale. After that moment, many Financial Crisis films and documentaries were produced to explain the unprecedented magnitude of the 2008 crash. Thus, the fall of Lehman Brothers was staged in two TV movies in the BBC and the HBO; and *Margin Call* was also inspired by Goldman Sachs, Lehman Brothers and Merrill Lynch (J. C. Chandor, 2011). Financial Crisis films such as *Margin Call* cannot be considered to inaugurate a new genre as they do not come out of a vacuum. Hollywood had previously produced other "Wall Street films" centered on the deeds of brokers and financial executives such as *Wall Street* (O. Stone, 1987) and *Boiler Room* (B. Younger, 2000). Financial Crisis films, however, do initiate a new cycle of cinematic productions concerned with the depiction of the decisive moment when Wall Street executives had to the face the inevitable financial meltdown.

Margin Call starts with a mass redundancy taking place in the firm. One of the employees who is laid off is Eric Dale (Stanley Tucci), head of risk management, who was working on the glitch in the money-making formula of the company that was going to spur the crash. Before leaving the premises, he gives a USB memory stick to one of the young members of his team while warning him to be careful. The film then revolves around the discovery of the problem that is going to give way to the events. After a tense meeting with the CEO and the top management of the firm, the bankers realize that the problem cannot be solved. Disaster is going to hit the company and, as a tsunami or contagious virus, will impinge on other firms and society at large not only in the USA, but also worldwide. The film cleverly uses generic conventions of thrillers, disaster and even horror films in its portrayal of a dark and claustrophobic mise-en-scène and tilted camera angles combined with bird-eye shots that enhance the vulnerability of people in the streets when having to confront the coming "financial disaster." Nevertheless, instead of presenting heroes that solve the difficult situation for the community – i.e. American society – and provide a happy ending to the story, *Margin Call* presents bankers that callously cling to their own positions of power and decide to only save themselves and survive on their own while the economy starts to sink. The film shows how the bankers get promoted, keep their jobs, or obtain large severance pays. At the same time, the selling of valueless assets to other companies or individual investors will have a tremendous negative effect on those at the lowest positions in the firm's hierarchy, who will lose their jobs and benefits. The film thus depicts the situation of unfairness that the Global Financial Crisis has brought. In Joseph Stiglitz's words:

> It was rightly perceived to be grossly unfair that many in the financial sector [...] walked off with outsized bonuses, while those who suffered from the crisis brought on by these bankers went without a job; or that government bailed out the banks, but was reluctant to even extend unemployment insurance for those who, through no fault of their own, could not get employment after searching for months and months; or that government failed to provide anything except token help to the millions who were losing their homes. What happened in the midst of the crisis made clear that it was not contribution to society that determined related pay, but something else: bankers received large rewards, though their contribution to society – and even to their firms – had been *negative*.
>
> *(2013, xliv; italics in original)*

Jeff Kinkle and Alberto Toscano point to the difficulty of portraying the complexity of economic matters on screen without falling into a Manichaean simplification of "families reuniting to overcome hardship, the machismo and malevolence of stockbrokers, the corrosive power of greed" (2011, 39). *Margin Call* does allow certain complexity to all the characters. Accordingly, J. C. Chandor's film departs from Oliver Stone's version of the crisis in *Money Never Sleeps*, where the polarization between the "good" and the "bad" banker is quite palpable. While criticizing the greed of speculators – Bretton James (Josh Brolin) and Gordon Gekko (Michael Douglas) – Stone includes the perspective of an "old-school" banker, Louis Zabel (Frank Langella), who commits suicide after realizing his firm is in bankruptcy due to the highly speculative activities of late capitalism that he does not fully understand nor agree with. Furthermore, *Money Never Sleeps* also provides a hero, Jake Moore (Shia LaBeouf), who offers some insights to reverse the damaging effects of the crisis in society by turning back to the "original" role of finance: a tool to fund productive ventures that could be not only profitable for investors but also beneficial for society.

Characters in *Margin Call*, in contrast, are neither heroes nor victims. One of them, Sam Rogers (Kevin Spacey), head of the trading floor, finds himself in a critical moment when he has to make a decision that could have turned him into the hero of the film. He is the only character who is shown to have doubts about selling their valueless assets to their clients. Nevertheless, all the characters, Sam included, finally decide to save themselves. There are also several scenes in the film that may make the audience think that some of these characters are going to commit suicide, recalling the years of the Great Depression with bankers jumping from the top of their offices. Yet none of them has the least intention of putting an end to their lives: their goal is to survive, even if it is at the expense of the weak.

Margin Call offers the point of view of the so-called one percent of society or the powerful "transnational overclass." The financial executives in the film are always backed by their power and money, and literally protected by remaining either at the top floors of the tower where their offices are located, or inside their cars when on the street. Such portrayal of the main characters reveals a social order in which the excessive polarization between the overclass and the precariat prevents social mobility and the American dream from becoming a possibility. As Stiglitz states:

> We are in fact paying a high price for our growing and outsize inequality: not only slower growth and lower GDP but even more instability. And this is not to say anything about the other prices we are paying: a weakened democracy, a diminished sense of fairness and justice, and even…a questioning of our sense of identity.
>
> *(2013, liii)*

The film shows how those members of the overclass do not fall from their "ivory towers" while they literally dump their toxic assets and transfer their risky business to those they call "normal people" (Giroux 2011). The result is that the precarious living conditions of vulnerable groups in society increase, while those at the top of the social scale are protected enough never to fall to the disadvantaged stages of society. As Bauman and Bordoni put it:

> But if we allow the economy and the markets to steer our lives, we will find ourselves in a globalized society that has marked social differences, composed of an impoverished majority that is deprived of guarantees and services and crushed down into a sort of equality, alongside a privileged minority: privileged not only because of their high income, but also because they enjoy certain concessions and the opportunity to access all kinds of benefits.
>
> *(2014, 148)*

This widening gap between the overclass and the precariat is insightfully portrayed in *Margin Call* by centering the plot and narrative on the way the financial executives react when facing the moment of crisis while, at the same time, deliberately portraying the marginality of characters belonging to vulnerable groups that will actually suffer the major consequences of the crisis and the recession. This is revealed in several scenes showing cleaning staff in the office at the background when the financial executives are nervously discussing the critical situation in the firm. The cleaning staff remain invisible to the eyes of the bankers but, interestingly enough, the unskilled workers do not seem to care either about what those members of the overclass are saying, in spite of the fact that they see the top management arriving for a meeting at night. Invisibility, therefore, goes both ways, to the point that they inhabit completely different worlds in spite of sharing the same space. However, it is the working class that is at risk of falling into an underclass status when unemployment hits. In the event of the company's bankruptcy, the powerless cleaning staff will not have the "choice" of accepting huge severance payments.

Such polarization is also present in the Spanish film *Justice&Co*. In contrast to *Margin Call*, this low-budget film depicts the effects of the crisis from the point of view of the precariat. Set in a mining region of Spain, the film tells the story of Justino (Hovic Keuchkerian), an unemployed miner who is the only survivor of a mining accident caused by bad management. Having probably accepted a bribe, the sub-secretary of the Department for Business, Energy and Industrial Strategy had authorized a private company to work in the mine using defective and cheap machinery. As a consequence, seven workers died in the accident, Justino's father and brother among them. When the powerful and influential politician is suspiciously acquitted of all charges, Justino decides to take the law into his own hands. With the help of Ramón (Álex Angulo), an unemployed, homeless, solitary old man, also a victim of the crisis, Justino kidnaps corrupt businessmen and politicians. Their purpose is to frighten them and make them confess their corruption-related crimes in front of a camera. Justino and Ramón send the recordings to a journalist to be broadcast on television. Their brave decision to publicly denounce corruption – and show the criminals in powerless and humiliating situations – turns them into national heroes. Even though effective violence is never perpetrated against the kidnapped, the camera shows their feeling of fear and suffering. The portrayal of the criminals in a state of vulnerability reverses the powerful-overclass versus powerless-precariat dichotomy which is often represented in the media.

Justino and Ramón travel in a van from the north to the south of Spain until they finally meet the sub-secretary of the Department of Industrial Strategy. Justino tries to explain to him the enormous harm done to his family. But, far from showing empathy, the politician verbally humiliates the miner from his powerful, godlike position. Out of rage, Justino kills him and runs away to the beach, where Ramón is waiting for him. Looking nostalgically at the horizon and metaphorically at their broken Quixotic dream of bringing justice back to the current recessionary Spanish society, the two friends remain together until they are caught by the police.

Justice&Co could be labeled as a Great Recession film, since it depicts the consequences of the Crash on the so-called 99 percent. In contrast to *Margin Call*, the narrative in *Justice&Co* is presented from the perspective of the members of the underclass and its action takes place in the street, more concretely, on the road, far away from financial centers. While *Margin Call* makes constant references to the global impact of the crisis from a financial perspective, *Justice&Co* emphasizes the local particularities of the global crisis in Spain, namely the pervasive corrupt activities which invade the political, social and economic system and prevent the country from recovering from the crisis. Estaregui's film follows the trend of other Spanish cinematic productions which engage with the effects of the economic crisis and the government's austerity measures on the population such as *Amador* (F. León de Aranoa, 2010), *Here's the Deal* (Somos gente honrada, A. Marzoa, 2012), *Yesterday Never Ends* (Ayer no termina nunca, I. Coixet, 2012), *As Luck Would Have It* (Chispa de la vida, A. de la Iglesia, 2012), and *Five Square Meters* (5 metros cuadrados, M. Lemcke, 2012), among others.[6] According to Dean Allbritton:

> These films' perpetually scrappy protagonists, unlike many who are paralyzed by sensations of precarity, find recourse in unorthodox actions that theoretically undermine the institutions that have placed them in such states. When the bank, the banker and capitalism at large are crushing one's potential for living out the "good life" as it has been imagined, the institution must be brought down – albeit safely, on screen, and in a manner so surreal that it has likely lost any potential radicality.
>
> (2014, 4)

In spite of the films' lack of "radicality," Allbritton also insists that the portrayal of vulnerability onscreen contributes to critically denounce the impact of the Global Financial Crisis and Great Recession on the precariat. In fact, the cinematic representation of collective groups hit by austerity measures in Spain – and by the recession in other countries – results in a vindictive desire for public recognition of private matters which are inevitably linked to the local consequences of a global crisis. The representation of shared personal experiences of vulnerability within a context of collective suffering, not only in cinema but also in other cultural practices such as literature, theater, television and social networks, may create a sense of community through bonds of interlinked transnational recessionary cultures. Consequently, "[t]he pain of being a vulnerable citizen can be then transformed into a practice that releases hope and a way to mitigate one's individual devastation onto the shoulders of a collective" (Allbritton 2014, 4).[7]

Justice&Co gives an overview of the precarious situation of many Spanish citizens in a country set against the Great Recession, by alluding to everyday scenes in quotidian Spanish settings. The first scene in the film shows the demonstration of the miners demanding justice after the accident. The scene recalls the *indignados* (indignants) movement in 2011 in Spain, which organized a number of demonstrations that condemned austerity measures.[8] The critical situation of the Spanish economy also gave way to a wave of foreclosures that mercilessly hit many families, most of whose members were unemployed. The film also makes indirect reference to this by showing blocks of apartments full of "to let" or "for sale" signs and with one of Justino's neighbors committing suicide at the beginning of the film. Although no specific explanation is given, the editing of the first scenes indirectly connects the event with the actual suicides of people in Spain who were to be evicted from their houses.[9]

The beginning of the film thus reflects the way in which risk has been transferred from those on top (the global overclass represented by the financial executives of *Margin Call* as well as politicians and powerful businessmen in *Justice&Co*) to "normal people" who literally and metaphorically inhabit (and fall down to) the lowest social positions at the street level. Dean Allbritton explains that all members of society except for the overclass experience the risk "of being made vulnerable," which means that "a citizen may be not only politically but also physically exposed by the law," as cuts in the welfare state diminish the social protection of citizens in a recessionary period (2014, 1). Although such risk of vulnerability may be experienced transnationally by those citizens whose countries have been hit by the crisis, Allbritton describes the acuteness of the situation in the Spanish context:

> This is particularly so in the case of Spain, where the austere political measures that purportedly safeguard the economy continue to intensely affect its populace in deep and meaningful ways. The precariousness of Spain's socioeconomic state heightens the sense of physical vulnerability of citizens and creates a spiraling system of increasing physical peril (and the recent deep cuts to government-provided health care only serve to increase the sense of one's physical vulnerability to the political system).
>
> *(2014, 1)*

Such vulnerability is clearly portrayed in *Justice&Co*, which includes in the very first scenes a reference to the suicide problem in Spain related to evictions and the precarious conditions being imposed on the population during the recession. This is to be contrasted with the reaction of the financial executives in *Margin Call* when they learn about the firm's bankruptcy: for all their concern about the situation, they find a way out to keep their positions of wealth and power in society and have no intention of committing suicide; they even joke at the idea of jumping from the top of the building in one of the scenes of the film.

Deeply affected by the image of his neighbor jumping out of a window, Justino visits his sister, who takes care of their old ill mother. Far from being a reassuring encounter, Justino's sister complains about her fate as caregiver while denouncing the Spanish healthcare system, which has collapsed after the Conservative government cuts. While cooking, she bitterly criticizes Justino for worrying about his Quixotic dreams to fight for social justice while she is the one who is taking care of their mother de facto. The film actually evokes Cervantes's novel through its episodic narrative, which is led by two characters that resemble the idealist Don Quixote – Justino – and his down-to-earth and faithful squire Sancho Panza, Ramón. Similarly to Cervantes's characters, Justino and Ramón set out on a trip in the search for justice, to defend the weak against the overclass, just to crash into giants that are too powerful to be fought. This is well illustrated in the scene where the protagonists travel from the north to the south of Spain and drive across the region of Castile: several long-shots show the landscape with the typical mills scattered over the hills, hinting at the "giant" mills from *Don Quixote*'s well-known passage. Apart from references to *Don Quixote*, the film alludes to other particularities of the Spanish cultural context. For example, the protagonists are also compared to Curro Jiménez, a character in the very successful eponymous TV series of the 1970s, which was based on the Spanish popular nineteenth-century literary tradition of good-natured bandits who fought for justice and survival in a polarized society.

In spite of this emphasis on the local particularities of Spanish culture, *Justice&Co* also includes other cinematic strategies that link the plot with American and European filmic traditions, thus pointing to the transnational dimension of the recessionary context. It shares with other Financial Crisis and Great Recession films a pervasive sense of inherent pessimism and lack of hope for regeneration in the future.[10] The widening gap between the transnational overclass and precariat, the growing power of the global economy and the sense of powerlessness of the common citizen is leading to hierarchical societies with a lack of opportunities to social mobility. This situation questions the idea of the welfare state and social democracies in Europe and also puts to the test the myth of the American dream. The use of filmic conventions from both European and American traditions re-embedded in the idiosyncrasies of the Spanish context helps establish a sense of shared recessionary experiences represented transnationally on the screen.

To begin with, the film could be categorized as a road movie, which is a genuinely American genre. More specifically, it recalls John Ford's *Grapes of Wrath* (1940), which was also set in a context of economic difficulties with a family losing their home and traveling to a place where they can find a job. At the same time, *Justice&Co* aligns with the Spanish "timid realist" tradition of road movies which deal with socio-economic issues, such as Miguel Hermoso's *Fugitives* (Fugitivas, 2000) (Quintana qtd. in Indurain, 2015). Similarly, the unglamorous portrayal of the harsh realities in contemporary Spain links the film to the British social-realist tradition of Ken Loach, Mike Leigh and Stephen Frears. British low-budget politically engaged films consciously depart from Hollywood-like fantasy and sweetened stories and show, just as *Justice&Co* does, the inevitable defeat of the working-class characters in their films in order to criticize the ills of social realities.

Apart from the obvious allusion to the road movie genre, *Justice&Co* makes intertextual references to other mainstream American movies of heroes and vigilantes seeking justice which, in the Spanish context, reappear with an ironic twist. For example, at some point in the film, the main characters refer to their old, cheap van as Batmobile and, to themselves, as Batman and Robin. After realizing that his defeat is a matter of time, bitterly and ironically, Justino says: "I was going to become the Spanish Charles Bronson." At the end of the film, the Spanish police joke about their lack of resources as compared with US police in the movies: "Why do you act like this is New York? This isn't fucking New York!" The influence of American culture is also present in the commodification of the funny nose-glasses disguise the characters wear when kidnapping their victims, which are sold in gas stations as soon as they become heroes in the media.

Set against the Spanish context, these references to American popular culture bring about moments of comedy which nevertheless end in the tragic defeat of the protagonists. The parodic inclusion of intertextual references to American cinema within the Spanish cinematic tradition and cultural context contributes to criticize the general, transnational effects of the Global Financial Crisis. On the one hand, as

Allbritton explains, such surreal and comic hints to American films may undermine the potential criticism of the film; but, on the other hand, the continuous references to other cinemas, precisely connect the local suffering of the precariat in the Spanish recessionary context with the global origins of the Financial Crisis and its pervasive effects at a transnational level.

The dialectics of the global and local dimensions of the Financial Crisis and Great Recession are also portrayed in *Freefall*, a British film concerned with the representation of the local effects of the recession in Britain while trying to explain the global causes of the financial meltdown as it hits the City of London. *Freefall* thus stands in between Financial Crisis films and Great Recession films. It revolves around three interlinked stories that involve characters affected by the Crash: Gus (Aidan Gillen), a successful investment banker from the City who panics when the stock exchange collapses in September 2008; Dave Mathews (Dominic Cooper), an unscrupulous real-estate broker who obtains large profits by selling subprime mortgages to high-risk customers; and a working-class family who becomes the victim of the mortgage meltdown. While the crisis was focalized by the financial elite in *Margin Call* and by the precariat in *Justice&Co*, *Freefall* includes the perspective of both groups and also adds the point of view of the broker, who connects these two distant social spheres.

While US cinema can trace back some instances of "financial" or rather "Wall Street" movies, British cinematography does not have a tradition of "City of London" films.[11] With the exception of *Rogue Trader* (J. Dearden, 1999), which does tell the story of a British banker but who works and trades in Asian markets and not in the City, British cinema seems to follow the "code of silence" that seems to rule the world of finance in London (Luyendijk, 2015). Financial executives fear that any leak in classified information or any misinterpretation of the news could affect the fluctuations of the financial market. This is why all information must be supervised and mediated by the company's public relations/communications department.[12]

As a "financial film", *Freefall* can thus be only related with *Rogue Trader*. However, lacking a tradition of "City of London film genre," *Freefall* could actually be framed within the British social-realist tradition in Ken Loach's vein as it also portrays the vicissitudes of a working-class family that cannot face the mortgage payments when interest rates increase and the breadwinner loses his job. The critical dimension of the British social-realist tradition, which was echoed in *Justice&Co*, is also present in *Freefall*, as the film denounces the unethical behavior of the real-estate agent and the lack of legal protection of families who could not afford the subprime mortgage payments.[13] The film is also influenced by the British documentary style:[14] some of the scenes are shot with an intrusive hand-held camera that invades the office space of the real-estate agency, the investment bank in the City and the working-class family house.

The film apparently follows a Manichaean construction similar to that of *Justice&Co*: the evil financial elite who are responsible for the crisis and the victimized working-class families. The British film, however, allows the audience to sympathize with the bankers, especially with one of the main characters, Gus (Aidan Gillen), who is a solitary workaholic divorced man who suffers tremendously when losing his job after the firm goes into bankruptcy. In contrast to the natural-born survivors in *Margin Call*, Gus cannot admit his own professional failure and commits suicide by jumping from a bridge in the City.

The character who is portrayed from a completely negative light is Dave, the mortgage salesman who has no scruples about providing loans to families that will not be able to afford them. He even sells one of those mortgages to his school friend Jim (Joseph Mawle), a security guard who is married and a father of two small children. Representing the entrepreneurial class, which has been promoted since the 1980s by the Thatcherite neoliberal discourse, Dave climbs the social ladder by stepping on others. The unethical social mobility he represents is portrayed in a very negative light in the film. Dave is shown as a *nouveau riche*, similar to American entrepreneurs, who does away with the moral values traditionally associated with the British social system which, in turn, are symbolized by the integrity embodied by the upper and lower class characters in the film. Showing no remorse, Dave is the ultimate survivor, who undertakes another business venture when the housing market bubble explodes. The film ends with a scene that is similar to the beginning, Dave singing happily in his car after having successfully sold new bubble products to families. With this, the film questions the neoliberal system implemented in Britain by the forces of globalization, originating in the Thatcher era. The film therefore criticizes the new global socio-economic order of late capitalism and the way in which it has negatively impacted on the British socio-economic and cultural system.

In the context of the subprime mortgage meltdown, both Financial Crisis and Great Recession films recurrently represent the dichotomy "house" versus "home."[15] The greedy search for a big house that stands for a higher social status, together with the unquenchable thirst for wealth and power of the financial elite, contributed to create the housing bubble. The house trade became a highly profitable business, only at the expense of the "home," which symbolized the values of the family or, by extension, those of the community, which were being lost. In all these films the cold bluish colors of the workplace are frequently contrasted with the cozy warm colors of the scenes depicting home spaces. "Home" represents the sense of community that is difficult to attain in increasingly individualized capitalist societies (Lasch 1991, Collier 1991). Zygmunt Bauman explains that people feel safe when they form part of a community as all the members can count on each other in difficult times: "When we fall on hard times [...] people won't ask us for collateral before deciding to bail us out of trouble; they won't be asking us how and when will we repay, but what our needs are" (2008, 2). The neoliberal discourses on "individual freedom" and the rise of individualism at the expense of community have generally reduced the stability and reliability of human bonding. Nevertheless, both Financial Crisis and Great Recession films show that, in times of crisis, the lack of a proper community and human reliable bonds is acutely missed.

In *Freefall*, Gus commits suicide because he cannot make sense of his lonely life after the bank, his only source of identity, crumbles. He finds himself alienated from his ex-wife, daughter, girlfriend *nouveau riche* and colleagues. In contrast, the working-class family remains united by bonds of affection. They lose the house of their dreams, but they go back to their council estate apartment where they still find a "home." Similarly, the main characters in *Justice&Co* lack both a home and a house at the beginning of the film but their lives change in their journey: they develop close bonds of friendship and their van not only becomes their "house" but also their "home." In the last scene in the film, which shows the characters' final defeat of their impossible pursuit of justice, both characters embrace, revealing the ultimate human connection in the small community they created when fighting for the common good.

In contrast, *Margin Call* develops the "home" versus "house" tension in quite a different manner. The film cleverly manages to depict the *absence* of family and community, with individuals reduced to figures and numbers (their earnings, profits, expenses *nouveau riche* and algorithms) which are repeatedly mentioned in the film. The main characters show no commitment to human relationships and they are never portrayed at home with their family but always at work or in the street. When in trouble, families remain absent;[16] the most compelling example is the last scene of the film, when Sam Rogers buries his dog in the yard of his ex-wife's house, while she coldly threatens him to call the police if he does not leave the place. The darkness of the night and the sound of the spade against the earth enhance the loneliness and despair of the character. The dog was the only being to which Sam showed affection, but the pet is now dead, which recalls the character's metaphorical death after having given up his ethical principles in the firm in exchange for money.

In the depiction of the dismissal of the head of risk management, Eric Dale, at the beginning of the film, the human resources team acts with politeness, however, the whole scene is characterized by impersonal coldness. In spite of having been working for nineteen years in the firm and feeling part of it – as he shows his concern about the project he was working on – Eric Dale is fired by someone who does not personally know him and only three of his workmates come to say goodbye. He is actually treated as a potential criminal, as he is escorted to his office by a threatening security guard and his communication with the firm is immediately cut off by closing his email account and disconnecting his mobile phone.

The firm thus represents the individualistic ethos of late capitalism which links people through technological networks instead of the cohesive human bonds of a community (Bauman and Bordoni 2014), which is particularly acute in the corporate culture of Wall Street firms (Ho 2009, 83–87). This first scene also portrays the dichotomy between networked individuals and caring human relations. Dale's office decoration reveals some hints of personal affection in the portraits that he has of his family and family-related objects scattered through the room such as a photograph of him and his wife in the countryside and a picture of a woman in a wedding dress. The wooden furniture in the office creates a cozy atmosphere as the character is surrounded by warm colors. This is clearly contrasted with the aseptic white room where he is fired, the dark blue and grey colors of the characters' suits, together with the bluish light of the computers illuminating the setting which create a cold atmosphere. The coldness of the room enhances the distant behavior of the human resources staff who fire him. They are shown to be completely disconnected from his job and personal life.

Just as technology easily helps connect individuals and facilitates communication in a networked society with the Internet, intranet *nouveau riche* and smartphones, it can also contribute to instantly disconnect individuals from their network, in an impersonal and almost cruel manner.[17] Employees seem to impersonate the very numbers bankers deal with every day, those rational calculations the firm is grounded on which rule the life of individuals. In just an instant, Dale is expelled from the network of top managers and is forced to abandon the upper floor of a Wall Street skyscraper to be left alone in the street. Dale, however, will not remain there for long, nor will he become a member of the precariat: he will return to the top floors of the building to receive economic compensation for his discovery and subsequent silence.

Margin Call, *Justice&Co* and *Freefall* thus show that the risk of vulnerability has been transferred to the vast majority of "normal people" while the global overclass remains isolated within their invulnerable spheres of power. The precariat, however, is portrayed as the only social group which is able to create or maintain the cohesive human relations of a community, either in the traditional family unit, as in *Freefall*, or in the bonds of friendship that keep the two main characters together in *Justice&Co*. The three films intertwine elements from different modes of filmmaking as well as specific socio-economic situations of their filmic locations within the general framework of the Global Financial Crisis and Great Recession. They attempt to explain the causes and consequences of the new global scenario of late capitalism and the way the gap between a transnational powerful overclass and vulnerable precariat is widening. From different perspectives, the three films also question the house-home dichotomy put forward by the mortgage crisis and reflect the growth of individualism in late capitalism. The films manage to depict on screen the way individuals are connected globally through a network system but, at the same time, personal relationships based on human bonding are difficult to maintain. As Zygmunt Bauman states, the most frightening impact of fear is the fear of powerlessness, the fear of having to fight back individually, "each one of us using our own and in most cases sorely inadequate resources" (2007, 21). In this light, without the support of a community looking for the common good, the search for justice will become a task very difficult to attain. The transnational dimension of Financial Crisis and Great Recession films may, however, contribute to create a sense of community in the common lived experiences of suffering on the part of the precariat. The intertwined stories of this cycle of films produced and set in different places and contexts may foster the proliferation of new transnational cultures of connectivity, which question the extent to which the finalization of the economy is actually eroding the principles of social mobility that are grounded in the discourses of "capitalism."

Notes

1 Research toward the writing of this chapter has been funded by the Spanish Ministry of Economy and Competitiveness, project no. FFI2013-40769-P and the Aragonese Government (reference no. H12).

2 The National Bureau of Economic Research in the United States indicated that this recession lasted eighteen months and officially labeled it "Great Recession," explaining that "The NBER does not define a recession in terms of two consecutive quarters of decline in real GDP. Rather, a recession is a significant decline in economic activity spread across the economy, lasting more than a few months, normally visible in real GDP, real income, employment, industrial production, and wholesale-retail sales." (NBER 2010). It has also been described by economists as a double-dip recession, lasting from 2007 to 2012 (Rosenberg 2012).

3 This term has widely been used by economic institutions such as the NBER and IMS, as well as economists such as Stiglitz (2010), Rajan (2010), and Roubini (2010), among others. This is also the term used by Miriam Meissner in the cultural and film analysis of films dealing with this topic (2012).

4 For the use of the expression "Great Recession" in the media, see Rampell, 2009.

5 According to Richard Rorty, the "transnational overclass" threatens to establish new global plutocratic states and displace democratic societies (in Bauman 2007, 146).

6 These films could also be inserted in what Alice Bardan has denominated "Cinema of Precarity," referring to a transnational cycle of films dealing with precarious and vulnerable lives in contemporary recessionary culture in Europe (see Bardan 2013; Kourelou, Liz and Vidal 2014).

7 Allbritton carries out an in-depth analysis of this idea of shared vulnerability in what he calls Spanish "crisis cinema" and questions the "spaces of hope" that such networks may offer when the precariat is confronted with the devastating effects of the Great Recession (see Allbritton, 2014).

8 The *indignados* movement also denounced the dangerously widening gap between the overclass and the precariat at a global scale while condemning the increasing cases of corruption and unethical activities carried out by politicians and businesspeople who were actually profiting from the crisis. The movement ultimately questioned the extent to which any political party in Spain represented the citizens who had been critically hit by the crisis. The demonstrations in the film also indirectly echo the Occupy Wall Street movement which also condemned the crisis caused by the deregulated measures of financial markets and excesses of late capitalism and advocated a change towards a fairer society.

9 For more information about the relationship between evictions and the increase in the suicide rate in Spain see Flesher Fominaya 2014; Gili et al. 2012, and press news such as Roberts 2012 and Davies 2012.

10 As Bauman and Bordoni put it, the current recession differs from the Great Depression in that the latter was caused by an industrial crisis and solved with the help of Keynesian theories, while the present recession has been caused by the excesses of global finance, and it therefore needs the implementation of a global strategy to improve the situation; otherwise, the measures applied by local governments, rather than solving the problem, exacerbate it (2014). Besides, in 1929, there was a strong State that could insure "all citizens against the vagaries of fate, individual misfortunes, and fear of indignity in any of the many forms (as fear of poverty, exclusion and negative discrimination, ill health, unemployment, homelessness, ignorance)" (2014, 8). Since the implementation of neoliberal policies in the 1980s thanks to the Thatcher-Reagan tandem, the weakening of the State in favor of the liberalization of financial markets has contributed to increase the sense of powerlessness experienced by a precariat unprotected after the dismantling of the welfare state.

11 The BBC actually produced *The Last Days of Lehman Brothers* (M. Samuels, 2009), which portrays the moment this firm was hit by the crisis, similarly to HBO's version, *Too Big*

to Fail (C. Hanson, 2011). Although it could certainly be categorized as a British film within the "Financial Crisis Films" group, Samuel's film actually portrays Wall Street and not the City of London.

12 In his book *Swimming with Sharks: Inside the World of Banking*, journalist Joris Luyendijk explains how difficult it was to find information about the daily life of bankers and financial executives in the City of London due to an unwritten "code of silence" that prevents bank employees talking about their job unless mediated by the bank or firm's PR (see Luyendijk 2015). In the United States, the concern of Wall Street firms with classified information also makes it difficult for outsiders to carry out research on professional activities and corporate culture of investment banks. As anthropologist Karen Ho explains, it is crucial to have connections and adequate background to access the world of Wall Street (2009). It is worth noting that both Oliver Stone and J. C. Chandor's accurate knowledge of Wall Street came through their respective fathers, who work in the Stock Exchange.

13 Ken Loach's recent films could also be considered as "Great Recession cinema," particularly *I, Daniel Blake* (2016).

14 Tradition set up by Grierson's documentary movement in the 1930s in opposition to Hollywood's fantasy and escapism.

15 For an in-depth analysis of the trope "home" vs. "house" in the Financial Crisis film *Money Never Sleeps*, see Oliete-Aldea 2012.

16 Eric Dale (Stanley Tucci) is not found at home with his wife after his dismissal and Peter Sullivan (Zachary Quinto) notices that Sam Rogers (Kevin Spacey) never contacts his son to tell him about his problems.

17 As Bauman and Bordoni put it: "The essential distinction of 'networks' – the name selected these days to replace the old-fashioned, and putatively outdated, ideas of 'community' or 'communion' – is precisely this right to *unilateral* termination" (2014, 152; italics in original).

References

Allbritton, Dean. 2014. "Prime Risks: The Politics of Pain and Suffering in Spanish Crisis Cinema." *Journal of Spanish Cultural Studies* 15(1–2): 101–115.

Bardan, Alice. 2013. "The New European Cinema of Precarity: A Transnational Perspective." In *Work in Cinema. Labor and the Human Condition*, edited by Ewa Mazierska, 69–90, Houndmills: Palgrave Macmillan.

Bauman, Zygmunt. 2007. *Liquid Fear*. Cambridge and Malden: Polity Press.

Bauman, Zygmunt. 2008. *Community. Seeking Safety in an Insecure World*. Cambridge and Malden: Polity Press.

Bauman, Zygmunt and Carlo Bordoni. 2014. *State of Crisis*. Cambridge and Malden: Polity Press.

Boyle, Kirk and Daniel Mrozowski. 2013. *The Great Recession in Fiction, Film and Television. Twenty-First Century Bust Culture*. Lanham, Plymouth: Lexington Books.

Chomsky, Noam. 2012. *Occupy*. New York: Zuccotti Park Press.

Collier, James Lincoln. 1991. *The Rise of Selfishness in America*. New York, Oxford: Oxford University Press.

Davies, Nigel. 2012. "Spain Promises to Spare Needy from Eviction after Suicides." *Reuters* (November 12), www.reuters.com/article/us-spain-evictions-idUSBRE8AB0GY2012 1112; 12.1.2017.

Flesher Fominaya, Cristina. 2014. *Social Movements and Globalisation*. Basingstoke: Palgrave Macmillan.

Gili, Margalida, Roca, Miquel, Basu, Sanjay, McKee, Martin, and Stuckler, David. 2012. "The Mental Health Risks of Economic Crisis in Spain: Evidence from Primary Care Centres, 2006 and 2010." *European Journal of Public Health* 23(1): 103–108.

Giroux, Henry A. 2011. "Neoliberalism and the Death of the Social State: Remember Walter Benjamin's Angel of History." *Social Identities* 17(4): 587–601.

Grusky, David B., Bruce Western, and Christopher Wimer. 2011. *The Great Recession*. New York: Russell Sage Foundation.

Harvey, David. 2003 (2000). *Spaces of Hope*. Berkeley and Los Angeles: University of California Press.

Harvey, David. 2010. *The Enigma of Capital and the Crises of Capitalism*. London: Profile Books.

Ho, Karen. 2009. *Liquidated. An Ethnography of Wall Street*. Durham and London: Duke University Press.

Indurain, Carmen. 2015. "The Transnational Dimension of Contemporary Spanish Road Movies." In *Global Genres, Local Films. The Transnational Dimension of Spanish Cinema*, edited by Elena Oliete-Aldea, Beatriz Oria and Juan A. Tarancón, 141–155, New York: Bloomsbury.

Kinkle, Jeff, and Alberto Toscano. 2011. "Filming the Crisis: A Survey," *Film Quarterly* 65(1): 39–41.

Koselleck, Reinhart. 2002. *The Practice of Conceptual History. Timing History, Spacing Concepts*. Stanford: Stanford University Press.

Kourelou, Olga, Mariana Liz, and Belén Vidal. 2014. "Crisis and Creativity: The New Cinemas of Portugal, Greece and Spain." *New Cinemas: Journal of Contemporary Film* 12(1&2): 133–151.

Lasch, Christopher. 1991. *Culture of Narcissism. American Life in an Age of Diminishing Expectations*. New York and London: Norton.

Luyendijk, Joris. 2015. *Swimming with Sharks: Inside the World of Bankers*. London: Guardian Books.

Meissner, Miriam. 2012. "Portraying the Global Financial Crisis: Myth, Aesthetics and the City." *NECSUS. European Journal of Media Studies* 1(1): 98–125.

National Bureau of Economic Research. 2010. "US Business Cycle Expansions and Contractions". NBER's Business Cycle Dating Committee, 20 Sept. 2010; www.nber.org/cycles.html#announcements; 20.10.2017.

Negra, Diane and Yvonne Tasker. 2014. *Gendering the Recession. Media and Culture in the Age of Austerity*. Durham and London: Duke University Press.

Oliete-Aldea, Elena. 2012. "Fear and Nostalgia in Times of Crisis: the Paradoxes of Globalization in Oliver Stone's *Money Never Sleeps* (2010)." *Culture Unbound* 4: 347–366; www.cultureunbound.ep.liu.se/v4/a18/; 7.7.2016.

Rajan, Raghuram G. 2010. *Fault Lines: How Hidden Fault Lines Still Threaten the World Economy*. Princeton: Princeton University Press.

Rampell, Catherine. 2009. "Great Recession: A Brief Etymology." March 11, *Economix, New York Times* https://economix.blogs.nytimes.com/2009/03/11/great-recession-a-brief-etymology/?_r=0; 8.1.2017.

Roberts, Martin. 2012. "Spanish Banks to Restrict Evictions after Suicides." November 12, *The Guardian* www.theguardian.com/world/2012/nov/12/spanish-banks-evictions-suicides; 10.1.2017.

Rosenberg, Jerry M. 2012. *The Concise Encyclopaedia of the Great Recession 2007–2012.* Lanham: Scarecrow Press.

Roubini, Nouriel. 2010. *Crisis Economics. A Crash Course in the Future of Finance.* London: Penguin.

Stiglitz, Joseph E. 2010. "Lessons from the Global Financial Crisis of 2008." *Seoul Journal of Economics* 23(3): 321–339.

Stiglitz, Joseph E. 2013 (2012). *The Price of Inequality* London: Penguin.

11

PRECARITY AND VULNERABILITY

Documentaries on the crisis in Spain

Araceli Rodríguez Mateos

Introduction

The global financial crisis and its fallout across the international economic landscape has had a profound impact in social and political terms, especially in the countries hardest hit by the recession. This traumatic event and its aftereffects have been addressed in documentaries made for cinema, television and online distribution, as part of a broader range of multimedia narratives (or as web-based audiovisual productions). *Capitalism: A Love Story* (M. Moore, 2009); *Inside Job* (C. Ferguson, 2010); *The Shock Doctrine* (M. Whitecross and M. Winterbottom, 2009); *Let's Make Money* (E. Wagenhofer, 2008), and *Debtocracy* (K. Kitidi and A. Hatzistefanou, 2011) are among the most significant – that is, best known – works in this regard. In general, these films have taken on the challenge of interpreting and communicating in audiovisual terms the ins-and-outs of a complex, intangible economic mechanism, rendering the technical concepts of the workings of the financial markets comprehensible to a non-specialist audience. The analysis provided covers the factors that led to the real estate bubble in the US, as well as the financial effects of its bursting, which led in turn to the sovereign-debt crisis in Europe.

Experts exploring this range of documentaries have defined a set of thematic and formal lines of inquiry and interpreted their discursive frameworks. A significant proportion of these films may be categorized as examples of "committed documentary" insofar as they formulate critical political positions from a left-wing perspective, dissecting the global causes and effects of what they frame as a grossly unfair economic and financial system. Eder has studied these related viewpoints concerning the crisis, their generally marginal position in the broader panorama of a hegemonic media discourse, and their long-term political ramifications. He has also described the different documentary modes, rhetorical structures and audiovisual styles prevalent in such discourses (2016). Meissner, in turn, has addressed the matter from the point of view of the poetics of space: in particular, the centrality of the cityscape in filmic representations in the early stages of the global financial crisis, in a study that encompasses both documentary and works of fiction (2012). These two contributions, especially the former, set a critical standard for the present chapter, which also defers to Jeff Kinkle and Alberto Toscano's work on films relating to the financial meltdown (2011). Both Kinkle and Toscano take into account, from a historical perspective, the main difficulty facing narratives that aim to respond to different financial crises in the US: the challenge of representing the invisible, immaterial and abstract nature of modern economics in audiovisual terms.

Moreover, rather than being depleted, the scholarly attention such discourses deserve takes on even greater significance in Europe in general, and some Eurozone countries in particular, which continue to suffer the effects of the financial crash. As one of the countries derogatorily referred to as PIGS,[1] Spain is an especially illuminating example in this regard; not only because of the economic markers of the crisis there, but also because of the sociopolitical effects that have, to a certain extent, spread to neighboring countries. The current historical context in Spain is precarious, characterized by instability to some extent. The erosion of the Welfare State as a result of the austerity and cutback policies at a European level has called into question the political and institutional model inaugurated and implemented on the basis of the transition to democracy in Spain. Against this national backdrop, an analysis of how documentary practices are inscribed and operate in relation to the protest culture of indignation[2] and the political empowerment of those most seriously affected by the crisis seems especially pertinent. However, to the extent that the full meaning of such phenomena emerges within a neoliberal global economic context, reading documentary discourses in relation to the precarious and vulnerable situation of individuals as a result of that economic rationale is also relevant.

Crisis narratives in media and cinematic contexts: theoretical models

An understanding of the wider media context is key to any clear account of the import of documentary narratives about the crisis in Spain. A number of studies, drawing on different critical approaches and frameworks, have traced patterns in the treatment of the crisis in the press (Berrocal, Redondo and Torres 2015) and on television (Ruiz, Ruiz and Olmedo 2013; Ruiz-Muñoz 2015; Segado 2015). In broad terms, they come to similar conclusions that the Spanish media discourse in this regard has focused on the terrible tailspin of the recession and its social impact, as well as on the economic measures subsequently put in place. The press has provided special coverage of particular moments, such as the 2012 bank bailout; and new television formats have been devised specifically to deal with the crisis. At the same time, however, these studies have also noted a tendency in media coverage to sensationalize these matters, both as infotainment in the wider spectrum of the information hyper-genre and in entertainment, docudrama and fiction programs as such.

It is not easy to see how documentary practices concerning the crisis are related to media treatment in general. Nonetheless, they are not completely separate discursive events; rather, to a certain extent, they draw on such narrative contents and modes. Since 2011, documentary-makers have endeavored to offer a more in-depth look at the complex topic of the crisis, often adopting a critical approach in marked contrast to the treatment of the issue as spectacle in the dominant media outlets, as discussed in further detail below. The steady production of one or two feature documentaries per year has given sustained visibility to a subject that has begun to slip down the agenda of the mainstream media over the last two years. Moreover, documentaries have also functioned as a call-to-arms for political activism undertaken by particular social pressure groups that use them to draw attention to their claims about the effects of the crisis as well as to sustain their online presence and activity[3]. This strategy echoes the definition of the "Coalition Model" framework outlined by Whiteman (2004) and further developed by Christensen (2009). Alvarado and Barquero have also applied this model to their analysis of a number of political works on the 15-M protest movement in Spain (2013).

Most documentaries' voices have traced the tangible impact of the economic crisis on households and homes: the impoverishment of the middle class and the widening of social divides, mass unemployment, repossessions, emigration and the decline of the Welfare State due to cutbacks in education, health and social services. The specific causes of the crisis have been dealt with to a lesser extent. Nevertheless, a number of works have taken an awareness-raising approach in this regard. *Why?!: An Endemic Crisis* (Porqué?!: Una crisis endémica, M. Balaguer Puig, 2013) and *Eurofraud* (Euroestafa, G. Cruz, 2014) are documentaries that explain the financial, economic, social and political factors that have shaped the crisis in macro-and microeconomic terms. Other issues called for further attention, such as the widespread financial fraud in the Spanish banking system over the last ten years. *My Savings, Their Pickings* (Mis ahorros, su botín, B. Casal Martí, 2012) is a film produced by Asociación de Usuarios de Bancos, Cajas y Seguros (an association of bank, cooperative and insurance agency users in Spain), which maps the responsibilities of all those involved in the sector and calls for greater protection of consumer savings.

Narratives concerning the social effects of the crisis in Spain are thematically linked to the cinema of precarity. This trend explores the development of new cultures and subjectivities within an economic system that marginalizes the individual to a position of social and political precarity. Alice Bardan (2013) and Dean Allbritton (2014) have analyzed this phenomenon in European and Spanish cinema, respectively. This concern is crucial to an assessment of the documentary practices under consideration in this chapter. As will be seen later, the Spanish documentary-makers have contributed to reflect on this contemporary and transnational issue from critical perspectives, questioning the neoliberal paradigm.

However, another concept is key to understanding the narrative modes deployed in documentary filmmaking: *subprime life histories*. This idea was set out in detail by Germán Labrador Méndez in a paper published in the *Hispanic Review* (2012), a contribution that is a major source of inspiration for this chapter. In general terms, subprime life histories are stories that narrate the individual experiences of those most profoundly affected by the crisis. Labrador has documented the circulation of such histories in communication, social and political contexts, taking the emergence of the 15-M protest movement in 2011 as his reference point. From then onwards, subprime life histories have been shared in online forums and public assemblies, giving their narrators a public visibility, voice, authority and demand to be heard that they had never previously enjoyed. These stories recover personal histories from the purely private sphere and invest them with political significance as part of public discourse, because they begin to be interpreted as instances of larger structural problems. In other words, such life histories comprise a strategy to represent the crisis as such, because biography incarnates and renders collective experience visible. These stories have political potential insofar as they enable the audience to know more about lives of which they were unaware, and in which they may see themselves mirrored: individuality is socialized, a shift that plays a key role in constructing collective subjects capable of calling into question the economic, social and political system, in the spirit of the protest culture of indignation.

Labrador points out that the untrammeled circulation of such stories has attracted wider media attention. In fact, Ruiz-Muñoz has traced their influence on entertainment programming, as well as on programs that address the crisis directly (Ruiz-Muñoz 2015, 1131–1133, 1136). Thus, the question arises as to how such discursive creativity has been incorporated into documentary practices: that is, what are the key characteristics of the discourse in audiovisual terms and, as a result, what has its outcome been for the emerging sociopolitical context in Spain since 2011?

Subprime life histories in documentary practices

Unemployment, repossession and Spanish emigration overseas are the core themes of the documentaries discussed here, which have also addressed related issues such as personal debt and state cutbacks in public services. Films that explore the facts of the matter by telling life histories are of special interest. The personal approach has become a standard narrative technique in documentary filmmaking, as well as in other genres. Two key points ought to be clarified at this juncture. Although the line between life history and testimony may at times be a thin one (Labrador 2012, 564), the examples explored here may be read as the former because their protagonists voice their first-person experience of the crisis, thereby investing a broader existential dynamic with greater meaning. On the other hand, Labrador uses the expression "subprime life" to denote an existence that encapsulates "a situation of serious biopolitical risk caused by the most recent economic cycle" (2012, 570). The life histories of Spanish emigrants who moved abroad in the wake of the crisis recounted in some documentaries are not encompassed by such a definition of extreme experience (poverty, eviction, slavery). However, they ought to be taken into consideration as part of a broader understanding of precarious lives; they share certain characteristics at an emotional and psychological level, although the degree of physical vulnerability is not the same.

The documentary has also contributed to the general ferment concerning, in Labrador's words (2012, 563), "stories about the end of the Welfare State," which have begun to shape a specific collective imagination of the economic crisis. It is noteworthy that this narrative formula has become the defining pattern for describing the impact of the economic crisis in Spain. When Labrador discusses the 2012 phenomenon, linking it to the political reality around the 15-M protest movement, he argues that life histories became prevalent in response to a crisis in the representation of precarity:

> The testimonies of those days insisted on breaking a silence, a collective vacuum. It is important to communicate that shared lived experience; something that had remained unsaid was, all of a sudden, being voiced: that it does affect one's mortgage, the keys to one's house and precarious working conditions. If all those demands had already been there, if the people come to see the public square as recognition, it was because there was a crisis of experience and representation, which the sharing of life histories in public assemblies disrupts.
>
> *(Labrador 2012, 573)*

Although these life histories were incorporated into documentary filmmaking in a climate of sociopolitical activism, such narratives have persisted as a discursive strategy, as the social effects of the crisis have been publicized through the 15-M movement (social networks, public assemblies, blogs, webpages, alternative media outlets, etc.) and were even also being covered by traditional media platforms. Among the first of such films was *Indebted: About the Spider's Web* (Endeudados, sobre la tela de araña, F. Vidal Vicens), a documentary that as early as 2009 sounded a warning about people who had taken on too much debt by telling the story of a number of families. This was followed by documentaries released around 2011 (year zero for the 15-M protest movement) including *The Platform* (La plataforma, J. Herranz, 2012), which examines the mortgage problem in Spain and was produced by the NGO SICOM and Namuss Films in conjunction with the PAH; and other films in the last two years such as *Whoever's with Me* (A quien conmigo va, A. Mejías, 2014), *In a Strange Land* (En tierra extraña, I. Bollaín, 2014) and *La Granja del Pas*[4] (S. Munt, 2015).

The documentary makes evident that subprime life histories no longer comprise a narrative strategy devised to respond to a crisis of representation, as had first been the case. Such stories now constitute a pattern of representation capable of understanding and interpreting the economic failure, especially when filmmakers explore its social impact for the purpose of inspiring greater political awareness on audiences. This storytelling allows the magnitude of the crisis – a financial and economic phenomenon – to be measured on a human scale. In the screen, the failures in the abstract dynamics of modern economics are concretized through the problems faced by the individuals most affected by the crisis (debt, unemployment, evictions, among others).

The specificity of audiovisual mediation: between the experience of crisis and its narration

Three interrelated dimensions are relevant to the discussion of the subprime life histories as a mechanism to approach the economic context: lives of precarity (the reality of life), the life histories that are shared (narratives of life) and political action (Labrador 2012, 572). In this regard, it is worth exploring first of all how documentary as a genre may mediate as an audiovisual artifact between life experiences in a time of crisis and audience perception. In the direct, polyphonic and multidirectional ferment of the 15-M protest movement, Labrador noted that the life history of the individual shared in online forums and public assemblies was gradually displaced by the publicization of such experience:

> As a life history is told and told again and re-told, it begins to lose the individuality of the teller and take on narrative form as such, the story in itself, pared down to what may be communicated socially (...) Thus, when life histories begin to be heard as the lives of others, they spread more easily as anecdotes that are useful in accounting for social life, which compress and formalize contemporary historical experience in terms of the individual.
>
> *(Labrador 2012, 566)*

In documentaries, however, the enunciation of their experiences by each participant remains unique.[5] They get the whole viewer's attention. The power with which such stories come across on screen (verbally and non-verbally) cannot be easily replaced with a third-person account: the first-person voice is key to any understanding of their experience because the bond of empathy linking life-history speaker and viewer involves an emotional energy that is amplified in audiovisual media. The corporal language constitutes a decisive moment, a semantics of meaning (Eder 2016, 34). Hence, the work of the documentary filmmaker consists of selecting subjects living in precarious situations, accrediting authority at the critical points discussed above and shaping a narrative that reflects unique, personal – and at times, private – concerns so as to give them a collective and public form.

A number of films are discussed here in terms of the various discursive strategies they deploy; they were made by socially engaged filmmakers, who raised the funding required to cover production costs mainly from small production companies, television networks and – in a small number of cases – public bodies. They are usually shown at film festivals, and this has found them an audience outside Spain as well,[6] or on limited cinema release (albeit not in all cases), before later distribution via a range of digital content platforms. The popular impact of these films may have been limited, but no more so than for other productions in the genre.

Icíar Bollaín uses the standard interview-based rhetorical model in her film, *In a Strange Land*, which deals with the lives of emigrants from Spain – people driven overseas through redundancy or the shrinking of the labor force, who have moved in search of employment prospects abroad. About 20,000 people have made their way to Edinburgh, the city that Bollaín centers on in her documentary. The film brings together a variety of voices, although most of those featured are recent university graduates and those who have worked their way through a series of poorly paid internships. Driven into exile, as they see it, they describe their experiences of precarity: the working conditions they left behind in Spain (temporary contracts, low salaries, the undervaluation of employees), and the uncertainty generated by the effort to make professional progress through a series of posts that fall far below an individual's qualifications (waiters, cleaners, kitchen porters, shop assistants, child-minders) motivated by the goal of proving one's own worth. One of the main contributors, Raquel, sums up the common denominator in Spanish emigration to Scotland:

> There are no opportunities open to me, and no clear future. I can't settle down with my partner, nor work in what I'd like to work at; in fact, I'm not even sure I can make a living by working in a job I don't like. I'm not back in Spain because I need to move forward.

The interwoven stories of the emigrants' lives comprise the discursive heart of the documentary, securing an unquestionable authority vis-à-vis the viewer, an effect that is likewise generated by other documentaries presenting subprime life histories. Expert opinions, in this case limited to the contribution of Joaquín García Roca, a sociologist and theologian, and graphs and captions showing emigration statistics frame individual experiences in the broader global context of – to use García Roca's words – "collective shipwreck." Within this narrative framework, Bollaín endeavors to sketch private lives by interviewing the emigrants in a neutral space so as to highlight the shared features of their exile in symbolic terms: their interpretation of their situation and the feelings it inspires. Only the private space of the main contributor is shown on screen; and the audience is given a glimpse of the workplace (a takeaway restaurant) of another young Spanish man. Other than that, the day-to-day life of the Spanish emigrants in Edinburgh is depicted in their wandering the cold streets of the city. Such shots function as a kind of punctuation that signals the sense of alienation that arises in exile, as though the emigrants themselves were or are somehow lost.

By contrast, other documentaries adopt a different rhetorical strategy by going behind closed doors, so to speak, into the private lives and spaces of their contributors. In *Whoever's with Me*, Amparo Mejías explores the plight of people who have been evicted from their homes by looking at the story of Lola, an emblematic example of thousands of similar situations in Spain in recent years, and the experience of Maria, an activist who works with those at risk of social exclusion. Significantly, the narrative opens with the preparations for a live broadcast on a morning magazine program, which touches on a protest led by Lola and other evictees in Alcalá de Guadaíra (Seville). The reporter sets up the segment, deciding whose voices will be heard. When questions are put to her on camera, Lola briefly tells her story: two attempts have been made to evict her, and she has two daughters (one a teenager, and another who is older and unemployed). This documentary approach enacts an

FIGURE 11.1 Still from *In a Strange Land* (2014).

implicit criticism of the televisual presentation of such experiences in programs of that kind, which tends to be superficial and sensationalized. In fact, this critique becomes more explicit over the course of the film and encompasses media discourse in general, whose treatment of the crisis is chided for being awkward and hackneyed, failing to detail the full social impact of the economic recession.

Mejías's approach, therefore, is to address the problem in depth by telling the stories of Lola and Maria and their daily struggles. Her project is a discreet form of direct cinema, based on observation not on participation, except for the scene in which Lola's parents, over whom an eviction order also hangs, speak straight to camera. Viewers witness the occupation of a property by people whose houses have been repossessed. With neither running water nor electricity, and with only a bare minimum of furniture at their disposal, Lola and her family struggle to move forward while their problems continue to pile up. On the other hand, Maria feels that she herself is fortunate and is committed to standing shoulder to shoulder with others, a position she finds hard to combine with her work and raising small children. Thus, the contributors also become the protagonists: they adopt a principal position regarding the filmmaker's camera, instead of the subordinate position imposed on them by the television camera before. Aware of the filmmaker's ongoing presence, and the continuous recording of their private lives to which they have granted her access, the contributors take control of the public narratives of their lived experiences. They do not need to put their suffering into words; in fact, at times, they are unable to do so. Nor do they have to present a standard autobiography as such. By tracing their footsteps, seeing how they interact with others and reflect on their own situations, their life histories begin to take shape.

Mejías draws on this material to weave a story by threading together sequences that evince the human complexity of the economic problem and generate a range of meanings. The following example may be illustrative in this regard: scenes in the homes of Lola and Maria are interwoven at nightfall. Lola, her husband and teenage daughter eat sandwiches and talk about their day in a house unlit by electricity; their actions reveal the strain involved in maintaining some degree of normality in what is a very precarious situation. In contrast, Maria has arrived home late after

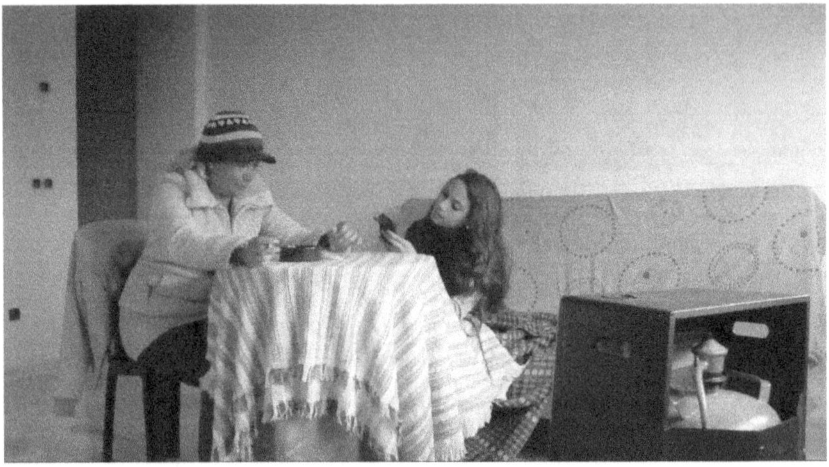

FIGURE 11.2 Still from *Whoever's with Me* (2014).

work and an advisory session for those whose homes have been repossessed, just in time to read her children a story and put them to bed. When she talks with her mother later, she reflects on the sacrifices she makes and the political and social reasons that motivate her endeavor: to defend the rights of the citizen in the face of an abusive financial system. In short, this sequence shows the value of an observational narrative style in interpreting the effects of the crisis; it is a form of mediation in which an avowedly more discreet technical and rhetorical strategy succeeds in giving viewers the sense that they have direct access to the subprime life histories described.

The domestic sphere and what may take place there in subprime lives is also rendered especially meaningful in Silvia Munt's *La Granja del Pas*, another film that aims to depict the crude reality facing those most negatively affected by a crisis that shows no signs of easing. To this end, the filmmaker focuses on the PAHC, an organization which was set up in Sabadell (Catalonia) in 2009 and that has spread throughout the country. Munt's narrative strategy combines two approaches. On the one hand, a direct, observational style is used to show how PAHC meetings unfold in a space that is both real and symbolic because it represents the process of empowerment among those who participate in the organization: the *La Granja del Pas* building. The social and racial diversity of those affected by subprime conditions are on display there. On the other hand, the personal interview technique is seen in conversations between the documentary-maker and a number of PAHC members. These interactions take place behind closed doors, within the four walls of the private properties occupied by the dispossessed. Having been buffeted by the financial storm and lost almost everything, they have begun to rebuild their homes, in moral and material terms. This occupied private space proves the best set on which to discuss indepth the life histories of those involved in PAHC. The subjects themselves voice their own experiences in conversations and at public assemblies.

Munt grants them authority in this regard, while she plays the more discreet role of selecting stories from the assemblies, steering private conversations and stitching together their experiences so as to make them meaningful in the broader context of the economic crisis.

These three films illustrate how documentaries may build a bridge between subprime subject and viewer, a bond in which emotion plays a key part. Such emotional engagement is intensified by narrowing the gap between experience and audience because the experience in itself and its enunciation in first person by the protagonist come across powerfully on screen. Indeed, one of the challenges facing these documentaries may well have been to ensure that their consideration of the social crisis was not overwhelmed by the emotional energy it generates. This is an

FIGURES 11.3 AND 11.4 Still from *La Granja del Pas* (2015).

important key for enabling viewers to draw conclusions from the subprime life histories in a critical and analytical sense.

Silvia Munt's film is particularly relevant in this regard. A few sequences from the documentary may exemplify the point. One such set-piece relates one of the most serious cases presented at a meeting of PAHC: Nadia, a young Moroccan woman who is mother to a small daughter and seven-months pregnant. Her husband is in Morocco. They know no one in Spain and are about to be evicted. Her situation is so desperate that she struggles to find the words to describe it. Having heard her story, another person at the gathering offers them shelter in her home, which is likewise at risk of repossession, and the crowd applauds her gesture. In another sequence, a montage framed as a conclusion to the film, Munt cuts between the contributions of the main speakers in which they outline how they have tried to deal with the situations they face. One of the contributors, Antonio, epitomizes the power of these voices and its devastating emotional impact on viewers: he has a job, he has begun to recover his enthusiasm for life, and he is about to buy himself a pair of trainers. Nevertheless, he will never be the person he was before the crisis, nor does he want to be: he has learned how to show solidarity to others, to be less selfish, "to love others more," as he says choking back tears.

International documentaries on the financial crisis continue to deploy "strategies of engagement and emotionalization" (Eder 2016, 38). In the same way this emotional dimension is an inherent aspect in the depiction of the human cost of the economic crisis made by the Spanish films. Even if some viewers did not feel involved by the life histories they see on screen, such stories would force them to face the hardship caused by the poverty that persists despite the apparent improvement in the country's macroeconomic indicators.

The cinematic construction of contemporary precarity

The success of these documentaries in terms of their political perspective depends on their power to convert the viewer's emotional involvement into empathy, rather than simply compassion. Labrador points out that this idea was key to understanding how the sharing of subprime life histories functioned in the political context of the 15-M protest movement and the anti-repossession/eviction organizations that preceded it. By broadcasting social experiences common to many people in crisis-stricken Spain, viewers identified with stories that gave greater meaning to their own lives, thus contributing to the further construction of a political body (Labrador 2012, 571). The documentary, too, added to the audience's self-recognition in subprime life stories. However, it is worth noting in this regard that the process of identification may be more significant in social, political and cultural terms when viewer does not share the life history depicted on screen, but rather when viewers realize that they too are vulnerable subjects to a greater or lesser degree within the same socioeconomic framework.

Therefore, while documentary filmmaking parallels other discourses articulating concerns about vulnerability and precariousness, not only in relation to the global financial crisis, but also with regard to the dysfunctional nature of late capitalism, such interests overlap at several points. In labor terms, precariousness, characterized by instability, contingency and the loss of labor achievements, arises within the reset of the employment system in Europe. To extend this further, precarious existence results from being jobless within the austerity program set on in the recent financial and economic crisis. This experience places the affected at risk of social exclusion, which can be portrayed as insecurity of access to basic resources and a limited or total lack of social protection. Dean Allbritton holds that a state of precarity is the result of neoliberal practices that place the individual in a situation of vulnerability insofar as (s)he may be subject to harm:

> Considering "precarity" as something more than just a new class formation is fundamental, particularly because it has become intricately linked to contemporary modes of being. That is, precarity does not coalesce only around a specific group of (more or less poor) people, as evidenced in the diversity of situations, but into a whole contingent of the vulnerable. In its current configuration, "precarity" seems to most often denote the neoliberal labor practices that have placed citizens in socioeconomic states of vulnerability; vulnerability, in contrast, often speaks generally of a susceptibility to harm, physical or otherwise. In this ideation, vulnerability leads to precarity; that is, if one is vulnerable a priori, one can be placed in a precarious situation.
>
> *(Allbritton 2014, 102)*

According to Allbritton, a number of Spanish fiction feature films produced in the crisis years have addressed the experiences of vulnerable citizens in physical, economic and social terms. He cites a wide range of films in this regard, including *Amador* (F. León de Aranoa, 2010), *To the Cold Door* (A puerta fría, X. Puebla, 2012), *Yesterday Never Ends* (Ayer no termina nunca, I. Coixet, 2013), *The World Is Ours* (El mundo es nuestro, A. Sánchez, 2012), *Died beyond Their Means* (Murieron por encima de sus posibilidades, I. Lacuesta, 2014), *As Luck Would Have It* (La Chispa de la vida, Á. De la Iglesia, 2012), and *The Last Days* (Los últimos días, D. Pastor and A. Pastor, 2013). More recent films such as *Food and Shelter* (Techo y comida, J. M. Del Castillo, 2015) might be added to the list. The basic characteristic of these films is the endeavor to frame individual experience of precarity and vulnerability against the backdrop of community or social experience. Drawing for the most part on genres such as drama, comedy, and even post-apocalyptic allegory, the main characters are portrayed as teetering on the edge, struggling to deal with the shock of having lost their jobs, homes and lifestyles. Workers, rich and poor, old and young, Spanish and foreign: all are looking for some kind of work. The bottom line is clear: the crisis can affect anyone, the crisis affects everyone (Allbritton 2014, 103–104).

The most serious consequences do not stem only from the financial collapse itself or the political efforts to reverse it through austerity measures (cutbacks to key areas of the Welfare State, for instance, and changes to working conditions and job security). Emergency measures like these amount to little more than an accelerated decline in the global economic model, which had already exacerbated the individual's vulnerability. Such is the radical material and existential dilemma facing individuals: a paradoxical system that imposes and promotes materialistic values while simultaneously failing to create the basic conditions required to ensure a dignified way of life. The individual's sense of frustration and exposure in this context calls for new models. Luis Moreno-Caballud has pointed out how even before the crisis, Spanish film and literature foreshadowed darker times to come in such films as *Mondays in the Sun* (Los lunes al sol, F. León de Aranoa, 2002), *Smoking Room* (J. D. Wallovits and R. Gual, 2002), *Mataharis* (I. Bollaín, 2007), and the movies of Joaquim Jordá (Moreno-Caballud 2012, 539).

This line of argument is also reflected in documentary filmmaking. Most of the life histories presented in *La Granja del Pas* concern middle-class individuals and families once in relatively stable financial circumstances. However, having lost their jobs or seen their businesses fail, they find themselves in an unimaginable situation, as they acknowledge on camera. The filmmaker takes care to communicate the reality of those who have fallen to a subprime condition, into a state of biopolitical risk, resisting the temptation to offer simplistic and/or tendentious views of the type of people involved. As noted above, Munt cuts between extreme experiences (the situation of immigrants, for example, an especially vulnerable social group) and other, no less desperate circumstances experienced by people who appeared to enjoy a more stable position in society. Both types of life history attract the identification of different target audiences. Other documentary productions have drawn on this dynamic to narrate and interpret the effects of the economic and financial bubble. Such is the case of *No Job Land* (G. Pecot, O. Calvo and E. Filgueira 2013), a multimedia story (video and photography) that explores the phenomenon of unemployment in terms of its human cost: the vulnerability and the risk of social exclusion faced by many families in Spain. The filmmakers open the doors into the private spheres of homes, enabling people to voice their frustrations, and document the process of political empowerment these victims undergo as they set out to find solutions.[7]

Across Europe, fiction feature films and documentaries have dealt with the problematic of contemporary precarity, encompassing job insecurity, the instability of temporary and part-time contracts, and poor working conditions. This situation impacts on the lives of ordinary individuals by preventing them from planning for the future or making provisions for long-term personal projects. This keen focus on the modes of production has led to the use of the new term "precariat", coined from a combination of "precarity" and "proletariat", to denote the segment of the working class that has borne the brunt of the neoliberal doctrine that insists on the need to foster greater flexibility in the labor market (Standing 2011, cited in Bardan 2013, 72). Bardan has drawn up a list of films that she refers to collectively as "the new cinema of precarity" (Bardan 2013, 71), because they articulate a cinematic account of the present state of precariousness on the basis of the distinctive features of this unique moment in history. In line with Lauren Berlant, Bardan argues that the "cinema of precarity" figures the present as a transitional moment in which, to a certain extent, the dreams of what constitutes a good life handed down from one generation to the next can no longer be fulfilled (Berlant 2011, 201, cited in Bardan 2013, 72). That these films have been made over the last ten years in the economic context of late capitalism, before and after the global crisis, is no coincidence; they have been produced in recent times not because precarity is a phenomenon new to Europe but because the current social structure is especially unstable (Bardan 2013, 72).

Within this overarching, transnational frame of reference, Bardan reflects on a number of European productions that belong to different genres and styles, made by filmmakers, video-activists or social collectives that have explored contemporary precarity in its various forms. Viewers may easily understand and, perhaps, recognize themselves in these films: they depict the victims of austerity in countries weighed down by increased sovereign debt, the restructuring of the labor market being implemented throughout Europe (outsourcing, re-distribution), the risks and effects of vulnerable situations, and the insecurities caused by the loss of social status associated with a decline in personal wealth. One of the most worrying phenomena explored by these productions in this context is the impact of precarity on young people. Italian and German cinema, especially the former, have presented the disillusionment and uncertainty felt by the younger generation, referred to variously as the "lost youth of Europe" and "baby-losers." They show young educated people trapped in temporary contracts, unable to make plans for the future. As a result, their ambition of having a "normal" life recedes and they begin to lose hope.

Drawing on the documentary precedent *Lost Generation?* (¿Generación perdida?, D. Martín de los Santos, 2011), which delves into the high unemployment rate among young people in Spain, Icíar Bollaín's film *In a Strange Land* deals with the precarious life experiences of young emigrants, and although it implies rather than directly depicts a transnational perspective on the phenomenon,[8] it prompts further reflection on the universal experience of immigrant life and the need to show solidarity to the displaced. Many of the people featured in the film acknowledge that they "now" understand the experience of Latin Americans in Spain and the struggles they face. As such, Bollaín's film may be categorized within the cinema of precarity, exploring how the lives of people in Europe have become more vulnerable, sharing some of the hardships faced by immigrants, thus giving rise to a kind of transnational fraternal bond. "Europe, in this vision, is no longer defined by a common identity and what 'others' are *not*. Rather, it is a territory united by a shared experience of structural uncertainty about the future" (Bardan 2013, 88).

Empowerment and political action

Bardan links the precariousness that stems from the prevailing economic forces to the emergence of "*new forms of political struggle and solidarity* that go beyond the traditional models of political party and trade union," which shape new cultures and subjectivities (Bardan 2013, 71). The *Indignados* protest movement in Spain is emblematic of the way in which a collective sense of vulnerability may be harnessed and converted into a call for political action. According to Labrador, the sharing of subprime life histories has played a key role in this process, and a study of their impact as a strategy of empowerment would be worthwhile. That is, they are intrinsically political by nature insofar as they herald the end of individual culpability: "(…) to have one's home repossessed or embargoed, to be made redundant, is no longer regarded as a source of shame, blame or punishment; rather, it is to be read in political terms. In contrast to the blame game, victimization may function as a counter-hegemonic strategy" (Labrador 2012, 563). Furthermore, by taking such life experiences out of family and local contexts so as to re-inscribe them within the collective paradigm of crisis, these stories assert the need for action on the audience's part.

Documentary narratives based on life histories of this kind have deployed that political approach. The individuals featured in them have taken an important step towards their own empowerment, overcoming any sense of shame in recounting their situation to a wider public. Overcoming the psychological barrier of frustration and a social culture that celebrates success and decries failure comes at a significant cost, a fact underscored by all of the films discussed here. Many immigrants in Edinburgh are unwilling to talk in public about their lives there because they are afraid of the harsh judgments of others. Similarly, many families living with the threat of eviction have kept their experience secret, literally behind closed doors, because they were ashamed of their plight and too embarrassed to reach out to others for help. In *La Granja del Pas*, some people are reluctant to talk about their situation in public assemblies; not until they hear the first-person testimonies of others do they dare to do so. *Whoever's with Me* also presents life histories as political dynamos: José Luis, Lola's husband, mirrors himself in the stories told by different people on his taxi's radio, and it is a moving experience for him. Thus, documentaries show the first stage of empowerment, whereby individuals take ownership of their situations and stop feeling ashamed of the circumstances in which they find themselves. There is a shift from a sense of defeat to a fighting spirit, from the weakness of psychological damage to a determined strength of will to challenge the economic system by which they have been victimized.

At the same time, these documentaries situate the subjective process in the broader context of collective awareness-raising, as part of the dynamic generated by the anti-eviction platform (PAH) and 15-M protest movement. According to Moreno-Caballud, the difference between the latter phenomena with their extraordinary socio-cultural capital and more traditional social movements is their "capacity to include many different types of people and their aim to move beyond mere protest to provide their own solutions" (2012, 539). In other words, the 15-M movement has blurred the distinction between citizen and activist. In line with the logic of events, the documentaries frame political acts of resistance to forced precarity as a collective drive to push in the same direction. The unquestionable subtext of all these narratives is that the individual will always come up against the wall of the real powers that, by action and omission, have been responsible for his/her downfall – that is, corrupt or permissive financial and political organizations which enable the injustices in the system. Only through collective mobilization, and the solidarity it entails, may individuals overcome their plight and rebuild their lives in a David-and-Goliath struggle between unequals. The protagonists of *Whoever's with Me* and *La Granja del Pas*, for example, are people without economic or financial training. Banks ignore their claims, because these isolated individuals are not considered a risk for the interests of the financial system. Subjectivity is likewise reinserted into the contemporary political, social and cultural contexts depicted in the fiction films that have addressed the status of the individual in times of crisis (Allbritton 2014, 11).

Thus, documentary filmmaking validates the empowerment strategies enacted by the new social movements referred to above. In the face of the legal vulnerability of individuals subject to repossession orders, these films make the case for the endeavor to find solutions that enable people to live with dignity. This struggle may also include such public actions as protests in front of banks and other institutions and, of course, the occupation of properties left empty as a result eviction orders. Both *La Granja del Pas* and *Whoever's with Me* return to this message again and again, amplifying the reverberations in the media of the initiatives of anti-repossession and eviction pressure groups.

In a Strange Land taps into the protests against the handling of the crisis and the political arguments articulated by the new organizations emerging from the 15-M movement – that is, the need to restore social rights, to stop evictions and to refuse to repay sovereign debt or to implement the Troika-imposed cutbacks. In the film, Gloria, a young teacher from Almería now living in Edinburgh, invites Spanish emigrants to gather together to show the government and public in general that they are not resigned to their fate. "Ni perdidos ni callados" ["Neither lost nor silent"] is the slogan that sums up their appeal for recognition as a political collective, a group of critical voices and votes, currently in exile. This intervention culminated at the doors to the Spanish embassy in Edinburgh on March 22, 2014, the same day that political events of even greater import took place in Spain itself: the marches for dignity. The parallel unity of the struggle is portrayed in a film that cuts between scenes of the popular protests on the streets of Spanish cities and images of unpaired gloves pinned to the fence of the Spanish embassy in Scotland, symbolizing the plight of migrants. In short, the documentary claims the need for "more participation, more democracy, for everyone to become human rights activists," in a direct appeal to the political views of the audience.

Thus, the political agenda of these Spanish documentaries lies further left along the social-democratic spectrum than international films dealing with the global financial crisis. The latter, *Inside Job* or *Capitalism: A Love Story*, for example, come down on the side of individual citizens whose rights and needs are opposed to the interests of the free market. To that end, therefore, they formulate a call for greater state regulation so as to prevent the systemic crises of capitalism (Eder 2016, 37). Although they share the same basic economic outlook as their international counterparts, the Spanish documentaries articulate a more radical approach at a national

FIGURE 11.5 Still from *In a Strange Land* (2014).

level that calls for the total transformation of the political system. From this point of view, the problem is not limited to the structure of an unfair economic system; it also involves a political class that is indebted to financial interests, and has ceased working for the good of the people or to protect them from corruption. Not even social democracy has taken on this duty. Instead, individuals have been abandoned to their precarious fate and feel that no one any longer represents their interests.

That the three films discussed here should foreground the common misinterpretation of the individual's sense of political alienation is no coincidence: it is not that the individual fails to take a political position; rather, (s)he feels no connection to the two-party political model prevalent until now. The empowerment of the citizen entails the abolition of corrupt political practices that can only lead to precariousness. *Whoever's with Me* and *In a Strange Land* are especially combative in this regard; these films unequivocally adopt the revisionist political outlook of Podemos[9] and its coalition allies, which decry a lack of real democracy in Spain by calling into question the institutional model brought into being by the transition to democracy. For example, Bollaín's film incorporates fragments of a play performed by the actor Alberto San Juan, who publicly supports Podemos. In his monologue, the actor plays a character – a kind of yuppie – impoverished by the economic crisis. He analyzes the current situation by reviewing the recent history of Spain in a critical perspective.

Notes towards a conclusion

This overview of the contribution of Spanish documentary-making to a clearer understanding of the global financial crisis and its impact in real economic terms has overlooked other noteworthy films. Among them are *Futures Market* (Mercado de futuros, M. Álvarez, 2011) and *The Building* (Edificio España, V. Moreno, 2014). Both films embrace a poetics of space as a metaphor for the human dimensions and cost of contemporary socioeconomic, political and cultural processes insofar as they are shaped by the rationale and values of the property market. Although both films comprise provocative visions, they have not been discussed here because they are only indirectly linked to the analysis of the devastating effects of the Spanish and global crisis on the lives of ordinary individuals.

At this critical juncture in history, the meanings articulated by documentaries complement the other forms of analysis that have identified the dynamics, mistakes and responsibilities pertaining to financial markets. As such, they comprise a set of audiovisual materials to be read in relation to other audiovisual narratives produced in different contexts, with different styles and approaches. They may be viewed as keys to the gradual disclosure and interpretation of the economic drift besetting the West in recent years. Most notable in this regard is that the documentary has established subprime life histories or stories of precarity as the definitive narrative genre of the crisis, which implies that such narratives constitute an alternative mode of political imagination insofar as they foster a self-reflexive reading of personal experience as part of a shared historical experience (Labrador 2012, 571). Thus, these stories have helped construct a collective imagination of the crisis that highlights the human cost involved by tracing the problems common to many and dismissing simplistic conclusions and clichés. Moreover, they also engage with the collaborative forms of political, social and cultural dynamics that have emerged in response to the dysfunctional system and the rationale on which it is based. Although the historical interpretative framework considered here is a national one – the situation of Spain – the issues raised and addressed in these documentary narratives have clearly prompted further reflection on the precariousness and vulnerability bedeviling contemporary personal and social experience throughout Europe.

There is a final point that ought not to be overlooked, and may be mentioned here with a view to seeing how it may develop in future productions or the cinematic histories of other countries and cultures. Discussion of the crisis has not been limited to female filmmakers, of course. However, the three films presented here as modeling the crisis narrative as such were made by women. These filmmakers are women who have written, directed and produced movies about the casualties of the crisis, the victims of the failed economic and financial system. Their work stems from an unwavering political commitment. Given their raw emotional content, and the concern to foreground the domestic sphere in considerable detail, the status of these films as melodrama may be worthy of further study.

However, more interesting still may be the way in which, albeit unconsciously, the work of these women documentary-makers evinces recent feminist thought on the multidimensional crisis, which was exacerbated by the 2008 crash but had been incubating before then within the neoliberal economic model itself. Amaia Pérez Orozco has proposed an alternative view of the crisis that diverges from the hegemonic approach that centers on the rationale and needs of financial markets, thus legitimizing an unsustainable and unfair system. She holds that the "modernizing project" must be called into question, along with such notions as development, progress and growth, which fail to live up to their names. She argues that the "financialization" of the economy has merely aggravated the conflict between capital and life; in other words, it amounts to a serious attack on the sustainability of life (Pérez Orozco 2010, 31, 33). Pérez Orozco's approach to understanding the crisis aims to situate the reproduction or sustainability of life, rather than the idea of production, at the heart of the socioeconomic system – that is, to focus on the conditions that ensure that life is worth living and sustainable as such. To Pérez Orozco's mind, the hegemonic values system must be overturned, prompting a return to the materiality of life and the body as a fundamental ontological principle: "Life is vulnerable and finite; it is precarious; if no care is taken, it cannot be sustained." Hence the need to ensure certain conditions of possibility; these are not automatic, they are predicated on other social and economic pre-conditions. Finally, "to acknowledge vulnerability is not to recognize a defect, but a source of potential: the capacity to feel affected by what happens to others, and the realization that life is always a shared life, an interdependent life." (Pérez Orozco 2010, 43–44).

In short, the documentary practices discussed here disclose how the conditions that assure sustainability in personal and social life have been affected, how they have become more intensely precarious, with the associated risk of social exclusion. As such, these documentaries inject new energy into a critical approach that is so necessary in these troubled times, especially for Europe.

Acknowledgement

The author is grateful to the academic colleagues, whose insightful works and comments have supported her research.

This chapter presents some results of the research project "Imaginaries of the crisis: Visual depictions of the economic, social and geopolitical collapse (1929–2012)." Reference: CSO2012-33782. Financed by the Spanish Ministry of Economy, Industry and Competitiveness, through the Fundamental Research Projects Program.

Notes

1 *PIGS* is an acronym that originated in financial media such as *Newsweek*, *The Economist* and *Financial Times* and used to refer to the economies of the Southern European countries of Portugal, Italy, Greece, and Spain. During the European sovereign-debt crisis of the late 2000s the term was popularized, including Ireland – *PIIGS*.

2 The idea of indignation relates to the dynamics of sociopolitical activism that critiques and rejects the processes of financial capitalism in general and the measures adopted by the State to comply to its demands, in particular. This line of argument gave rise in turn to a social movement that became publically visible for the first time through collective protests such as demonstrations and the occupation of public spaces in Madrid and other Spanish cities from May 15, 2011 onwards, which were later mirrored by similar actions in other countries. The media refer to the people in this movement as *indignados* ["the indignant"], a form of activism that has given rise to a range of political organizations that have since achieved official status in Spanish government institutions as well as the European Parliament. However, those involved in the 15-M protest refer to it as the 15M Movement or the *Democracia Real Ya* movement (DRY: Real Democracy Now).

3 The *Plataforma de Afectados por la Hipoteca* [PAH: an association of people affected by the pressure of mortgage repayments, operating in Spain] is a clear example in this regard.
4 The title refers to the place where the PAH in Sabadell, Catalonia, meets (PAHC).
5 Whether or not, of course, viewers later re-tell such testimonies, simplifying and turning them into the kind of anecdotes to which Labrador refers.
6 Such festivals include the San Sebastian Film Festival and Human Rights Film Festival, and the Sao Paulo Film Festival, for *In a Strange Land*; the Valladolid International Film Festival, where *La Granja del Pas* won the Tiempo de Historia Award for best documentary; and the Munich International Documentary Film Festival, where *Whoever's with Me* was first screened. *Sources*: www.imdb.com and www.filmin.es.
7 Olmo Calvo, one of the contributors to this multimedia project, had previously made a significant photographic portfolio on home repossessions in Spain. The series, entitled "Víctimas de los desahucios" ["Victims of evictions"], won the 16th Premio Luis Valtueña, awarded by the NGO Médicos del Mundo, in 2012.
8 Moreno-Caballud discusses the literary dimension of the "lost generation" in the Spanish novel (2012: 547).
9 Podemos is the main national political party that emerged from the 15-M movement. It was founded in January 2014.

References

Allbritton, Dean. 2014. "Prime Risk: The Politics of Pain and Suffering in Spanish Crisis Cinema." *Journal of Spanish Cultural Studies* 15(1–2): 101–115.

Alvarado, Alejandro and Concha Barquero. 2013. "Un despertar revulsivo: prácticas colaborativas en el documental sobre el 15-M." *Fonseca, Journal of Communication* 2: 316–337.

Bardan, Alice. 2013. "The New European Cinema of Precarity: A Transnational Perspective." In *Work in Cinema. Labor and the Human Condition*, edited by Ewa Mazierska, 69–90, New York: Palgrave MacMillan.

Berlant, Lauren. 2011. *Cruel Optimism*. Durham, NC: Duke University Press.

Berrocal, Salomé, Marta Redondo and Luis Miguel Torres. 2015. "La crisis como espectáculo: el infoentretenimiento en las noticias sobre el rescate bancario en la prensa española de referencia." *Communication & Society* 28(4): 1–16.

Christensen, Christian. 2009. "Political Documentary, Online Organization and Activist Synergies." *Studies in Documentary Film* 3(2): 77–94.

Eder, Jens. 2016. "Imágenes de la Crisis Financiera. Las intervenciones de las películas documentales." *Revista Latinoamericana de Estudios sobre Cuerpos, Emociones y Sociedad* 8(20): 27–40.

Kinkle, Jeff and Alberto Toscano. 2011. "Filming the Crisis: A Survey." *Film Quarterly* 65(1): 39–52.

Labrador Méndez, Germán. 2012. "Las vidas subprime: la circulación de historias de vida como tecnología de imaginación política en la crisis española (2007–2012)." *Hispanic Review* 80(4): 557–581.

Meissner, Miriam. 2012. "Portraying the Global Financial Crisis: Myth, Aesthetics, and the City." *European Journal of Media Studies* 1(1): 98–125.

Moreno-Caballud, Luis. 2012. "La imaginación sostenible: culturas y crisis económica en la España actual." *Hispanic Review* 80(4): 535–555.

Pérez Orozco, Amaia. 2010. "Crisis multidimensional y sostenibilidad de la vida." *Investigaciones Feministas* 1: 29–53.

Ruiz, María Jesús, Isabel Ruiz and Silvia Olmedo. 2013. "La representación de la crisis española en el discurso televisivo: formatos de entretenimiento, docudramáticos y ficcionales."

In *Narrativas audiovisuales digitales. Convergencia de medios, multiculturalidad y transmedia*, edited by Virginia Guarinos and Ana Sedeño, 139–162, Madrid: Fragua.

Ruiz-Muñoz, María Jesús. 2015. "La representación de la crisis en televisión. Análisis de España e Italia." *Opción* 31(5): 1119–1139.

Segado Boj, Francisco. 2015. "Amarillismo e infoentretenimiento en la información televisiva sobre la crisis económica: El caso de Cuatro TV (2012)." *Revista Internacional de Historia de la Comunicación Social* 5(1): 76–88.

Standing, Guy. 2011. *The Precariat: The New Dangerous Class*. New York: Bloomsbury Publishing.

Whiteman, David. 2004. "Out of the Theaters and Into the Streets: A Coalition Model of the Political Impact of Documentary Film and Video." *Political Communication* 21(1): 51–69.

POSTSCRIPT

Notes of a filmmaker

HOW TO MAKE A FILM ABOUT MONEY AND DEBT WITHOUT ANY MONEY AND WITHOUT FALLING INTO DEBT

Michael Chanan

1

What do children understand of money? This is how our film *Money Puzzles* (2016) begins, and what we find out is quite curious. Ten-year-old Lucy and her friend Sofia know that you need money to live, which comes from having a job. They know that you can keep money in a bank, and the bank pays you something called interest. They also know that a banknote is just a piece of paper, and Lucy comes to the conclusion that what it's worth is "in what you spend it on." Of course, whatever a child knows about money varies with their social class and location. A middle-class kid somewhere in the South of England will hardly think the same as, let's say, the child of a peasant family in an African country like Kenya. But this isn't just about the reach of the cash nexus. For the African child, who may not be used to seeing banknotes, money is nowadays likely to be something that its parents do with a mobile phone. It isn't just cash; cash may no longer even be the primary form of money. Of course, the English child may well be aware that you can also pay for stuff using electronic cards; that doesn't mean they understand, say, the difference between a credit and a debit card. But we can also be surprised. We cut from the children to a clip from Alexander Kluge's *News from Ideological Antiquity* (2008), in which the poet Hans Magnus Enzensberger deems that a twelve-year-old can hardly be expected to understand what a derivative is – and then comes a segue to a twelve-year-old on the podium at the US Public Banking Institute, asking sophisticated questions about the Canadian national debt.

Money Puzzles is a documentary about money and debt, austerity and solidarity, shot in 2015 in the UK, Greece, Spain, Belgium and Argentina, which sets out to question the way that money is represented, how it works, who controls it and to what effect. (Argentina is included as an example of what happens when a country's economy collapses and the national currency disappears from circulation.) In part the film is explanatory and in part reportage. Alongside the crushing effects of the neoliberal agenda of financial capitalism which holds Europe in its grip, the film reports on grassroots solidarity networks and ground-level anti-austerity initiatives which aim to construct an alternative social economics, including the worldwide movement for citizens' debt audits and the repudiation of illegitimate national debt.

2

The Premise. There is something strange about money. As a measure of value, it doesn't have a price of its own. If I give you a five-pound note for five one-pound coins, we both still have the same amount. To put it another way: money isn't like an ordinary commodity, which has a use value distinct from its price (exchange value). Money has no use value other than its being a certain amount of money. It is the form under which price (or exchange value) appears (what Marx called the "general equivalent"). On the other hand, it doesn't grow on trees. You have to work for it (unless you inherit it), or if you want to borrow some money, for example from a bank, you have to pay for it – whereupon it does behave like a commodity, but an odd one, because the cost is not in the here-and-now but a promise that accrues to the future. When I borrow I become a debtor, and what I pay for the money, for the use of it, on top of the value of the debt, is called interest. Conversely, the lender becomes a creditor. Interest, then, is the future product of using money to make money. Making money out of money once used to be called usury. Aristotle didn't approve of it. But capitalism naturalizes it.

What do such contradictory characteristics indicate about the fundamental nature of money? And how do you make a film about it? How do you picture something simultaneously ubiquitous and abstract? Search the web for videos about money and even excluding the stuff on how to manage your investments and other excrescences of the finance industry, you'll find a good many animated diagrams and quite a few cartoons. Some of these graphic and diagrammatic representations are quoted in *Money Puzzles*, but they don't actually explain anything. They function as iconic representations of something that remains beyond graphic portrayal, a totalizing system in which economic, political, ideological, social and cultural components fit together in complex, elusive, often counter-intuitive citizens debt audits and constantly shifting ways. Documentary, however, especially an essay film like this one, has other resources. Foremost of course is montage, to which Walter Benjamin attested in his description of "the shock effect of the film" (Benjamin 1969, 238), which prevents the spectator from contemplating the film screen in the same way as a painting because no sooner has the eye grasped a scene than it has already changed and the spectator's process of association is interrupted. But if this is what Benjamin calls the "technical structure" of film, then it also stimulates the "heightened presence of mind" he extols, by creating new associations – indeed it does so in the many different ways that Benjamin's slightly younger contemporary Sergei Eisenstein elaborated in both his films and his writings. The aesthetic premise of *Money Puzzles* is that economic reality is complex and dialectical in character, full of invisible forces acting and reacting, and this has to be reflected in any attempt to represent how it works. Instead of a stepwise linear exposition, then, *Money Puzzles* employs the techniques of montage, incorporating a multitude of materials in a variety of ways, from simple illustration and quotation to ironic interruption and dialectical juxtaposition, in order to map the circularity and self-referentiality of the money system.

This is an endeavor that cannot succeed, of course, because it's embedded in what Fredric Jameson calls "the dilemma of representation as such": because if capitalism is a totality, then "No-one has ever seen that totality, nor is capitalism ever visible as such, but only in its symptoms" (Jameson 2011, 4–6). Inevitably, then, there will be jumps and gaps in the explanations proffered, but instead of papering them over, the grammar of montage can prod the viewer's presence of mind. Better than the simplifications of the normal discourse of the documentary commentary, the disembodied voice that is supposed to know. And another advantage: it allows different but related themes to be intertwined. It enables the film to set up its own memes, so to speak, like the idea announced within the first few minutes that money = debt. Because cash comprises only 3 percent of money in circulation, almost the entire money supply nowadays consists in nothing more than "blips on a screen," and what these blips represent is not a store of value like the sovereigns we see being struck in the archive footage of the Royal Mint, but a digital register of debt issued by the banks themselves. This meme returns along the length of the film in different shape and form, from passing visual allusions and questions in street interviews to sequences on student debt, and at the international level, odious, illegitimate citizens debt audits and unpayable sovereign debt.

Because the imagery that montage hungers for is nowadays available in one form or another on the Internet, this method of construction is also a practical response to the basic mercenary question which faces anyone producing such a film as an independent filmmaker, including within academia. How to make a critical documentary on the matter of money boils down to the question "how to make a film about money and debt without any money and without falling into debt?" If you forswear commercial intent, then you can exercise your right to fair use of stuff you find on the web. Working this way, *Money Puzzles* was made with equipment belonging to the filmmakers, small tranches of academic funding, support in kind, and some crowdfunding. But it wasn't the first time this filmmaker has worked in this way.

3

When we set out to make *Secret City* (2012), an investigation into the Corporation of the City of London which governs the famous Square Mile, we wondered if it might be possible to get a television commission.[1] Made-for-television documentary is nowadays a very different business from my experience of the BBC in the 1970s and Channel 4 in the 1980s, when program editors were much more open to one-off independent productions. Consequently I was skeptical, but we went to see an independent producer, an old friend who was sympathetic to the idea.

We quickly reached the conclusion that it was an impossible prospect. There were three problems, all stemming from the conventions of television documentary. First, television would expect it to be narrated, on or off screen, by one of their own people, but we didn't want an explicit narration at all. We wanted to construct the film through dialogical montage to take the viewer on a journey of historical rediscovery. Second, television would want revelations, but there weren't any revelations beyond the very scandal of the City's secrecy – you cannot get information about the Corporation's private accounts, for example, from a Freedom of Information request, because it's a private corporation, not a public body like any other local authority. Third, the issue of "balance," the doctrine that "controversial subjects" are to be treated with due impartiality, which is often reduced to the idea of every argument having two sides and you have to show both, so we would need to give the Corporation a chance to respond. But this we believe is both a gross oversimplification and an ideological illusion, and it was not our purpose to produce that kind of account, which all too easily allows an entity like the Corporation to put up a smokescreen.

The Corporation of London is a crucial node in the global network of power. It has distorting effects, geographically on London's built environment, financially on the economy, politically through its influence on government, and ideologically through the plethora of media, including the financial pages of the newspapers, whose accounts of "economics" are largely just accounts of the interests of finance capital. The priorities of the Corporation animate British economic policy, and its voice is heard indirectly through the media all the time. They are so adept at the veiled expression of their ideological self-interest that we were sure we knew what they would say. Indeed, they had already said it in one or two corporate videos we found on the web, which we included in the film to represent their point of view – and throw it into relief. This was not only quicker and easier (as well as cheaper), but these clips took their place alongside a range of maps and archive imagery which we used to draw out the history of the representations of the City over the centuries.

Our purpose was to demonstrate how the institutional structures of finance capitalism are hidden in plain sight. The core problem in doing this is a variation on the issue indicated by Walter Benjamin in his "Small History of Photography," (Benjamin 1979) when he cited Brecht's remark that the simple reproduction of reality says very little about what it shows, and a photograph of, say, the Krupp works or AEG tells us almost nothing about these enterprises, because it cannot reveal the reification of human relations which is produced within them (Brecht 2000). Documentary is constantly confronted with this difficulty, especially when the object of investigation is already visually very well established by a repertoire of stock images with iconic status, precisely like the City of London, whose very familiarity is a façade that obscures what goes on within. Indeed the City has had centuries of cultivating this façade in the form of the ceremonial by which it has inscribed itself in the national imaginary. (In *Secret City* we used music – a jazz version of the old London nursery rhyme "Oranges and Lemons" – to ironize these images of the Lord Mayor's Show: the words are all about owing money and paying debts.[2])

However, Benjamin also spoke, in another context, of the dialectical image: the graphic representation which points to a larger historical truth, the emblematic trace whose historical resonance could be activated through montage, to which, according to Susan Buck-Morss, Benjamin afforded "special, perhaps even total rights" as a progressive form because it "interrupts the context into which it is inserted" and thus "counteracts illusion" (Buck-Morss 1991, 67). The crucial quality of the dialectical image is its historical resonance. The concept is a fuzzy one, because the dialectical image is necessarily ambiguous, but it points to the space of history because the image represents, as Benjamin sees it, a momentary aspect of a dialectical process – "the figurative appearance of the dialectic, the law of the dialectic at a standstill" (Benjamin 1973, 171).

The archive provides an endless source of dialectical images – images which lend themselves to dialectical expression through insertion into montage, cold and inert until juxtaposed with other images which throw them into relief. *Secret City* offers several examples, like a photographically undistinguished documentary from 1939 on the Port of London with an unintentionally revealing commentary, not because it nowadays sounds irredeemably pompous but because in setting London up at the start of the quoted film it throws up the phrase "We think of her as the city in which the British ideology evolved." The clip called out for inclusion in *Secret City* because of the way the word "ideology" jumps out at you, how it's being used quite correctly but in a sense unlikely to be employed in the mainstream media in the present day: ideology as a system of values and beliefs, of whatever ilk (the way Bakhtin construed it), rather than something you accuse your enemies of. Another example: a corporate documentary on the City from 1951 which presents the Corporation's Council in session while the commentary speaks of the Lord Mayor: "The head of a state within a state, for here he is monarch over all except his king. One of a line unbroken for 700 years – the Lord Mayor of London, presiding at this, his Common Council, a parliament older than Westminster." Here the archive was obligingly presenting our own thesis in direct and transparent language which would nowadays never be used in the kind of corporate video we found on the web.

What these snippets of archive do is to bring the past back and insert it into the present tense of the film, revealing history not as it was, so to speak, but as a persistent hidden truth, like the archeological substratum on which the city is built. Because London is a singular place which has been a subject for the film camera since the earliest days of cinema, we knew that this kind of footage would exist in some form or other. Long experience working with archive footage teaches that the premise of picture research is not to ask *if* it exists but that it most probably does, and your job is to find it. This used to mean going to an archive to inspect the holdings, going through drawers full of index cards, and then ordering up any likely looking items. This has now become very much easier. The index cards have become a database which can be consulted online, and increasingly the films themselves are available to preview. The problem for poorly funded independent production is the cost of full resolution copies. Sometimes it helps being an academic making a non-commercial film, and you get reduced charges or even pro bono access; sometimes it doesn't. But now there is the Internet as a source in itself, more like a constantly updated library than an archive. Ready access to recordings of television news, for example, allows the mediatized contemporary to be juxtaposed with the mediatized historical, but this also has a complicating effect on the play of representations in the film that does this.

4

The Internet has done more than make the archives more accessible, it has transformed the archive from a remote place into the active space of immediate access known as the virtual world. The result is a transformation of the audiovisual public sphere, of its "technical structure," which threatens to overwhelm the dialectical function of montage, because interruption happens randomly on almost any screen you watch, where it disrupts and fragments any semblance of coherence in the pictured world. (If the darkened space of the cinema remains a privileged site of viewing, even here you can be distracted by flickering phone screens around you.)

The media's manufactured, processed, artificial audiovisual representations of the real world have long become an active part of our everyday environment, and now we don't even sit down to watch them but carry them around with us and watch on multiple screens of different sizes – and with variable audio. The concomitant of this exponential mediatization is unequal fragmentation of a hugely expanded public sphere, with a hegemonic and increasingly concentrated corporate mainstream dedicated to the manufacture of "public opinion" facing off the multiplication of digital niches on the participatory platforms known as "social media," which are controlled by new corporate giants who allow content to circulate according to complex algorithms, seemingly outside anyone's control. But these digital platforms have contradictory characteristics. The Internet provides democratizing instruments for building new forms of public opinion and supporting new forms of social and political activity (as we see in *Money Puzzles*). But it also serves to amplify and exaggerate disaffected individual voices and narrow group-think through insidious forms of abbreviated utterance where confirmation bias has free rein and dialogue is displaced by verbal abuse and hate speech. The result is a network of networks of networks that becomes a free-for-all for every political tendency, whose social and cultural effects are highly unsettling. (Enter Trump.)

In response to this environment, *Money Puzzles* takes full account of it by borrowing from the widest range of sources, both historical and contemporary, most of them freely available on the web. This includes historical archive sources like an official documentary about the Royal Mint from the early 1950s, or the German agitprop film *Kuhle Wampe* (1932). There are clips from recent documentaries by well-known directors (Pino Solanas as well as Kluge); a French museum film; television news (from the BBC, Sky, C4, Al Jazeera etc.) and video streams (Ruptly, TRNN, and the UN); political satire from UK and Australian television; activist videos from Spain; cartoons from various sources. These clips carry diverse resonances and operate in different semiotic modes (sometimes emphasized by the film's DIY style of visual manipulation). They may be semantically specific and make particular discursive contributions to the argument, but will also sometimes be ideologically loaded and thus symptomatic of the speaker's positioning – like a pronouncement by the Governor of the Bank of England who claims the authority to speak untrammeled truth, but demonstrates the highly political nature of all utterances about money, debt, financial policy, in short, economics.

To judge by comments at screenings, clips like these have an iconic quality. They strike people like metaphors of the reality they encapsulate. Sometimes clips say something unintentionally revealing, like the former Tory politician Cecil Parkinson in a TV chat show: "And what it seems to me, if I may just make a point on that, is that the capitalists seem determined to destroy capitalism. It's a most peculiar attitude that they have, and the politicians have to defend them." But sometimes what seems like honesty is confounded by ambiguity. The clip most remarked upon at screenings is the BBC interview with a trader in New York in 2011, a certain Alessio Rastani, who speaks with unusual candor about making money. Asked how investors can be reassured about the economy, Rastani replies that "we don't really care about how they're gonna fix the economy…our job is to make money from it." He goes on to explain how recessions and depressions are good opportunities to make money for traders and speculators. The interviewer's response to this straightforward explanation of the real interests of financial speculators was "if you could see the people around me in the studio… jaws have collectively dropped at what you've just said."[3] Later, near the end, we come back to him, and his assessment of the recession:

> This economic crisis is like a cancer. If you just wait and wait thinking this is going to go away – just like the cancer it's going to grow, and it'll be too late. What I would say to everybody is: get prepared. This is not a time right now for wishful thinking that the government are going to sort things out. The governments don't rule the world. Goldman Sachs rules the world.

There are few better examples of the disjuncture between the idea of economics propagated by the mainstream media and the reality of traders and investors. Rastani's perspective as a trader is perfectly representative; it's the worldview of financial capitalism. But it doesn't fit with the ideological perspective of the BBC's newsroom – why else would jaws drop?

It wasn't only BBC jaws that dropped, and the following day, after the video went viral, the Corporation felt cornered into officially denying that the interview was a hoax.[4] In fact you can find the fellow at www.leadingtrader.com/alessio-rastani. In the ironic context of *Money Puzzles*, however, audiences seem to agree that it doesn't matter whether it was a hoax or not. What the fellow is saying, without the usual dissembling, punctures and disrupts the supposedly disinterested stance of the public service broadcaster, because no-one is supposed to publicly utter such truths.

5

Alternative thinking about economics and the economy is found in the film's fieldwork among grassroots solidarity networks in Greece and Spain, a sequence about the Bristol Pound which explains how complementary currencies work, a meeting in Brussels of the movement for citizen and public debt audits, along with the testimony of solidarity volunteers and activists, critical economists and politicians, journalists, even a bitcoin trader. The found footage quoted by the film is not merely illustrative or incidental, but reproduces the multidimensional public world in which the discourse of money takes confused and contradictory shape. However, the intention to produce a counter-narrative to mainstream economics can hardly be carried out except outside the mainstream media, where artisanal cultural production can be pitted like David against the Goliath of globalized cultural monopolies. I have found that academia has provided a workable base for the endeavor. Not merely for practical reasons, like helping to keep the costs of production down, but crucially, by providing a zone of intellectual and creative freedom – at least until now. Subject of course to legalities, but these nowadays include protection for the reproduction of publicly sourced material employed under the rubric of "fair use" in works intended for educational and non-commercial purposes (though perhaps independent filmmakers in the UK shouldn't take this for granted). *Money Puzzles* is accordingly available on the web at no charge – just go to www.moneypuzzles.net (you can watch it in one go or chapter by chapter). (*Secret City* can be found at www.youtube.com/watch?v=eHnwtkfX2k4.)

Digital video cameras and desktop editing means that production is not the problem it once was (and nowadays the independent filmmaker generally owns their own gear). The problem is dissemination. Excluded from commercial distribution because the film refuses the status of a vendible commodity (and has no budget for marketing and publicity), circulation can equally only take place outside the mainstream. There are websites dedicated to making political documentaries freely available, but when you launch a new film you are still subject to the unwritten law of the social media, namely, that the network you want to reach is always further away than the network you're able to reach from the network you start off in. In short, the dispersed and fragmented character of the Internet offers spaces for counter-discourses but only on condition of marginalization from the money-driven virtual mainstream.

Since *Secret City* appeared on YouTube the year after its premiere in 2012, it has clocked up over 166,000 hits at the last count (March 2017) and still rising, so it's proven to have what the retail end of the business calls a good shelf life; since *Money Puzzles* premiered in October 2016, it's too soon to know how it might compare. Importantly, over the year following its launch, *Secret City* had something like ninety screenings across the UK (and a few abroad). The direct encounter with the audience remains the best test of whether a film is working, so you take it out on the road, following the practice of independent filmmaking in the heyday of 16mm in the 1970s, which equally operated outside the mainstream. That practice was eclipsed by the rise of video in the 80s and the demise of 16mm distribution, but is now revived by small media DVD projection – even in a tent in the English countryside at an activist summer camp. More usual venues range from university lecture theaters to meeting rooms in pubs to small cinemas. Audiences for *Secret City* were largely comprised of sympathizers of the Occupy movement of autumn 2011, of all ages but mainly youthful, expressing a range of soft to hard left political sentiments, and belonging to three key and partly overlapping constituencies: academic audiences; political audiences; and general audiences which might include, for example at London's Frontline Club, journalists and other professionals. Since the film told most people stuff they didn't know about the way the City of London is governed, but refrains from suggesting solutions in the style of numerous campaign films of recent years, the reaction in discussion typically moved from initial astonishment to wide-ranging debate about financial capitalism and the democratic deficit of representative democracy.

Money Puzzles, on the other hand, offers various suggestions about the ways that financial capitalism needs to be brought under control, but they're not programmatic, and the response has been similar: wide-ranging discussion about the effects of the operation of globalized financial capitalism mapped out on the screen, effects which are recognized as common in all but one of countries where the film has been screened so far – Portugal, England, Scotland, Ireland, Denmark, and Spain. No matter that each country has its own political and economic configuration, the brands of yogurt in the corner-shops are the same, and so are the credit card providers.

The exception is Cuba, where the film was screened at the Havana Film Festival. An instructive experience. The festival audience is made up of both Cuban and Latin American cinephiles, who have different perspectives on the question of money. For the latter, the landscape of globalized financial capitalism is familiar territory, notwithstanding the film's European focus. (A viewer from Colombia remarked that the Argentine perspective was especially useful for understanding the euro crisis, but the same comment has been made by people in Europe.) For Cubans, however, the premise of the film is outside their experience: there are no private banks, no source of official financial loans, people aren't in debt. The everyday lifeworld has a different shape. This, of course, is totally missing in foreign coverage of Cuba, even when it reports on the government's intention to reform the dual currency monetary system, which seriously distorts the country's economy. But that's another story, yet to be told.

When we were traveling around for the filming, moving between different languages and local cultures but always recognizing the commonalities of different European countries, I kept wondering about their differences from my home territory, as if the UK somehow remained out of step with the European imaginary, not least in the political domain. Since this was then a speculative question, we left the Brexit agenda out of the film; it was answered while we were editing, and is sometimes raised in discussion. This also happens with other topics that people raise, in the process filling out some of the other gaps in the film. These gaps, ultimately due the impossibility of representing the totality, also arise because the totality is constantly evolving. New issues arise, like proposals for a Universal Basic Income which began to enter wider public debate while we were editing, and now also comes up in discussion.

In short, the screenings in this first phase of the film's dissemination bring together small audiences of people mostly already concerned and knowledgeable about the issues, for whom the film works as an open text which allows discussion to open out in turn. This is both the strength and the problem of any film that wishes to puncture the conventional wisdoms of dominant ideological discourse. On the one hand, a film may prove an effective trigger for an audience to share a moment of thinking certain questions through together. On the other, its wider dissemination is impeded by the contradictory structure of the culture in which it seeks to intervene, in which the public is presented with a world whose perception of it is hindered by the very forms of representation. I am paraphrasing Siegfried Kracauer's observation, in the 1920s, that in "illustrated magazines people see the very world that the illustrated magazines prevent them from perceiving" (Kracauer 1993, 432). The problem is rendered many times more acute in the twenty-first century, when a hugely expanded and multiplied apparatus of cultural consumption largely devoted to mass distraction, is also serving up "fake news" and "alternative facts." But another kind of alternative comprehension is also possible, and a film can help, providing a space to be able to start re-imagining the world, even if only for a couple of hours in front of a film screen.

Perhaps the most interesting screening so far has been to my own students in the class I teach to second year film students on forms of documentary. The class was ethnically diverse, with women outnumbering men, and very international, including several European exchange students and one from the USA. At the end, following a few moments of silence, the first to speak said he was shocked, he hadn't realized any of what the film showed, maybe it was his own fault for ignoring it. They then quickly began to compare notes on university fees and student debt, and how some countries didn't sell students down the river, and I sensed the collective dawning of a new comprehension of economic reality. Yet while the film connected with them, I was left with a feeling of frustration, the vexation of the independent filmmaker struggling for their film to find the audience that it's made for.

Notes

1 For a full account of *Secret City*, see Chanan and Salter, 2016.

2 "Oranges and Lemons, / Say the bells of St. Clements, / You owe me five farthings, / Say the bells of St. Martin's. / When will you pay me? / Say the bells of Old Bailey. / When I grow rich, / Say the bells of Shoreditch. / When will that be? / Say the bells of Stepney. / I do not know, / Says the great bell of Bow."

3 This can be seen in the full clip, which can be viewed at www.youtube.com/watch?v=9S48A0J7T84 (consulted 19.03.2017).

4 www.bbc.co.uk/pressoffice/pressreleases/stories/2011/09_september/27/statement.shtml (consulted 19.03.2017).

THE FILMS

Money Puzzles (Michael Chanan, 2016) www.moneypuzzles.net

Secret City (Michael Chanan and Lee Salter, 2012) www.secretcity-thefilm.com and www.youtube.com/watch?v=eHnwtkfX2k4

References

Benjamin, Walter. 1969. "The Work of Art in the Age of Mechanical Reproduction," in Arendt, Hannah (ed.). *Illuminations*. New York: Schocken Books.

Benjamin, Walter. 1973. *Charles Baudelaire: A Lyric Poet in the Era of High Capitalism*. London: New Left Books.

Benjamin, Walter. 1979. "A Small History of Photography," in Benjamin, Walter. *One-Way Street*. London: Verso.

Brecht, Bertolt. 2000. "The Threepenny Lawsuit" in Silberman, Marc (ed.). *Brecht on Film and Radio*. London: Methuen.

Buck-Morss, Susan. 1991. *The Dialectics of Seeing*. Cambridge, Mass.: MIT Press.

Chanan, Michael and Salter, Lee. 2016. "Secret City (2012): A Reception Diary," in Tzioumakis, Yannis and Molloy, Claire (eds.). *The Routledge Companion to Cinema and Politics*. London: Routledge.

Jameson, Fredric. 2011. *Representing Capital*. London: Verso.

Kracauer, Siegfried and Levin, Thomas Y. 1993. "Photography." *Critical Inquiry*, Vol. 19, No. 3, Spring.

INDEX

For Product Safety Concerns and Information please contact our EU representative GPSR@taylorandfrancis.com
Taylor & Francis Verlag GmbH, Kaufingerstraße 24, 80331 München, Germany

www.ingramcontent.com/pod-product-compliance
Lightning Source LLC
LaVergne TN
LVHW021123300926
849160LV00010B/840
9781138045286